POLITICS AND PROFIT

POLITICS AND PROFIT

A Study of Sir Ralph Sadler
1507-1547

BY

ARTHUR JOSEPH SLAVIN

Assistant Professor of History in the University of California, Los Angeles

CAMBRIDGE
AT THE UNIVERSITY PRESS
1966

PUBLISHED BY
THE SYNDICS OF THE CAMBRIDGE UNIVERSITY PRESS

Bentley House, 200 Euston Road, London, N.W. 1
American Branch: 32 East 57th Street, New York, N.Y. 10022
West African Office: P.M.B. 5181, Ibadan, Nigeria

Printed in Great Britain at the University Printing House, Cambridge
(Brooke Crutchley, University Printer)

LIBRARY OF CONGRESS CATALOGUE
CARD NUMBER: 66-12311

CONTENTS

TO CAMILLE

PREFACE

The intention of this history is a modest one suggested by what might well be called the problem of the 1540s. As Dr G. R. Elton has sufficiently proved, the character of Henry VIII's long reign varied with that of his ministers.[1] Without subscribing in advance to all of his views about the nature of the seven years after Cromwell's fall, it does seem true that Dr Elton has made his basic point. The wearisome failure of the last seven years of the king's reign will be understood only after we come to grips with the lives of the small number of men who guided England's foreign policy and administered the newly reconstituted organs of government at home.

That is a somewhat frustrating realisation, however. For Cromwell and a handful of other men, including the king, have by their very greatness tended to obscure the part played by statesmen and politicians of less celebrity. Hence there is no adequate published account of Sir William Paget.[2] The same holds for most of the privy councillors of the era, among them Wriothesley, the lord chancellor, and his one-time co-secretary Sir Ralph Sadler. While Mr F. G. Emmison, the learned keeper of Essex records, has recently published an excellent study of Sir William Petre,[3] the best study of Sir Edward Seymour, the Protector, is still that imperfect book by Pollard.[4] Lord Audley, Wriothesley's immediate predecessor in the chancellorship, remains a shadowy figure among the titans of the day, like most of his colleagues a paper man tightly bound between boards in the *Letters and Papers*. Even so dramatic and pivotal a figure as Sir Richard Rich remains less than well known, despite the recent efforts of Professor W. C. Richardson to cast him in a light more favourable than that used by Sir Thomas More's admirers.[5]

Thus it seems that Sir John Neale's voice has been more often heard

[1] See his masterful presentation of the problem in his Historical Association pamphlet *Henry VIII* (London, 1962).

[2] Dr S. R. Gammon's valuable doctoral dissertation 'Sir William Paget: The Master of Practises' (Princeton, 1953), will in all likelihood never be published, since Dr Gammon has become a career diplomat.

[3] F. G. Emmison, *Tudor Secretary, Sir William Petre: at court and home* (Cambridge, Mass.: Harvard University Press, 1961).

[4] *England under Protector Somerset* (London: Longmans, 1900).

[5] *A History of the Court of Augmentations* (Baton Rouge: L.S.U. Press, 1961), *passim*.

than heeded. His reminder that patient study of dozens of men not of the first flight is necessary if we are to replace the shadow with the substance of knowledge stands as a warning that we leave undone the lives of the men of rank and influence at a great cost. Our knowledge of offices and systems advances more rapidly than our understanding of the men filling the offices and making the systems work: and that is enough of a paradox for most historians. We have excellent studies of the making of the statute of artificers of 1563,[1] and brilliant expositions of the war in the exchequer of receipt under Elizabeth,[2] while offerings about the gentry as a class are a glut on the market. But concrete gentlemen who also happen to be officials are more often than not mere names in the pages of journals given to debates about a sort of history curiously abstract and having no clear human focus.

This study aspires to demonstrate that within the context of the questions raised by 'analytical' history the conditions of Henrician politics are illuminable in a biographical focus. Without claiming in any way that Sir Ralph Sadler's career was typical of that of the office-holding gentry in general, it is intended that some light be cast on the processes that made a career like his possible.

The choice of Sadler was not an entirely capricious one. It arose from an initial ambition to study the conditions of the Henrician political scene. That such a task was impossible for a novice became quickly apparent, while at the same time it also became apparent that a beginning could be made by a humbler design. Hence the choice of a man whose Henrician career stemmed from a place in Cromwell's circle and led in a kind of *cursus honorum* which included routine administrative and diplomatic work to the higher echelons of the principal secretaryship and the council board. In a career that spanned the lives of Henry VIII and each of his children in turn, Sir Ralph Sadler held dozens of offices, a handful at the highest level. Nominated for the secretaryship by Cromwell himself, a promotion which capped the Henrician part of his career, Sadler lived to serve Elizabeth I as a privy councillor, parliamentary leader, chancellor of the duchy of Lancaster and in a number of ambassadorial functions. Control over duchy patronage gave him a

[1] Samuel T. Bindoff, 'The Making of the Statute of Artificers', *Elizabethan Government and Society: Essays Presented to Sir John Neale*, Ed. S. T. Bindoff, Joel Hurstfield and C. H. Williams (London: Athlone Press, 1960), pp. 56–95.

[2] G. R. Elton, 'The Elizabethan Exchequer: War in the Receipt', *ibid.* pp. 213–49.

Preface

powerful place in Elizabethan politics.[1] On the parliamentary side, Sir John Neale pointed to Sadler as one of the great men of the mid-Elizabethan era, a veritable Nestor both for wisdom and longevity.[2] Even the duke of Norfolk, perhaps Sadler's worst enemy in politics, admitted that Sir Ralph was England's leading expert in things Scottish.[3] Some thought him to be the richest commoner in the kingdom.[4] Professor Richardson and Dr Elton agree that men like Sadler gave to Tudor government the stability and efficiency that it sometimes exhibited.[5] They have thus partially redressed the balance of opinion, which tends to see Sir Ralph Sadler wholly in terms of his Elizabethan career.

It is a fact that whatever accounts there are of Sadler's life stress the years after 1558 in a way not warranted by his story. Most modern writers have all but ignored the man to whom Tudors and Stuarts alike assigned a high place. While admitting that David Lloyd was given to hyperbole, it is to the point to recall his view of Sadler: 'Epaminondas was the last *Grecian*, and *Sir Ralph Sadler* was one of the last *English men*.'[6] A Victorian reviewer found him 'second to none' in the roll-call of Tudor statesmen, an estimate which seems disproportionate to me, while also putting his finger unerringly on a feature of Sadler's career which helps to explain his modern eclipse, at least in part. Sir Ralph seemed to avoid the centre of the stage:

> For lefer had he, in his country hall,
> Been reading some old books, with his hound
> Crouched at his hearth, and his old flask of wine
> Beside him.[7]

The lack of proportion which this study seeks to restore also stems from the accidents of survival. No great body of material exists apart

---

[1] The nature of such control forms a part of Wallace T. MacCaffery's theme in his 'Place and Patronage in Elizabethan Politics', *Elizabethan Government and Society*, pp. 107 ff.

[2] *The Elizabethan House of Commons* (London: Jonathan Cape, 1949), pp. 28 and 318.

[3] Hatfield House, Salisbury MSS. 231, fo. 209, Norfolk to Sir Wm. Cecil, 15 April 1560.

[4] J. D. Mackie, *The Earlier Tudors, 1485–1558* (Oxford: Clarendon Press, 1952), p. 400; Neale, *The Elizabethan House of Commons*, p. 222, notes Sadler 'amassing great wealth'.

[5] W. C. Richardson makes the point often in his *A History of the Court of Augmentations* and *Tudor Chamber Administration* (Baton Rouge: L.S.U. Press, 1952), while Elton specifically mentions Sadler in his *England under the Tudors* (London: Methuen, 1955), p. 410, n. 1.

[6] *The States-men and Favourites of England since the Reformation* (London: J. C. for Samuel Speed, 1665), p. 64.

[7] *The Times*, 3 Nov. 1877, in a review entitled 'An Elizabethan Statesman', testifying to the obscurity of his career under Henry VIII.

from the elaborate diplomatic correspondence relevant to Scotland, which is itself chiefly Elizabethan, to illuminate the early Tudor career. Despite his own statement that he 'booked' every expense and noted every event of his lifetime, there are today no long rows of folios at Standon comparable to those that draw the historian to Hatfield, Longleat and even to Plas Newydd. This necessitates that the Henrician career be reconstructed out of bits and pieces found among often un-yielding materials related to chancery, exchequer and state-paper office collections housed in London's Public Record Office and the British Museum.[1]

Nevertheless, within the initial resolve to make this book neither a complete biography of Sadler nor a story of the reign of Henry VIII seen through Sadler's eyes, several lines of investigation proved eminently feasible. It was decided that a series of dissolving views of Sadler's activities, each of them frustratingly incomplete in themselves, could be united in the hope that the series would tell us something useful about patronage, politics, and the pursuit of profit, which I think Sadler believed to be the chief objects and means of public life. Conventional questions about Sadler's birth, apprenticeship, connections and social advancement occasionally gave rise to some unconventional answers. And Sadler emerged as a first-rate man in the second flight of Henrician politicians, a man crafty but temperate, a pluralist anxious for advancement but also capable of imposing limits to that ambition that seem to me at least to accord well enough with a just estimate of his talents and the risky currents of his age. He also emerges as the victim of a bigamous marriage and the plotter of the murder of David Cardinal Beaton, the Scottish prelate who was England's staunchest enemy at the time of the 'rough wooing'. The more lurid elements have to compete with others easily familiar: the establishment of a family, a certain brand of fervent protestantism and the careful attention to detail so treasured in that era of revolution in the techniques of government. Taken together, these images of a man's career in Henrician politics are perhaps more revealing about the fabric of such a career than either the particulars of the administrative revolution or statistical abstractions about gentlemen office-holders. At least that is the premise of the book.

[1] Plas Newydd houses the Paget papers in the possession of the current marquis of Anglesey, Sir William Paget's descendant.

Preface

The marrying of the frames in the picture of Cromwell's affinity, Scottish diplomacy and adventuring in the Tudor land market could not have been accomplished without the help of a long list of people and institutions who materially aided me in the course of this study while often providing sustenance of another kind also. Without wanting to give the impression that the whole world of scholarship breathlessly helped in the production of this book, I would be delinquent if I gave those who generously helped me less than their due.

My greatest debts are to those teachers and scholars who provided encouragement and criticism, both of which were badly needed. Among the encouragers I must name Professors Walter C. Richardson, James E. King and Dr G. R. Elton. Professor Stephen B. Baxter, who directed the preliminary work on Sir Ralph Sadler, has exceeded his responsibility with regard to both criticism of the work itself and encouragement of the author. I owe similar debts to the professors and seminarians at the Institute of Historical Research in London and the Folger Shakespeare Library in Washington, D.C. Professor Mark H. Curtis and my fellow seminar members in the first Folger Post-doctoral Seminar in Tudor and Stuart Civilisation listened to my ideas with patience and made valuable suggestions about many matters.

In the gathering of material for Sadler's Henrician career librarians and archivists put me in the way of manuscripts and helped me in their interpretation. I want to thank the librarians and staffs of the following institutions in that regard: the Manuscript Division of the British Museum; the Round Room of the Public Record Office; the Hertfordshire Record Office; the Bodleian Library; the Library of Gonville and Caius College, Cambridge; Somerset House, the Principal Probate Register; the Bristol Archives Office; the Warwickshire Record Office; the Middlesex County Record Office; the Hackney Borough Public Library; the City of London Guildhall Muniments Room; Westminister Cathedral Muniments Room; the Victoria County History Office; the History of Parliament Trust Office; the National Portrait Gallery; the Department of Prints of the British Museum; the Louis Wilson Round Library of the University of North Carolina; the Ellen Clark Bertrand Library of Bucknell University and the Folger Shakespeare Library.

Special thanks are due to those who went beyond the normal limit of professional service in connection with my inquiries: Dr Kevin McDonnell, the keeper of Manuscripts at Westminster Cathedral; Mr Roy Strong of the National Portrait Gallery; Miss Clare Talbot of Hatfield House and Dr Marjorie Blatchford Bindoff, who let me see the proofs of her work on the calendar of the Bath MSS. at Longleat.

I gratefully acknowledge the financial support of the following funds and foundations, without whose subvention this work would have been impossible: the Woodrow Wilson Fellowship Foundation; the Southern Fellowship Foundation; the Smith Fund of the University of North Carolina—all of which contributed to the sustenance of my work as a doctoral candidate between 1958 and 1961. The Committee for the Encouragement of Faculty Research of Bucknell University provided me with a generous grant for the Summer of 1964, thus affording me the opportunity to complete the preparation of this manuscript. Finally, the Director of the Folger Shakespeare Library, Dr Louis B. Wright, encouraged me to apply for membership in the Folger Post-doctoral Seminar of 1964, not only thereby insuring me of additional financial support but also of the excitement of the Library, its staff and the scholars working there.

Some of the material of chh. 8 and 10 appeared in *BIHR* and *Huntington Library Quarterly* articles in 1965. I wish to thank the editors of those journals for their permission to use that material in this book.

I must not omit mention of the fact that several friends and colleagues took time off from their own labours to read parts of this manuscript, offering invaluable criticism without thereby inculpating themselves in my sins of commission and omission. I want especially to thank Ned Partridge of Bucknell, Drs G. R. Elton of Cambridge and S. B. Baxter, and Mark Curtis, now President of Scripps College, in that regard. Finally, I want to thank my research assistant, J. Michael Phelps, of the Center for Medieval and Renaissance Studies, U.C.L.A., for his help in reading the proofs and making the index.

A. J. S.

Lewisburg, Pennsylvania
January 1965

ABBREVIATIONS

APC	*Acts of the Privy Council,* ed. J. R. Dasent
APS	*The Acts of the Parliaments of Scotland,* ed. Thompson and Innes
BM	British Museum
Brewer	*The Reign of Henry VIII from his Accession to the Death of Wolsey,* by John Sharon Brewer
BIHR	*Bulletin of the Institute of Historical Research*
CHJ	*Cambridge Historical Journal*
CSPD	*Calendar of State Papers, Domestic*
CSPSp	*Calendar of State Papers, Spanish*
DNB	*Dictionary of National Biography,* reissued 1908–9
EcHR	*Economic History Review*
EHR	*English Historical Review*
Foedera	*Foedera, conventiones, litterae, etc.,* ed. Rymer and Sanderson
HP	*Hamilton Papers,* ed. Jos. Bain
L & P	*Letters and Papers, Foreign and Domestic, of the Reign of Henry VIII,* ed. Brewer, Gairdner and Brodie, 1862–1929
PCC	Prerogative Court of Canterbury, Probate Registers
ScHR	*Scottish Historical Review*
SP	*State Papers of the Reign of Henry VIII,* ed. by The Record Commission, 1830–.
SR	*The Statutes of the Realm,* ed. by The Record Commission, 1810–28
SSP	*Sadler State Papers,* ed. Clifford
TRHS	*Transactions of the Royal Historical Society*
VCH	*Victoria County History*
VE	*Valor Ecclesiasticus*

MANUSCRIPTS

Manuscripts preserved at the Public Record Office, London (PRO), are quoted by the call number there in use, according to the following key.

Chancery

C 1	Early Proceedings
C 3	Proceedings, Series II

C 38	Reports and Certificates
C 47	Miscellanea
C 48	Miscellaneous Papers
C 49	Parliament and Council Proceedings
C 54	Close Rolls
C 55	Additional Close Rolls
C 66	Patent Rolls
C 67	Supplementary Patent Rolls
C 82	Warrants for the Great Seal, Series II
C 84	Ecclesiastical Petitions
C 89	Certiorari Bundles, Rolls Chapel Series
C 142	Inquisitions *post mortem*
C 192	Miscellaneous fiats
C 218	Petty Bag Office, Returns of Members of Parliament

Exchequer: Treasury of Receipt

E 24	Wolsey's Patents
E 34	Privy Seals for Loans
E 36	Miscellaneous Books

Exchequer: King's Remembrancer

E 101	Accounts Various
E 114	Bonds
E 115	Certificates of Residence
E 118	Conventual Leases
E 122	Customs, Accounts of Collectors
E 135	Ecclesiastical Documents
E 149	Inquisitions *post mortem*
E 164	Miscellaneous Books, Series I
E 179	Subsidies
E 192	Private Collections
E 210	Deeds, Ancient Series 'D'

Exchequer: Augmentations Office

E 303	Conventual Leases
E 304	Conveyances of Crown Lands
E 305	Deeds of Purchase and Exchange
E 315	Miscellaneous Books

E 316   Particulars for Grants
E 318   Particulars for Grants
E 321   Proceedings of the Court
E 323   Treasurer's Accounts
E 326   Deeds, Ancient Series 'B'

Exchequer: Lord Treasurer's Remembrancer
E 351   Declared Accounts

Exchequer: Exchequer of Receipt
E 403   Issue Rolls
E 405   Receipt Rolls
E 407   Star Chamber Diets

King's Bench
KB 8   Baga de secretis

Land Revenue Office
LR 10   Particulars for Grants
LR 13   Rental Surveys
LR 14   Deeds, Modern Series 'E'

State Paper Office: Foreign Transcripts
PRO 30/2   Milan Archives
PRO 30/3   Paris Archives
PRO 31/9   Rome Archives, Series I
PRO 31/10   Rome Archives, Series II
PRO 31/11   Spanish Archives
PRO 31/18   Vienna Archives

Court of Requests
Requests 2   Bills of Complaint

Special Collections
SC 6   Ministers' and Receivers' Accounts
SC 11   Rentals and Surveys, Rolls
SC 12   Rentals and Surveys, Portfolios

State Papers Office: The Reign of Henry VIII

SP 1	Letters and Papers
SP 2	Folios
SP 3	Lisle Papers
SP 4	Signature by Stamp
SP 6	Tracts
SP 7	Wriothesley Papers
SP 49	Scotland, Series I, Henry VIII

NOTE ON STYLE AND DATES

Figures after references to *L & P* are to numbers of documents; the same is the case with regard to *HP*. In all other cases pages are referred to by arabic number, preceded by volume indications in roman numerals, where necessary. In transcripts from manuscripts, abbreviations have generally been extended and punctuation modernised, whenever it seemed necessary to render to a modern reader the sense of the original, with the result that capitals have been occasionally added where there are none in the documents. With these exceptions, the style and spelling of the manuscript material have been preserved.

All dates are given in New Style. Hence an event dated by Sadler 25 February 1539 appears here in the narrative under the year 1540. Wherever documents have been dated from the internal evidence of regnal years, that is made clear in my citations. No other calendar adjustments were made.

HEIR TO A FAIR INHERITANCE

I have no othre cumforte or helpe to call upon when I have nede, but
onlie you syn my olde mastre Belknapp departed...

HENRY SADLER to Thomas Cromwell

The search for Sir Ralph Sadler's origins can properly begin with the
Hertfordshire visitation made by Richmond Herald Henry St George
in 1634. He was investigating pedigrees and warrants to quarter arms;
the descendants of Sadler of Standon naturally occupied a good deal of
his time, since they were a very prominent county family. He was,
however, unable to trace the family beyond the early Tudors, a somewhat puzzling fact in the light of the genius of that age for inventing
ancient family trees. For heraldic purposes, Sir Ralph was the first of
his line.[1] No pedigree-hunter between 1572 and 1664 had any better
luck in that regard.[2]

Where the efforts of contemporaries and near contemporaries failed,
Canon Thomas Fuller, antiquarian and chaplain to Charles II, succeeded.
Sadler, it turned out, had been born at Hackney in Fuller's own county
of Middlesex, to the east of London, and was 'heir to a fair inheritance
there'.[3]

That Ralph Sadler was of a good Middlesex background thus became an 'historical' fact in so far as later writers were concerned.[4] The
fullest version of the story came from the hand of Sir Walter Scott, who
repeated the tale of comfortable and gentle origins in his contribution
to the *Sadler State Papers*.[5] Glossing Fuller's line, Scott assured his
audience that Sadler's birth 'was neither obscure and ignoble, nor so

---

[1] BM Harleian MSS. 1504, fos. 3–5, the Hertfordshire Visitation of 1579, added to in 1634.
[2] There are several Hertfordshire 'Visitation Books' in the British Museum, copies of the
Heralds' College originals under Anthony R. Wagner's custody. They are in Harleian MSS. 1546,
fos. 31–5v (1572); 1547, fo. 27 (1634); 1234, fos. 133r–156v (1664); 1565, fo. 61v (no date). The
last listed is the fullest for Sadler's marriage and his heirs. In the Hackney Public Library, London,
there is a fourteen-volume manuscript collection of armorial bearings of Hackney families,
beautifully done in colour on vellum: Thyssen MSS. 30/2, fos. 114a–136b, provide the details of
Sadler's arms, crest, lineage, etc. But pedigrees in the British Museum are silent on his parents.
[3] Fuller, *The History of the Worthies of England* (London: F. G. W. I. & W. G. 1662), p. 183.
[4] Especially, Lloyd, Scott, Fuller and Col. Stoney.   [5] I, ii.

much exalted above the middling rank of society as to contribute in any material degree to the splendid success of his career in life'.[1] Hackney came to be the place 'where his family had been for some time settled'.[2] Ralph Sadler was in fact the son of one Henry Sadler, a man

> not exempt from professional labour, and even from personal dependence... It does not, therefore, contradict what has been handed down to us concerning Henry Sadler's rank and estate, that he seems to have acted in some domestic capacity, probably as steward or surveyor to a nobleman, proprietor of a manor called Cilney, near Great Hadham, in Essex.[3]

At this point, familiar as we are with the nice points already scored in the 'storm over the gentry', we ought to take a closer look at Scott's social and genealogical commentary. A fair reading of his remarks makes Sadler out to be precisely one of those 'new men' whose rise in politics will serve as a classic example of at least one part of the gentry thesis: the steady climb of a man of good but humble birth into the chambers of the mighty. Like so many sons of Caedmon, the Sadlers of English history seem to have risen from the soil to be king's secretaries, if not kings. And along with responsibility came enough of power to provide the means toward a vast estate.[4]

It is a shame to say so, but much of what we are now learning of Tudor society is undermining our confidence in the myth of the new men, be they 'gentry' or 'middle class'. Their place in Tudor history is being carefully reviewed, with the consequence that John Sharon Brewer's durable theory of their rise being mirrored in the rising number of signet bills and privy seals, with its concomitant notion that they took their place by stepping over the bodies of fallen churchmen, no longer seems acceptable.[5] On the one hand, it is enough to recall that Henry VIII's council always contained at least four bishops.[6] Moreover, on the other hand, no sixteenth-century politician could readily subscribe to the idea of novelty, partly for intellectual reasons deeply

---

[1] *SSP*, I, i. See also Nicholas Sanders, *De origine ac progressu schismatis Angliae* (Cologne: Aggrippinae, 1585), p. 112: 'non obscuri nominis vir'.

[2] *SSP*, I, i. [3] *Idem.*

[4] R. H. Tawney, 'The Rise of the Gentry', *EcHR*, XI (1941), 27–8.

[5] See the classic statement of John Sharon Brewer, *The Reign of Henry VIII from his Accession to the Death of Wolsey*, 2 vols. (London: Longmans, 1884), I, 68, no longer acceptable in that form.

[6] On this and related points of ecclesiastics in politics see the study by Lacey Baldwin Smith, *Tudor Prelates and Politics* (Princeton University Press, 1953), *passim*.

rooted in Tudor thought and partly for the more obvious reason that attention to a man's affinity or connection was necessary before passing judgement on the individual. Our own awareness of the increasingly complex nature of social and political connections as the Tudors themselves understood them is now producing a new outlook in Tudor studies, an outlook in which the mutuality of dependence between master and man appears as the prerequisite of most careers. Dr Elton has admirably summed up the burden of work done by Richardson, MacCaffery and Neale, to name but a few of the main contributors to this revised picture, when remarking:

Everywhere, patronage organised the hierarchic social system. The old relations of master and man, of lord and servant, always dependent as much on the sentiments of duty and respect as on mutual interest, came to be crystallised in an extensive network of gifts and services ranging through the ranks of society.[1]

With regard to Scott's tale, three elements of it can be tested in the light of the new perspective mentioned above: the idea of the Hackney background and the fair inheritance; the notion that Henry Sadler was indeed part of some baronial connection centred on Essex; and, last of all, the view that Ralph Sadler's rise owed nothing to his father's place and function in the social hierarchy.

A single letter supplies the crucial hints which enable us to provide more satisfactory answers to these questions of origins and affinity. It is in Henry Sadler's Gothic hand and carries Thomas Cromwell's name as the receiver:

Ryght worshypfull and my syngler good mastre Crumwell I hertely recommende me unto you. And I thanke you for the grete cumforte and goodness to me and myn shoyd at all tymes. At my laste beynge with your mastreshyp ye saied that you wold be so good lorde to me to gett me the rest of the xxviii^{lis} of Mastre Shelley at hys returne out of Sussexe. If ye have not receyvd yt, I pray you hertely and in the way of charyte gett hit unto your handes. For then I reckyn hit as sure as yt were in my owne purse. Syr, I shoyd your mastreshyp howe I have boughte a howse in Haceney. It is xl^s o^d yere to be lett, and the quytrent is viii^d by the yere. And I thanke almyghtty God I have payde for hit with yn viii^{lis} ii^s. That payde I trust I my

---

[1] See Elton, *Reformation Europe, 1517–1559* (London: Collins, 1963), p. 300, as well as Sir John Neale's masterful Raleigh Lecture 'The Elizabethan Political Scene', delivered in 1954 and printed in his *Essays in Elizabethan History*. The notes to the Preface above supply other basic references.

1-2

wyfe and our childryn shall inioye the saied howse with the appurtenences to godly plesure. And with oughte the helpe of God and your mastreshyp I can make no shyft for the aforesaied payment. Wherfore good Mastre Crumwell have me in good rememberaunce to Mastre Shelley for my money, whiche is xxiiij^lis xiii^s iiij^d. Thus I am bolde to put your mastreshyp to prayer. I have no othre cumforte or helpe to call upon when I have nede, but onlie you syn my olde mastre Belknapp departed whose soull God pardon. And thys ys undeservyd in my behaulfe. But your mastreshyp hath and shal have me for one of your dayle orators duryng my lyfe as God knowithe who ever preserve you in mych worshyp with long lyfe and good helthe. Wrygttyn at Tiltey the fyrst daie of June. By your orator duryng lyfe Henry Sadleyer.[1]

It is important to keep in mind the matters of substance in the letter, if the problem of Sadler's origin is to be dealt with satisfactorily. It was addressed to Thomas Cromwell. A man named Shelley apparently had some business in Sussex, from whence he would soon return. Shelley owed Henry Sadler a sum of money great enough to enable the latter to get clear of a debt contracted in the form of a house newly purchased at Hackney. The appeal to Cromwell stemmed from the fact that Sadler's former master, one Belknapp, had died, apparently recently, leaving Henry Sadler no option but to press boldly a favour with another more powerful than either himself or Shelley. Finally, the most critical for the case to be made here, the date of the letter is incomplete, lacking any mention of the year of its origin.

James Gairdner, in the course of his work on the *Letters and Papers*, assigned the letter in question to 1531.[2] His reason for doing so seems to have been the existence of another letter begging Cromwell's favour, written by Henry Sadler from Tiltey and internally dated 1531.[3] But Gairdner's attribution is demonstrably wrong. In fact, it is safe to say that the discovery of that error in itself enables us to understand Henry Sadler's place in Tudor society, his relationship to Cromwell and, consequently, the basis of Ralph Sadler's political career.

It is implicit in our document that Shelley and Belknapp were men normally within the circle of Cromwell's friends or official acquaintances. Further, Henry Sadler apparently had some expectation of seeing Cromwell in the normal course of events. And in the light of the

[1] PRO, SP 1/66, fo. 47, Henry Sadler to Thomas Cromwell, 11 July 1521.
[2] *L & P*, v, 279.
[3] *Ibid.* p. 333, Henry Sadler to Thomas Cromwell, 11 July 1531.

reference to the new house at Hackney, it seems that the Sadlers were trying to move up a notch by getting established in one of London's very fashionable suburbs. It is further implied that Sadler's children still were under his own roof, where it is hoped more pleasant circumstances would prevail, if only the house could be paid for. Now it is hard to reconcile these statements with the 1531 date for the letter. Ralph Sadler, the oldest of Henry Sadler's two children, would be twenty-four years of age in 1531, and thus hardly describable as a child under his father's care. More to the point, we know that Ralph Sadler was placed in Cromwell's service at a very early age.[1] It is incredible that he would have described himself as Cromwell's dependent, 'as to him that hath hitherto from the yeres of discressyon nurisshed broughte up and admyryd me' had he lived with his father in 1531. Nor is it likely that in that year Henry Sadler would have overlooked his son's good offices as an intermediary in a suit with Cromwell, since by 1526 Ralph was one of Cromwell's senior clerks.[2]

The name Belknap argues even more strongly against the date assigned by Gairdner. If Henry Sadler's recently deceased master was a man whose business about 1531 was of the kind to bring him into contact with Cromwell frequently, he ought to be easily identifiable with the circle of courtiers, politicians or administrators with whom Cromwell dealt at that time or in the immediate past.[3] But the only Belknapp or Belknap of any note in early Tudor government circles was Sir Edward Belknap, the great revenue administrator whose career under Henry VII and his son Professor Richardson recently rescued from oblivion.[4] The trouble with that Belknap is simple: *he died in 1521.*[5]

Although it is wise to avoid the 'lucky dip' principle, the temptation to fit Sir Edward Belknap into the frame of our picture proved to be a fruitful one. That Belknap had a brother-in-law named William Shelley.[6] Shelley was a government man, a justice of the court of

---

[1] *SSP*, II, 618, where the epitaph of Sadler is transcribed.

[2] PRO, SP 1/127, fo. 250, Ralph Sadler to Thomas Cromwell, Oct. 1537; see also SP 1/235, fo. 67, undated, for another remark of Ralph's addressed to his mentor.

[3] *L & P*, III, i, 331 and 920, which show Belknap's work for Wolsey.

[4] *Tudor Chamber Administration*, pp. 201–5, and various index entries.

[5] *Ibid.* p. 204.

[6] *L & P*, III, i, 1,203. See also Belknap's will among the Canterbury probate records preserved at Somerset House, London, PCC 17 Maynwaryng.

common pleas whose eyre took him to Sussex.[1] Hence the connection between Cromwell, Belknap and Shelley becomes meaningful on the assumption that our letter was truly written about 1521 rather than a decade later. While that in itself does not tell us anything about the Tiltey problem or about the exact nature of the relationship between Henry Sadler and his patrons, it does put us in the way of the facts necessary for the clarification of such relationships.

Belknap's activities as an administrator are reflected in accounts and other administrative records which also show something of Sadler's work for his old master. As early as 1517 prests of money[2] were given to Henry Sadler at Belknap's order.[3] In the same year Sadler is mentioned as a collector of the impost on wine arriving in London from France; Belknap was England's chief butler.[4] On other occasions between 1517 and 1520 Ralph's father performed other routine tasks involving the collection or expenditure of royal funds, sometimes in harness with Shelley.[5] The obvious conclusion from all this is a simple one: failing to find evidence of Sadler's employment in such offices prior to the entry of Belknap into the accounts, we must assume that Henry Sadler was one of Sir Edward's clerks.[6]

Other accounts demonstrate that Henry Sadler was a man of some importance in Belknap's entourage. A book of royal payments for 1519–20 has entries proving that Sadler received over £700 for the purchase of canvas and buckram earmarked for the building programme for the Field of Cloth of Gold.[7] Richard Gibson of the Revels office, with whom Sadler did some business as early as 1517,[8] recorded Sadler as the receiver of goods for the work at Calais.[9] The declared accounts of Robert Fowler, the undertreasurer there, indicate that Sadler constantly received prests to facilitate the preparation of the splendid pageantry planned for 1520.[10] Belknap was the administrator of the

[1] *L & P*, III, i, 1,203 thus serves to clarify Shelley's 'coming out of Sussex'.
[2] Simply used to indicate an advance for official purposes.
[3] *L & P*, II, ii, 3,862.
[4] PRO, E 101/86/5, fo. 105 v.
[5] PRO, E 351/455–6, Belknap's accounts for 1519–20, where Sadler is frequently mentioned. See also BM Royal MSS. 14 B XI for other notices as early as 1515.
[6] PRO, E 101/613/8–9 and E 36/183.
[7] PRO, SP 1/29, fos. 170–80, 'The Kinges Booke of Paymentes anno 11–12 Henry VIII', calendared in *L & P*, III, ii, 3,695.
[8] See note 3 above.   [9] PRO, E 36/217, fo. 156r.
[10] PRO, SP 1/20, fos. 79–82.

entire project,[1] a fact sufficient to explain Sadler's employment as chief purveyor for the artists charged with making a convincing display of England's might and Wolsey's magnificence.[2]

It also seems likely that Belknap's patronage saved Henry Sadler from the threat of Wolsey's displeasure when the work in France almost came to a halt. It availed nothing to complain that funds came too slowly.[3] Despite assurances by Belknap to his fellow commissioners, Sir Nicholas Vaux and Sir Edward Sandys, to the effect that all that was humanly possible was being done to speed the works, they were less than convinced. Henry Sadler, for one, had failed to declare his accounts on time.[4] Vaux, anxious to spare himself the cardinal's wrath, which was only slightly less terrible and much more immediate than the king's, asked Wolsey to threaten Sadler and the artisans with imprisonment, a fate from which they were spared by virtue of Belknap's intercession.[5]

It is clear from what has already been said that Belknap's influence on Sadler senior was considerable after 1517. It can also be shown that before that date the same was true. The place of the earliest connection was Warwickshire, where Belknap had a large estate, although he was Kentish by birth.[6] Most of his lands were in the Shakespeare country, and it was there that he served in local government on many occasions. His head manor, 'le Stiewardys place', was located in Barlichway hundred and it served as the focal point of his estate management, as the name itself implies. He was a great man thereabouts.[7]

Little wonder, then, that we find Henry Sadler settled in that county. There were a number of Sadlers in Knightslow and Barlichway hundreds, the locale of Belknap's real power. On the Belknap lands themselves several Sadlers were rated to the subsidies imposed by Henry VIII, including one 'Harry Sadler' of Astley rated at £5 *pro bonis*.[8]

---

[1] See Sydney Anglo, 'Le Camp du Drap d'Or et les entreveres d'Henri VIII et de Charles-Quint', *Les Fêtes de la Renaissance*, ed. Jean Jacquot, 2 vols. II, *Fêtes et cérémonies au temps de Charles Quint* (Paris: Centre National de la Recherche Scientifique, 1960), esp. p. 129.

[2] BM Cotton MSS. Caligula D VII, fo. 218a cites Sadler's position by name.

[3] *Ibid.* 218b.   [4] *L & P*, III, i, 825.

[5] Sydney Anglo, 'Public Spectacle in Early Tudor Policy, 1485–1547' (unpublished doctoral dissertation, The University of London, 1958), p. 231.

[6] See the account given in BM Add. MSS. 5509, fos. 2d, 8d and 9; also 5937, fo. 32d.

[7] *Tudor Chamber Administration*, pp. 202–6.

[8] PRO, E 179/192/117a and 120, subsidy rolls for 1505 and 1519–20 respectively. For a guide to the interpretation of these rolls see A. Peyton, 'The Village Population in the Tudor Lay Subsidy Rolls', *EHR*, xxx (Apr. 1915), 234–50, where *pro bonis* and *in terris* are explained as interchangeable terms used to express the wealth of a subject.

That figure accords well enough with the status of Henry Sadler, who spent the early years of the sixteenth century serving Belknap as a steward on his Warwickshire estates, lands eventually acquired by Sir Ralph Sadler.[1]

This identification is made all the more probable in the light of the utter failure of Hackney records to mention any Sadlers whatsoever. Apart from the Hackney letter of 1521 already cited, there is not a shred of evidence placing Henry Sadler in the beautifully wooded London suburb of Fuller's account.[2] The court rolls of the manor of Grumbolds, an episcopal estate of the bishopric of London, fail to reveal any Henry Sadler or indeed any other Sadler before Sir Ralph among the freemen called to frankpledge.[3] Only in the 1540s do we find Sir Ralph himself well established in both the manorial and town records.[4] Middlesex heraldic records know nothing of any Sadler before Sir Ralph; nor do the subsidy rolls for Hackney, which was taxed as part of Osultone hundred, reveal that name. In fact not even Sir Ralph was assessed there. While he served as chief assessor in 1541 and again in 1546, he was rated with the king's household.[5] No Sadler was ever rated in the hundred at an earlier date.[6] The only Henry Sadler liable to assessment there was Sir Ralph's son, not his father.[7] Parish records, not systemati-

[1] The evidence is found in the *Victoria History of the Counties of England: A History of Warwick-shire*, ed. William Page and others, 6 vols. (London: Constable, 1906–51), III, 152; IV, 167 and 219; V, 70; VI, 225. (All volumes hereafter cited simply as *VCH*.)

[2] Hackney was an upper class suburb, *extra muros* in the sixteenth century. The list of prominent Tudors living there included the earl of Lennox, Lady Margaret Douglas, Sir Richard Cromwell and Sir Francis Bryan. The town was 3½ miles north-east of St Paul's and 5 miles from West-minster. See John Stow, *A Survey of London*, ed. Charles Letherbridge Kingsford, 2 vols. (Oxford: Clarendon Press, 1908), II, 74.

[3] Hackney Public Library, Thyssen MSS. Y 150, pt. 1, m. 13, for a notice of Sir Ralph Sadler 'de Hackeny in comitu Middlesesiensis'; for a similar mention see also PRO, E 315/213, fo. 15 b.

[4] Various views of frankpledge mention Sadler in relationship to Hackney lands upon which services were owing. Often he is listed with the defaulters: Hackney Public Library, Thyssen MSS. Y 150, pt. 1, mm. 13 a, 13 d, 14 a and 14 d; Y 235, where he is called 'firmarius domini regis ibidem' with regard to the manor of King's Hold (20 Apr. anno 34); see also Middlesex Record Office, Acc. 193/1–10 and Acc. 282/2, covering Hackney for the period 1513–72. The Thyssen MSS. deal with 1542–52.

[5] PRO, E 179/141/113 (1524), 141/116 (1525), 141/127 (1542), 141/131 (1546), 141/134 (1541), 141/137 (1543), 141/138 (1542–3). More ancient rolls were also searched, covering the period 1330–1443 (E 179/141/23) and 1460–1516 (E 179/141/164).

[6] PRO, E 179/238/98, 141/141, the entire surviving collection for Middlesex assessments in 1524, especially complete for Westminster.

[7] Such certificates were *fiats* issued by the exchequer allowing the persons named to be taxed in a place other than that in which they had their principal residence. They were usually granted to merchants and government agents required to move about in the course of their work: see PRO, E 115/337/71, 343/18 and 359/27 for Henry Sadler of Standon.

cally kept before 1550, to be sure, record no Sadler as born, baptised or buried there before 1650.[1] The extensive collections of wills at Somerset House, the London Guild Hall and the Hackney Borough Library show no hint of Henry Sadler's existence.[2]

The conclusion is forced upon us. If Henry Sadler lived at Hackney he must have been a mean man, surely less than able to provide a fair inheritance for his first-born son. He must have been unable to bear the rate imposed on every soul worth twenty shillings in either land or goods. He was either unfree or otherwise unworthy to frankpledge. Apparently, if he ever lived at Hackney, he made no will there. Even allowing the biggest of margins for the accidents of the survival of documents in several series which tell continuous stories about the Herons, Alingtons and Elringtons, all old Hackney families still very much alive under the early Tudors, Henry Sadler would have had to be an obscure man to have remained so well hidden from public view.

Given our Belknap connection, the truth appears to be that Henry Sadler was a Warwickshire man at loose ends after the death of his master and patron. That he bought a house in Hackney soon after the blow of Belknap's death seems to indicate some hope or expectation that he would soon enter government service in some capacity. The fact that he was renting a house there on a very nominal rent, with his son as his landlord, in 1542, may even be taken to indicate that he never

[1] Hackney Public Library, Thyssen MSS. Y 221, a complete transcript of the registers of St John's at Hackney, covering the years 1550–1832. The originals are now in the possession of the London County Council.

[2] For the wills relating to Hackney preserved at Somerset House see S. A. Smith and E. A. Fry, *The Index Library: Index of Wills Preserved in the Prerogative Courts of Canterbury, 1384–1558*, 2 vols. (London: British Record Society, 1898). The same wills are excerpted in Hackney Public Library, Thyssen MSS. Y 210. The City of London Guildhall Library has very extensive holdings of wills not proved in the PCC registers, since in theory such registers dealt only with testators who held land in more than a single county. Middlesex landholders owning land nowhere else had to prove wills either in the bishop of London's archdeaconry court or in his commissary court. Both register series are preserved at the Guildhall. Guildhall Library MSS. 9051/1–19 contain 'Probate archives, register of the wills of the Archdeaconry Court of London, 1393–1807'. Omissions in that series are supplied by 9052/1–50, the 'Probate archives, register of the wills of the Archdeaconry Court of London, 1524–1807', of which box no. 1 has the originals from 1524 to 1602. The bishop of London's commissary court registers are in 9171/1–54, of which set volume 11 covers 1539–48 and volume 12 1548–53, while volume 13 covers 1553–8. The wills themselves were examined in the originals (9172/1–3). Dr Kevin McDonnell of Queen Mary's College, University of London, tells me that the Consistory Court register kept by the bishop of London has no will for any Sadlers. On the basis of his thorough study of Hackney landholding, he assures me that Sadler was not of an ancient Hackney family.

managed to make good his suit to Cromwell.[1] But that is sheer speculation. All that we know for sure is this: the family did live there during
the 1530s and they seem to have settled there in 1521.[2]

What remains puzzling is the exact nature of the link that connects
Belknap, Cromwell and the lord of Tiltey abbey with Henry Sadler
after 1521.

In that pivotal year in Henry Sadler's fortunes the Crown directed
him to pay a certain sum of money to William Shelley, whom we have
already identified as Belknap's brother-in-law, and who was the
principal executor of that knight's estate. The money was owed to
Belknap in connection with his work as butler under Henry VIII and
was to be paid into the estate in order to compensate the dead administrator for his diets at Calais.[3] The carrying out of that task brought
Henry Sadler once more into contact with Shelley; in fact it had
brought him back to Warwickshire even before his master's death, as
Belknap gathered his family, friends and servants when he knew himself to be dying. The Crown directive found Henry Sadler sadly
thinking out the future that would await him should he remain masterless for long in a world that measured men by their masters' position.
Not that he was unprovided for: Belknap favoured him in his will,
singling him out as 'my most trusted servaunte who shall have for the
payns he hath alwaies done for me in times past fowre pounds yerely
duryng hys lyfe out of my manor of Dorcette in Warwyckshyre'.[4] But
the £4 a year was scant comfort when measured against his loss of place.

It was precisely in that sense that the Belknap patronage was to
rescue Henry Sadler. The Belknaps were cousins of the Grey family,
especially close to the Ferrers–Grey line descended from Sir Edward
Grey, Elizabeth Woodville's first husband. That family was in turn
related to the Dorset–Grey connection, which then gave England its
second ranking peer, the marquis of Dorset.[5] It was doubtless that

---

[1] BM Add. MSS. 35824, fos. 24b, 26a and 27b, parts of the 'Account Book of Gervase Cawood,
Receiver General to Sir Ralph Sadler'.

[2] BM Cotton MSS. Titus B I, fo. 153, Henry Sadler to Ralph Sadler, 16 Dec. 1531.

[3] PRO, SP 1/23, fo. 123a, a warrant dated 20 Nov. 1521: 'That of suche our monie that re-
mayneth in the handes of the executors of the saied Sir Edwarde of the arrearages and issues of
our pryse of wyne and also customes called butlerage or in the handes of Henry Sadler late
servaunt to the saied Sir Edwarde...'

[4] Somerset House, PCC Register, 17 Maynwaryng.

[5] *Idem*, for the relationship between Belknap and Ferrers. See also BM Add. MSS. 5509,
fos. 2d and 9; *DNB*, article 'Thomas Grey'; *VCH Warwickshire*, VI, 225.

relationship which accounts for Henry Sadler's entry into the Dorset service, for the letters from Tiltey, not 'Cillney' as Scott's copyist had it, reveal that Sadler was a Dorset steward in 1521, since Tiltey was their head manor in Essex. Indeed, Henry Sadler remained in their service until 1531, at which time he left that employ due to the declining fortunes of the family.[1]

Having resolved in this way the Belknap–Tiltey–Dorset connection, it merely remains to show in what manner Cromwell fitted into the picture. Naturally, the fact of Belknap's political activities at a time when Cromwell was already Wolsey's factotum is enough to allow us to suppose that Henry Sadler would know Thomas Cromwell. No doubt that was their first connection. But the Dorset affinity bound them in a common service of a different sort. The Grey family had fallen upon misfortunes and in their necessity from time to time fell back upon the services of their attorney. While it might prove galling to do so, they could not really manage their affairs without seeking the patronage of Thomas Cromwell.[2] He had served the marchioness and her son, the second marquis, in various legal capacities while also managing a part of Wolsey's business.[3] That was in itself not startling, if we recall that the first marquis lifted Wolsey from obscurity as an Oxford don late in the fifteenth century, bringing him into the family

[1] *L & P*, v, 279, 333 and 584 for the letters in question. Here some remarks about Scott's 'Cillney' are in order. Sir Walter believed that Henry Sadler served a nobleman whose seat lay at Cillney, Essex. He was unable to identify the magnate for the very good reason that the site did not exist. Sir H. Ellis, in the course of editing his *Original Letters Illustrative of English History*, 3rd ser. 4 vols. (London: 1846), II, 144, presented a copy of Henry Sadler's letter of 16 Dec. 1531, noting the error made by Scott's copyist. He then asserted that Sadler worked for Thomas, Lord Audley, who was of course lord chancellor. But Audley took possession of Tiltey as late as Apr. 1542, as a result of the death of the dowager marchioness of Dorset. For the details of Audley's tenure and the subsequent history of Tiltey see Folger Shakespeare Library MS. Z. c. 12, fo. 13, an indenture made in 1588, by which Thomas Howard, the second son of the duke of Norfolk, conveyed the land for a sum of £5,000 to Henry Maynard. He was given the reversion reserved to the Crown as a means of keeping the estate in the Dorset family, since he had married Elizabeth Grey, the youngest daughter of the marchioness, in 1538. Sadler's rise could not be laid at the lord chancellor's door, short of a critical anachronism. By 1542 Ralph had been in Cromwell's service at least sixteen years, up until that minister's death in 1540. The connection of Tiltey with the Greys is beyond doubt: see *L & P*, IV, i, 1,611; v, 279, 333, 584, 1,539, 1,557 and 1,584. The grant to Audley is in *L & P*, XVII, 285 (2).
[2] The troubles of the Dorset family may be followed in *L & P*, IV, i, 1,611 and the other references given in the note immediately preceding this one, covering the years 1525–32.
[3] *L & P*, III, ii, 2,437, Cecily Dorset to Thomas Cromwell, 14 Aug. 1522, identifies Cromwell as 'my sonne Marquys servaunt'. Cromwell's nephew, Richard Williams, alias Cromwell, also served the Dorsets: see *DNB*, article 'Thomas Cromwell'.

service as a chaplain.[1] In 1521 Henry Sadler merely read the omens well. Knowing that he could not count on his new master for much, he turned for help to their attorney, who also happened to be an old acquaintance from government days as well as the cardinal's man. Whereas the Dorsets were declining, Cromwell was on the rise.[2]

Again and again, Henry Sadler revived that connection. In the 1520s he used it to become involved in the royal service in a capacity that remains obscure. On one occasion he wrote to Cromwell about some problem related to money owing to the king.[3] Later on, when his worst fears about the Dorset fortunes were only too fully realised, he sought Cromwell's help, carefully using as an intermediary his son Ralph, in an attempt to secure a place in the royal administration in lieu of that at Tiltey. Complaining of the injustices he had suffered, Henry Sadler begged Ralph's help with Cromwell:

Desyre him to be good to me son Raff. Where as I sholde have had of my lorde at thys tyme xx markes I can gett nevar a pennie but feyer wordes with whyche I cannot lyve. My lorde hath putt awaie hys yeomen at thys tyme and dothe intende after Christmas to putt awaie more. Therefore I pray you I may be recommendid to your good mastre and desyre hym by your humble suyt to gett me thoffice of the Toure or some othre so that I shal be nyghe London.

Both the hopes and the fears, it was added, were to be frankly conveyed to Ralph's mother, who lived at Hackney.[4] It is certain that Henry Sadler shortly thereafter left the Dorset service, although we cannot state that he secured a government post in 1531, the true year of this second letter.[5] Thus the only link in a chain of dependence stretching

---

[1] Pollard, *Henry VIII*, p. 29, n. 2; *Wolsey*, pp. 12 and 304, stresses that connection, as does Charles Ferguson, *Naked to Mine Enemies* (Boston: Little, Brown and Co., 1958), p. 52.

[2] *L & P*, XIII, ii, 732. In 1507 only Stafford, duke of Buckingham, outranked Thomas Grey, the first marquis of Dorset. The Greys never managed to shake the onus of their Yorkist birth, though for a time the second marquis was a tournament favourite of Henry VIII.

[3] PRO, E 101/519/7, a warrant dated 5 Sept. 1525, permitting Sir William Holgill, master of the Savoy and farmer of the revenues arising out of the hospital lands in Hackney, to take Sadler's account. See also BM Cotton MSS. Titus B I, fo. 153, where Henry Sadler claims that Cromwell will no doubt 'knowleige I doe owe to the kinges grace but iiij^lis and all in monie if it plese hym to loke upon my boke'. PRO, SP 1/66, fo. 183, Henry Sadler to Thomas Cromwell, asked the latter's intervention with Holgill in order to get him to take Sadler's account earlier than usual.

[4] BM Cotton MSS. Titus B I, fo. 153.

[5] This statement is based on the fact that from 1521 to 1532 there are letters from Henry Sadler to both his son and Cromwell mentioning the Dorset connection and seeking some other position. After 1532 no further talk of the Grey affinity appears.

over a generation was now Henry Sadler's son Ralph, given into Cromwell's service as a boy.

On these grounds it is impossible to agree with Scott, who sums up the 'traditional' story of Sadler's rise. Obviously, Henry Sadler's connection had everything to do with his son's place in politics, which was to depend completely on his place in Cromwell's household. If, as Dr Elton has wisely remarked, it was terrifying to be masterless, it was equally true that having the *right* master was crucial.[1] Despite the efforts and success of Henry VII in striking out against the worst elements of connection and affinity, especially livery and maintenance, social security still in large measure hinged on remnants of bastard feudalism, which, stripped of any pejorative connotation, and seen in the context of a shifting society, supplied the thongs that bound master and man in ties of mutual service. In an age only imperfectly cured of the disease of private warfare, that vestige of an older society which still infected the autumn of English chivalry, Henry Sadler and his son both hoped to escape the worst uncertainties of life by virtue of their connection.[2]

While head-smashing bullies still prowled the countryside giving their private brand of justice, Henry Sadler did well in his reliance on Belknap, Dorset and Cromwell.[3] The gradual movement toward a less militant concept of service was not then fully matured, and the rise of Sir Ralph Sadler by virtue of his father's shifting connections is itself a proof of the gradualness of the change. The Sadlers, father and son alike, provided their masters with services that were a far cry from that done in some earlier affinities, which were hardly more than schools for brawlers and bawdy men, so mightily laughed at in the persons of Nym and Pistol.

[1] *The Tudor Revolution in Government* (Cambridge University Press, 1953) p. 81.

[2] Kenneth B. Macfarlane, 'Bastard Feudalism', *BIHR*, xx (1943–5), 161–80, for this interpretation of dependence and the decline of tenure by serjeanty.

[3] That this statement is no exaggeration can best be seen by glancing at the *Discourse of the Common Weal of this Realm of England*, ed. Elizabeth Lamond (Cambridge University Press, 1929), pp. 39 and 47. See also BM Lansdowne MSS. 827, nos. 6 and 830, item 13, for two cases of murder in Wiltshire attributed to armed retainers during Elizabeth I's reign.

2

THE SORCERER'S APPRENTICE

And what was Ralph Sadler but a clerk of Cromwell?

SCOTT, *Kenilworth*

The obscurity of Henry Sadler's life which was so gracefully disguised by Scott's *dicta* brought something beyond uncertain connections to him. He had two sons, Ralph and John.[1] Nothing of any note about the childhood of either of them is known, a fact that ought not to surprise us in the light of the dearth of material about the early years of Tudor statesmen in general. The material that might flesh out the bones of state papers and later recollections has more often than not vanished, if indeed it ever did exist in recorded form. Apart from isolated and often fanciful tales, we begin to know most politically important sixteenth-century people only when they are already public figures. Hence Ralph Sadler's youth and apprenticeship are capable of study only in a most oblique way in the years before we find him at work within Cromwell's household.

Sir Walter Scott, for whom Sadler held a certain interest which we shall return to again, correctly noted Sadler's station in *Kenilworth*, where the notorious Ralph Varney passes this comment on Ralph Sadler's low origin: 'And what was Ralph Sadler but a clerk of Cromwell? and he gazed eighteen fair lordships.'[2] Setting aside Varney's annoyance over the fact that Sadler escaped Cromwell's fate, we may once more take our departure from Scott and trace Sadler's rise in Cromwell's service.

We know from Sadler's funeral monument that he was born in 1507 and entered Cromwell's service when the future statesman and reformer was still little more than an aspiring lawyer and merchant:

This worthie knighte in hys youthe was browte up with Thomas Cromwell ...and when he came to mannes estate he became his secretaire, by meanes whereof he did many thinges touchinge matiers of state and by that meanes he in continuance of time was knowne to King Harry...[3]

[1] See the *DNB* for John Sadler.   [2] *Kenilworth* (London: Murray, 1856), p. 113.
[3] *SSP*, II, 618.

How old was Ralph Sadler when he entered Cromwell's household? We cannot be sure, although we may suppose that he was a mere boy. Sadler once described himself as 'nurisshed . . . and admyryd' by Cromwell from the 'yeres of discressyon',[1] which we may take to mean the canonical 'age of reason', that is the seventh year, or even the common confirmation age of twelve. Beyond that, the only other sure reference to Ralph Sadler before 1526 is that general mention of his children made by Henry Sadler in 1521.

From 1526 on, however, the details of the future secretary's career are supplied by a variety of letters and papers of an official kind. Even the earliest of these imply that before he was twenty-one Sadler was Cromwell's trusted clerk, fully aware of the details of Wolsey's ministry and self-aggrandisement. And the very first letter touching Sadler's work for Cromwell relevant to the cardinal's affairs warrants the assertion that he had had a careful grooming, while also illustrating the operation of what we may well label a system of administrative apprenticeship with its centre in the household of the king's chief minister of the day and the chief minister to be. For that reason alone the text is worth quoting in part:

Woorshypful Syr it may please you to be advertysed that I have receyvyd your lettre with my lorde hys warrante for John Abell therinclosed wherewith accordyng to your commaundement Stephan Vaughan and Richard Swifte ben now repayred to Mr Doctor Stubbes at Yorke Palace there to receyve such soomes of monie as in the asme ys contayned. And as touchyng Ric Morgan hys matyer the trowthe ys that Doctor Dolman, Doctor Bennett and Doctor Bell have shewyd hym as much favour as to them was possyble and have promysed that whatsoever ye wyl devyse to be doon in the advancemente of the same they wyl use such polyce therin that your purpose shal take effecte. . . All othre commaundementes conteyned in your said lettre I truste to use such dyligent service in thaccomplishmente of the same that no defaute or negligence in me shalbe espyed. At London thys present Satersdaie your humble servaunte Rafe Sadeleyer.[2]

[1] PRO, SP 1/127, fo. 250, Ralph Sadler to Thomas Cromwell, Oct. 1537.

[2] PRO, SP 1/235, fo. 67, same to the same, undated. The letter appears to belong to 1526. A badly mutilated paper seal with the *chi rho* monogram in use in Wolsey's household is plainly visible. Internal evidence makes a Fall 1526 date certain, since all the persons referred to were then in correspondence with Wolsey and his agents about the extraordinary receipts (*recepta forinseca*) taken at York Palace over a period of 14 months by Swift and others: see *L & P*, iv, ii, 2,538 (2), item 8.

Sadler, aged nineteen, was clearly already working in a secretarial capacity to Cromwell.[1]

The key to that letter just cited and to similar ones is Merriman's statement describing Cromwell as the executor of Wolsey's building programme in the mid-1520s. The Cromwell correspondence of those years rests on the details of the dissolution of several monasteries to facilitate the erection of colleges witnessing the cardinal's power and magnanimity.[2] Cromwell and his clerks attended to the valuations, deeds of sale and the acts of surrender in Wolsey's behalf. We meet Stephen Vaughan and William Brabazon as well as Sadler, all of them brought up to administrative work by Cromwell's service to Wolsey;[3] as Cromwell was brought to royal service by the cardinal, so he was to repeat that pattern and insinuate his own men into the king's affairs in the 1530s.[4]

Thus Ralph Sadler began his career as the double beneficiary of the nature of Tudor affinities, kept busy with the details of his immediate master's work in Wolsey's entourage, which Cromwell had entered in 1514, when we may suppose Sadler was taken into his own patron's household.[5] Sadler learned how to make surveys, the techniques of land transfer and the mysteries of seisin.[6] He accompanied his master when this or that priory was dissolved.[7] He gained from Wolsey the grant of powers of attorney in recognition of his newly gotten skills, and used his warrant to take possession of Essex and Suffolk lands held by the dean and canons of Cardinal's College, Oxford.[8] One of Wolsey's deftly tricked patents emblazoned with the Norfolk arms as well names Sadler as the agent in the surrender of Felixstow Priory to Wolsey's use.[9]

---

[1] Somerset House, PCC Register 23 Stephens, where Sadler's will clearly implies a 1507 birthdate, an implication confirmed in the official inquisition *post mortem* in PRO, C142/215/259.

[2] Roger B. Merriman, *The Life and Letters of Thomas Cromwell*, 2 vols. (Oxford: Clarendon Press, 1902), I, 51.

[3] For Vaughan and other Cromwellians of his day see Walter C. Richardson, *Stephen Vaughan, Financial Agent of Henry VIII* (Baton Rouge: Louisiana State University Press, 1953), a valuable work on the administrative and diplomatic career of a man of some prominence in the Wolsey-Cromwell era.

[4] Florence M. G. Evans, *The Principal Secretary of State* (Manchester University Press, 1923), pp. 26–7, and esp. p. 33, n. 2, as well as *The Tudor Revolution in Government*, pp. 81–2.

[5] See the *DNB* article on Cromwell.

[6] See *L & P*, IV, i, 989, for typical business falling to Cromwell in this regard.   [7] *Ibid.* II, 4,623.

[8] PRO, E 24/23/15, a collection of Wolsey's patents in which Sadler and Nicholas Gifford are often styled 'nostros veros et legittimos attornatores' by Wolsey's draftsmen.

[9] See the mention of this in PRO, SP 1/52, fos. 101–3; for the original patent see E 24/23/21.

Sadler was clearly not the cardinal's agent in any direct sense; in all he was Cromwell's man.[1] That comes through in the surrender of Mountjoy priory in Norwich, where Sadler is described as Cromwell's witness.[2] The point is clearly made by Ralph himself in relating Wolsey's wishes to Cromwell at the time of the cardinal's fall. In a fit of anxiety about the fate of his colleges, Wolsey urged Ralph to remind Cromwell that 'they are in a manner *opera manuum tuarum*'.[3] The king could not be moved, however, and the lands were put to other use.[4]

The routine work done before 1529 could not have prepared Sadler for the crisis of that year and the extraordinary tasks that fell to him as a consequence of Wolsey's fall. Chief among these was the role he had to play in extricating his own master from the disaster suffered by the king's minister. When the gathering resentment of churchmen, courtiers and politicians finally brought Wolsey down, Cromwell at first worked to save his master, using his own funds in that effort, even if he did subsequently send Sadler to urge the necessity of reimbursement on the good grounds that Wolsey could not claim poverty, whatever problems he did have.[5] Cromwell was badly shaken, a fact implicit in his drafting his will in that year for the first time, an instrument in which Sadler figured as both beneficiary and executor: he was to receive 200 marks and his master's library in the event of Cromwell's death. That he was named to execute the will urges his primacy among Cromwell's clerks at a difficult time.[6]

1529, it is well known, was the year in which Cromwell declared that he would 'make or mar' his future.[7] As the reaction against Wolsey gathered momentum, Cromwell, always the brilliant pragmatist, realised that he had himself reaped a crop of 'abundant hate'.[8] To

---

[1] PRO, SP 1/42, fo. 146a, undated notice of a murder case in which the men of Cromwell and Wolsey figure prominently, including John Williamson, Cromwell's brother-in-law and Thomas Avery, Sadler's lifelong friend and agent.

[2] *L & P*, IV, iii, 5,411, 1 Apr. 1529.

[3] Jesus College MSS. 674, fo. 170.

[4] *L & P*, IV, iii, 6,076, Thomas Cromwell to Thomas Wolsey, 12 July 1529.

[5] Idem, undated, Ralph Sadler to Thomas Wolsey, 12 July 1529.

[6] PRO, SP 1/54, fos. 269–78, 12 July 1529. The editor of *L & P*, IV, ii, 5,772, attributed the draft to Wriothesley, with corrections made in Cromwell's hand. Sadler and Wriothesley, however, wrote not very similar hands. Hence, the evidence of fo. 275r is important, for there 'Ralph Sadler' is written with the flourishes peculiar to Sadler's hand.

[7] George Cavendish, *The Life of Cardinal Wolsey* (London: Dent, 1885), p. 185.

[8] Philip Hughes, *The History of the Reformation in England*, 3 vols. (London: Collins, 1950–54), I, 224.

transform that into capital would require the skills of the sorcerer and the services of devoted apprentices.

But that is what Cromwell did. Wolsey was down; some said openly that he was betrayed by his favourite, Stephen Gardiner. Du Bellay, the French ambassador, informed his sovereign in words to that effect.[1] Sadler surely thought that to be the case. His letters to Cromwell warn against depending on the king's secretary, urging his master to look elsewhere in order to escape Wolsey's fate.[2] His estimate seems to be a just one, as even Gardiner's biographer admits.[3] Cromwell, for his part, shared Sadler's opinion of Gardiner and acted circumspectly with regard to him, while at the same time marking Sadler for a vital role in the plans then being formulated as a safeguard against the plots of the Norfolk-Boleyn faction and the supporters of the queen as well.[4]

The stratagem unfolded itself slowly. On 1 November Cromwell rode to Esher in order to talk with Wolsey. He promised the cardinal that he would return to London to recoup his patron's losses. Cavendish, who reported the interview, also noted that Sadler accompanied Cromwell back to London.[5] Cavendish also understood that Cromwell meant to seek a seat in Parliament in order to put Wolsey's cause before the Commons.[6]

It is not true that Sadler went with Cromwell to Esher on All Saints' Day. He had remained in London, where his presence was required by virtue of his own master's designs. It fell to him to effect the most

[1] *L & P*, IV, iii, 5,945, 9 Oct. 1529, where Wolsey's *protégés* are said to have betrayed him: 'luy ont tourne la robe'. Gardiner and Tuke are obviously intended, according to Brewer, *Reign of Henry VIII*, II, 369.

[2] *L & P*, IV, iii, 6,112, undated.

[3] James A. Muller, *Stephen Gardiner and the Tudor Reaction* (London: Macmillan, 1926), pp. 35 ff. for Cavendish's distrust of Gardiner. J. S. Brewer, who found the bishop of Winchester guilty of nothing worse than seeking safety in a storm, nevertheless confessed it to be difficult to decipher Gardiner's role: *The Reign of Henry VIII*, II, 369. Wilhelm Busch declared Gardiner was Wolsey's Judas in his *Der Sturz des Cardinals Wolsey* (Leipzig: Historisches Taschenbuch, 1890), pp. 62–3, 71–2, 99.

[4] James Gairdner, 'The Fall of Wolsey', *TRHS*, 2nd ser. XIII (1899), 75–102, tried to demonstrate that Gardiner let Wolsey take the entire blame for the failure of a policy partly of his own design.

[5] *Life of Cardinal Wolsey*, p. 157.

[6] Pollard commented critically on Cavendish's account of Cromwell's entry into parliament (*Wolsey*, p. 262), while accepting him on the whole. Elton, on the other hand, thought Pollard's treatment of the All Hallows events too critical and arbitrary, while maintaining the 'general precision and fullness of detail' in Cavendish as proof that Wolsey's clerk kept notes (*Tudor Revolution in Government*, p. 75, n. 6). I cannot agree altogether with either authority: Elton, for example, does not believe Cromwell approached Norfolk.

delicate deception upon which Cromwell's hopes rested, as we gather from the letter which he wrote to Cromwell from London on the first:

Worshypful syr it may please you to be advertysed that a lyttle befor the receypte of your lettre I cam from the courte where I spake with Mr Gage[1] and accordynge to your commaundement moved hym to speke with my lorde of Norfolk for the burgeses rowme of the parlyament on your behaulfe and he accordyngly dyd so withoute delay lyke a faythful frende. Whereuppon my saide lorde of Norfolk answered the saide Mr Gage that he had spoken with the king and that hys hyghnes was veray well contentyd ye shoulde be a burges so ye woulde order yourselfe in the saide rowme accordynge to the instruccyons as the saide duke shal give you from the kinge. Advertysyng you further that the saide duke in any wyse willeth that ye do speke with hys grace to morrow for that purpose. In token whereof hys grace sent you by Mr Gage your ryng with the turques whych I do now send you by thys berar. *As touchyng Mr Russhe[2] I spake wyth hym also at the courte. If I had then knowne your pleasure I could now have sent you answere to the same. Howbeit I will speke with hym thys nighte God willinge and knowe whether ye shalbe burges of Orforde or not. And yf you are not electyd there I will then accordynge to your ferther instruccyons repayre unto M Pawlet[3] and requyre hym to name you to be one of the burgeses of one of my lordes townes of hys bishoprycke of Winchestre accordinglie. Syr methinketh it were gud so it may stande with your plesure that ye dyd repayre hither to morrow as soon as ye convenyentlie may for to speke with the duke...*Assuringe you that your frendes wolde not have you to tarrie with my lorde[4] there as little as myghte be for many consideracyons as Mr Gage will shew you who much disireth to speke with you...

Divers of my lordes servauntes are sworne the kinges servauntes. Mr Gifforde[5] and I came from the courte together but he saide he had now newes. London All Saynctes Daie 4 paste noone. Your humble servaunte Rafe Sadleyer.[6]

We must pay careful attention to the chronology of events and the exact wording of the letter, if we are to understand the part played by

---

[1] Knighted and made vice-chamberlain of Henry VIII's household, a post he filled 1528–40. Although long a friend of Cromwell, he joined the factions that overthrew the earl of Essex in 1540.

[2] A servant of Wolsey and lifetime friend of Cromwell. They had worked together in the administration of Wolsey's colleges at Ipswich and Oxford.

[3] An important household official throughout the Henrician era, later he became lord treasurer of England and the first marquis of Winchester.

[4] This must refer to Wolsey himself.

[5] See note 13 for Gifford as an agent of Thomas Cromwell.

[6] BM Cotton MSS. Cleopatra E IV, fo. 178. Merriman printed the letter in full, but misread 'Oxforde' for 'Orforde' (*Life and Letters of Thomas Cromwell*, I, 67–8).

Sadler in Cromwell's manoeuvres. He had apparently been ordered to remain in London for the purpose of representing Cromwell's interest to Gage on the first of November. Having done what he was charged with, he returned from court to find new plans having to do with Rush and Paulet. This necessitated talking with Rush a second time. Hence his promise to return to court that very night, to expedite the matter at hand. Meanwhile, as a devoted servant, he found it necessary to warn Cromwell about the rapidly changing situation at court in so far as Wolsey was concerned. In fact, it seems likely that it was on Sadler's hint that Cromwell left for London 'to make or mar'.

The fact that Cromwell visited Esher alone, while Sadler carried on in London, makes the entire series of negotiations intelligible. Merriman, who thoroughly disliked Cromwell, emphasised the dealings with Gage, thus elevating the importance of a suit made to the duke of Norfolk, Gage's master and Wolsey's foe. He chose to believe that Sadler was urged to curry favour with the duke while Cromwell falsely placated the cardinal. But he missed the timing of events, holding with Cavendish that Ralph had been at Esher with Cromwell.[1] That error in a crucial detail led Merriman to underestimate Cromwell's finesse and to overestimate his reliance on Norfolk. It is clear from Sadler's letter that the price of unswerving obedience to the duke was too high for Cromwell's taste. Only in the ultimate necessity would he join Wolsey's enemies.

What in fact Sadler was about Pollard grasped completely. There was a brisk trade in seats in the Reformation Parliament. Hence the fact that by 1 November most members were already duly returned lends urgency to Cromwell's situation, for he had been pinched into seeking a seat at an inconveniently late hour. It was for that reason that he was reduced to seeking Norfolk's aid through Gage, while Sadler carried forward other parts of the main plan. Pollard erred in attributing to Sadler the initiative in discussing the issue with Rush, whose son was already elected for Orford and who was an old friend of Cromwell. He also erred in believing it to be Sadler's idea to work on Paulet, just in case Rush's seat could not be had. Paulet, of course, was Wolsey's steward and as such quite capable of disposing of one of the few pocket boroughs commanded by the cardinal. Taunton was a case in point:

[1] *The Life and Letters of Thomas Cromwell*, I, 66–7.

Paulet had surveyed the borough for Wolsey some months earlier.[1] Since it is a fact that Cromwell sat for Taunton, Pollard concluded that Sadler had made a brilliant bargain for his master with a duly elected member, assigning a major share of the credit for Cromwell's success to his clerk.[2]

While this flattering thesis does take into account the complexity of Sadler's mission, the image of brilliant initiative must be sacrificed in the interest of truth. First of all, Pollard relied throughout on the calendared version of the letter, which at a critical juncture reads: 'If you are not elected there (Orford) I will desire Mr Paulet to name you.'[3] But it is clear in the original of the letter that Sadler was acting under cover of specific instructions in contacting Paulet, orders received from his master too late to be put into effect during his trip to see Gage.[4] While we must not minimise the delicacy of Ralph's work, it will not do to assign to him the genius for manoeuvre that was Cromwell's.

This telling of the story enables us to understand the true sequence of events. Cromwell had apparently evolved three schemes, each to be executed by Sadler.[5] His agent was to assay the cost of a Norfolk seat, which does cast doubt on Gairdner's view that Cromwell's loyalty to Wolsey never wavered.[6] In the event that the duke's price was beyond paying, Cromwell would face a genuine dilemma. He wished to help Wolsey while at the same time saving himself. Hence the attempt to get a seat on the open market from Rush. Failing that, the least eligible alternative would have to do, and an effort would be made to get one of the cardinal's pocket boroughs through the good offices of Paulet. The last choice might not save Cromwell, since he hardly wished to sail under Wolsey's colours in the light of the circumstances in which he found himself. The Wolsey seat seemed a sure thing, since the cardinal badly wanted an advocate in Parliament.

The difficult task of executing these orders fell to Sadler in his capacity

---

[1] *L & P*, IV, ii, 5,407, Sir William Paulet to Thomas Wolsey, Apr. 1529.

[2] Pollard, 'A Changeling Member of Parliament', *BIHR*, X (1932), 20–7, especially n. 1, p. 24, for Sadler's supposed role.

[3] *L & P*, IV, appendix, 238. Oxford appears, but the manuscript in BM Cleopatra E IV, 178, clearly reads Orforde.

[4] The text of the letter leaves no room for doubt on this point.

[5] Despite my slight disagreement with Dr Elton as to Cavendish, it is obvious that my account rests on his brilliant reconstruction of these events in *The Tudor Revolution in Government*, pp. 76–82.

[6] 'The Fall of Wolsey', p. 99.

as Cromwell's confidential clerk. He had to bait all the hooks without frightening the potential catch. That required him to deal earnestly with Gage, to try to buy up the Rush seat, while reserving for Paulet his special skill in dissembling, where the seat was actually found. In that bit of court diplomacy Sadler well merited Lloyd's description of him: 'Close and industrious; able to discover others' will while masking his own.' He also proved himself worthy of hire as the sorcerer's apprentice, fit to serve the man Father Hughes laboriously hailed as the one genuine political genius of Tudor England.[1]

In the events of 1530 the clever efforts of 1529 were both frustrated and rewarded. On the one hand, Cromwell's efforts in Wolsey's behalf met with scant sympathy in Parliament. Gardiner, working behind the scenes, baulked those efforts. Well might Sadler remind his patron that all went for nothing, that Gardiner held the whip hand and professed ignorance of Wolsey's affairs while also undermining Cromwell. Furthermore, Gage, with whom Sadler conferred, was ordered by the king's secretary, and would recount little beyond the fact that the Cromwellians had no luck in gaining the king's ear.[2] The enemies of Wolsey, Gage alleged, were dominant, despite the hopes of all good men that their plots 'shal take small effecte'. Sadler's efforts to cut the fog of generalities resulted in his going to Gardiner directly. But to no avail. The king's secretary denied that he was any better informed about Wolsey than was Gage. Sadler was hardly taken in by the palaver. He described Gardiner as a liar, remarking to Cromwell that he would do nothing to help Wolsey but would instead attend only to what advanced his own career. The principal secretary was not to be trusted on any account.[3]

The passage of time revealed the rectitude of Sadler's judgement. While Cromwell spent time, energy and part of his wealth, by Sadler's version of the events, others made capital out of the cardinal's errors. The attempts to restore Wolsey's fortunes were doomed.[4] Yet something of importance did take place in that crisis of 1529–30, at least from

---

[1] *The History of the Reformation in England*, I, 195; see Lloyd, *Statesmen and Worthies*, p. 64.

[2] This must refer to either Sir William Fitzwilliam, treasurer of the household, or Sir Brian Tuke, treasurer of the chamber. I think Tuke is the better choice, since he was closely tied to Wolsey, although Du Bellay, who must be cited with caution, linked him with Gardiner when giving his opinion that Winchester was the chief traitor (*L & P*, IV, iii, 5,945).

[3] BM Cotton MSS. Titus B I, fo. 370, Ralph Sadler to Thomas Cromwell, undated.

[4] *L & P*, IV, iii, 6,076, Ralph Sadler to Thomas Wolsey, undated.

the point of view taken here. Cromwell recognised Sadler's service, stating succinctly to Wolsey: 'I assure your grace is much bounde to this gentilman for his good reporte in everie place...who has not lefte in everie presence to say of you as by lykehod ye have given hym cause.'[1] When put to the proof, both master and servant had exhibited qualities of courage and loyalty in a lost cause. That could hardly escape the king's notice. And whatever his immediate reaction might be, those were virtues treasured by Henry VIII.

Left to their own devices, those who survived Wolsey found life good beyond their expectation. Cromwell, who had laboured at the first remove from power under the cardinal's tutelage, was well placed in the struggle for power that followed hard upon the cardinal's fall. For him only the frail life of an old patron had stood between the substance and the shadow of power. Now it had been snuffed out, and Cromwell had managed to retain his credit with the king. Sadler, for his part, had also arrived at court in the household of the astute commoner who was destined to forward reforms that were in fact revolutionary. The chair left vacant by the man who was once an obscure Oxford don was beckoning and proved to be not beyond the reach of a quondam lawyer.

Little time for contemplation of those events was afforded either Cromwell or Sadler, as the crisis first deepened and then dissolved. The early 1530s were to be filled with a never-ending series of routine tasks related to the administrative and political business of the realm, as Cromwell engrossed power in a way more solid though less splendid than Wolsey before him. It is for that reason that our knowledge of Sadler's rise cannot be distinguished from the processes of government attesting to Cromwell's influence and eventual omnicompetence.

Until 1535 legal work of one sort or another occupied the major share of Sadler's time. He acted for the Crown in matters of property surrendered to the king's use in 1531, when the prior of St John's Hospital gave way to Henry VIII.[2] It was clearly the case, however, that Sadler's powers of attorney stemmed from Cromwell's ministry.[3] As his own power waxed he involved Sadler in official affairs: witness the occasion on which Ralph Sadler inquired into the murder of one

---

[1] *The Life and Letters of Thomas Cromwell*, I, 329.
[2] *L & P*, v, 285, 5 June 1531.   [3] *Ibid.* pp. 406, 619, 622 and 1,360.

Aubrey Gates on behalf of the king, though he was no law officer of the Crown.[1] Again, we find him at the London Charterhouse, interrogating monks in the matter of the royal supremacy,[2] a visit the official character of which is attested by the presence of Richard Rich, king's solicitor, a rapier-minded man who could not prevail upon Friar Lawrence to deny his faith.[3] The darker side of the stage could not be avoided; we find Sadler involved in the prosecution of Sir Thomas More and the learned Bishop Fisher. Among Cromwell's notes in June 1535 is this one: 'to know his (the king's) pleasure concerning Mastre More, when Mastre Fisher shall go to execution...To send the king by Raffe Mastre Fishers behaviour.'[4] From the records that remain, it is impossible to show that this work caused any more difficulty for Sadler than the more orderly business he usually did for his master.[5]

Throughout this period Sadler's circle of friends grew gradually to include men connected with the court through Cromwell, the presiding genius of his life. Like himself, they were drawn into the vortex of power and influence flowing about the king's powerful minister. Such a man was Stephen Vaughan, with whom Sadler made a survey of the king's jewels.[6] Vaughan was to be Sadler's friend until his death.[7] The same can be said of others who often begged to be remembered to Sadler, a fact that also is evidence of his growing influence in Cromwell's service.[8] Tudor bureaucrats and courtiers knew their place and how to improve it; and there one's circle of friends might mean everything. Hence, while Sadler was in reality only Cromwell's clerk before 1535, performing household duties as well as government tasks,[9] those with whom he was in contact did not care much about that distinction. When he delivered certain bonds or obligations to an official like John

[1] *L & P*, VI, 294, 30 March 1533.

[2] PRO, SP 1/92, fos. 34–47, 20 Apr. 1535.

[3] *L & P*, VIII, 566.

[4] BM Cotton MSS. Titus B I, fo. 474, undated. This paper seems to belong to June 1535, since More was obviously under indictment at the time. His trial was concluded on 1 July 1535.

[5] *L & P*, VIII, 962 (22), 25 June 1535; IX, 914 (5), 12 Nov. 1535.

[6] BM Royal MSS. 7 C XVI, fo. 48, 13 Feb. 1532.

[7] Somerset House, PCC Register 5 Coode, for Vaughan's will bearing an expression of gratitude for 'mi lovynge friende Sir Ralph Sadler'. The friendship can be traced at least as early as 1526, when the two men were employed by Cromwell: see PRO, E 101/518/14, fo. 4*b*, 'The Booke of Cromwell's expenses'.

[8] *L & P*, V, 461 and 1,593; VI, 394; VII, 1,340.

[9] PRO, SP 1/72, fos. 88–97, Dec. 1532, Brabazon's 'hoole receite' as Cromwell's receiver-general.

Gostwick[1] or received small sums earmarked by Gostwick for Cromwell,[2] it mattered little whether Sadler acted as a household agent or a royal servant. In an age that often was imprecise about the conditions of service in particular what was never lacking was the realisation that this man was near the centre of power and therefore of some influence.

That Sadler did routine work could not disguise the fact that he also did much more. He was in fact his master's secretary. He was on that account alone becoming skilled in the craft of politics, with every expectation that he would graduate from minor matters to those of policy. Between 1532 and 1535 the surviving evidence testifies to that transformation; routine work plays a smaller and smaller part in Sadler's service to Cromwell. And by 1535 the change that had commenced with the scramble for a seat in Parliament in 1529 was complete.

Increasingly, notices of Sadler in the early 1530s indicate his special place in Cromwell's household. Thomas Heritage, a priest and building agent of Cromwell, begged that 'Ralph Sadler or othre your clerks write me a few words'.[3] While some might fail to distinguish Sadler from the other clerks employed by Cromwell, among them William Brabazon[4] and James Horsewell,[5] others as early as 1533 clearly found that Sadler held a position of exceptional trust not equalled by the others.

In that respect a very illuminating incident concerning the possession of the king's signet seal is specially worthy of notice. Thomas Derby, one of the signet clerks, wrote to Sadler as follows:

Bicause there is muche haste made by oone Mastre Norres servauntes for thre bond men to whom the kinges highness hathe graunted manumission and as he telleth me my mastre Crumwell is privie to the signature of the bille, I sende my warraunte to be sealed with the signett by thys berar who cometh to be sped spedelie...I pray you deliver the signett bille to thys saide berar agayn to bring unto me. From London thys crastino Michalmis... Post scripta. I have received the fees of the signett.[6]

[1] BM Royal MSS. 7 C xvi, fos. 75 b–76 a, 19 July 1533.
[2] *L & P*, IX, 65, 11 Aug. 1535 and *ibid.* p. 125, 19 Aug. 1535, both letters from John Gostwick to Thomas Cromwell.
[3] *L & P*, V, 1,461, Thomas Heritage to Thomas Cromwell, undated.
[4] *Ibid.* p. 1,593.
[5] *L & P*, VI, 394, James Horsewell to Richard Cromwell, 28 Apr. 1533.
[6] PRO, SP 1/79, fo. 114, 30 Sept. 1533. The letter is addressed to 'Master Sadler or Mr Richard Crumwell, being at Hamptoncourte or at Master Heneges or in their absens to some of Master Crumwelles servauntes there'.

It is clear from Derby's letter that he expected either Sadler or Richard Cromwell to have the king's signet. Since Derby referred to Cromwell as 'my mastre', a problem arises in the interpretation of the letter. Derby had his place at the signet before Cromwell rose to prominence. We would thus normally interpret his reference to Cromwell as meaning that he was responsible as a signet clerk to the principal secretary of state. But Elton was clearly of the opinion that Cromwell did not become chief secretary until April 1534, on the grounds that Bishop Gardiner continued to endorse warrants as late as February of that year, while the *first* warrant countersigned by Cromwell is dated 15 April 1534.[1] Taking advantage of the fact that this was not the only time when Sadler had custody of the signet in 1533,[2] Elton explained the facts in the following way. Gardiner was on mission in France from 3 September 1533 until early in 1534. In his own absence, he gave the signet into Cromwell's hands. Cromwell was thus merely acting as Gardiner's deputy at that time and had not yet become the king's secretary. When it was necessary for Cromwell himself to be away, he put the seal in Sadler's charge, as a mark of special trust in his agent.

Here *pluralitas non ponende sine necessitate* seems an admirable rule. A check of the signet bills shows that the manumission mentioned took place in September 1533 and that it was endorsed '*per me* Thomas

[1] See Elton, *The Tudor Revolution in Government*, p. 124, as well as Gairdner's signed *DNB* article on Cromwell.

[2] The signet warrants are filed in PRO, C 82; for 1533 the bundle C 82/674 is pertinent. The bill referred to in Derby's letter is no. 23 of that bundle, the only manumission bill for either 1533 or 1534, which supplies formal detail about the manumission dated 'ultimo die Septembris anno regni vicesimo quinto' and superscribed 'receptus iiij Octobris'. The regnal year, of course, began on 22 Apr. and ran until 21 Apr. next ensuing. In addition to this evidence, warrants at the signet office were drawn under Cromwell's supervision as early as 9 Sept. 1533 (see C 82/674/7), when an annuity for John Dudley was superscribed with his autograph. The draft is in a hand resembling Sadler's. It was distinctly the task of the secretary to sign warrants authorising the signet bill to go forward to the privy seal. Additional support comes from another document, which shows Sadler in charge of the signet as early as 1533. SP 3/7, fo. 120, Leonard Smith to Lord Lisle, 15 Dec. 1533, was erroneously calendared in *L & P*, addenda, I, i, 886, which may help to set the problem in context (see Elton, *The Tudor Revolution in Government*, pp. 124–5). The *L & P* version reads: 'I have a bill signed by the king for your license...Knowing that all things done in the chancery are very chargeable, and that Mr Cromwell, when he delivered it unto me ...said he had no power to make it pass freely, but as the signet is in his keeping in the absence of the secretary, Mr Sadler, he would remit the fee for the signet.' Sadler was not secretary in 1533. The text reads as follows: 'Notwithstanding bi cause the signett is in hys kepyng now in the absens of the secretarie Raufe Sadleyer wolde take nothinge for the signett...' Cromwell was the absent secretary. After delivering the signet bill authorising the warrant, he left the seal in Sadler's hands. Smith could get no favour from Sadler, who had no power to pass things without charge.

Cromwell'. In the absence of a warrant appointing the secretary to his office, and the office was not at that time bestowed by patent, it seems likely that Cromwell was not merely acting for Gardiner but that he was already the *de facto* secretary even though the bishop was not relieved of his duties immediately upon his return from France. It is a simpler explanation of the facts, throwing light on Sadler's custodianship and also explaining Derby's talk about Cromwell being his master. An absentee secretary of state was of less than no use, a fact that Sadler perhaps ruefully recalled ten years later, when he was himself removed from that office while on the king's business in Edinburgh.

Whatever the truth of the matter is, the enhancement of Cromwell's stature signalled also a basic change in Sadler's position. There is evidence for that assertion beyond the assignment of the signet. It was in 1533 that Sadler first drafted fair copies of state papers: a letter from Cromwell to the king;[1] instructions for Richard Forster's mission to Ireland;[2] a copy of a curious tract about the vicious life led by curates and bishops;[3] and a translation of a Latin tract touching the wool staple at Calais.[4] All of the documents mentioned suggest a new role for Sadler and reflect Cromwell's ministry. They were of the essence of the secretarial office,[5] concerns from which Sadler never strayed until his own appointment to the secretaryship in 1540.[6]

The work of the Cromwellian secretariat to which Sadler fitted himself at the time brought two advantages. It introduced him to high politics. It also provided him with steady access to the king's chambers. Whatever the matter that came to Cromwell's attention, Sadler dealt with it in the course of time. He worked into the small hours of the night on a variety of papers and tasks for his master. He translated an heretical and seditious tract Henry VIII wanted 'Englisshed'.[7] If the

---

[1] PRO, SP 1/238, fo. 117, undated, but apparently of 1533.

[2] PRO, SP 1/238, fo. 117v.   [3] PRO, SP 6/IV, fos. 4–31.

[4] PRO, SP 1/239, fo. 9.

[5] For examples see the following: PRO, SP 1/239, fo. 79 and fos. 219–29; SP 1/49, fos. 54–9; no. 36/118, fos. 92–7, 98–101 and 150–2; SP 1/109, fos. 58–9; SP 1/133, fos. 262–9; BM Cotton MSS. Cleopatra E VI, fos. 272–93.

[6] See ch. 4 below for a full analysis of Sadler's tenure of the principal secretaryship.

[7] The books cannot be identified with any certainty. William Marshall sent some works of heretical import to Cromwell on 1 Apr. 1534, including *The Gifte of Constantine, Defensor Pacis* and *De veteri et novo deo* (see *L & P*, VII, 422–3). We know for certain that Sadler did some work on the Constantine tract, but another candidate is the book John Mason described to Thomas Starkey as 'a newe booke against the Pope', referring to the tragedy which began with a marriage (*L & P*, VII, 945, 3 July 1534), meaning of course the Boleyn marriage.

French ambassador complained about the lack of good plate provided him, the king's goldsmith wrote apologetically to Cromwell, not knowing whether 'his frende Ralph Sadler' was about to handle the matter.[1] John ap Rice, one of the most ubiquitous of the Cromwellians, also made his excuse to Cromwell for bothering him with a short note. It was his habit to send everything 'in a packet to Mastre Sadler'.[2] Even Sir William Fitzwilliam, the lord treasurer of the household, recognised that Sadler cared for the details of Cromwell's business,[3] while Lord Lisle and his agents knew that Sadler was an effective agent in Cromwell's control of the patronage machinery of the day.[4]

It was his position in regard to patronage especially that made him a man of some influence at court. We may even go so far as to say that beyond his ordinary duties Sadler was a sort of patronage secretary for the king's chief minister. Hence it is not surprising to see Sadler himself gathering rewards for his industry and vigilance in the affairs of men dealing with his master.[5] While Sadler's own profit will be treated extensively elsewhere, it is not amiss here to notice that he received cash rewards,[6] reversions to offices,[7] and ecclesiastical annuities made over to him by Cromwell,[8] all as a function in part of his own access to the king himself.

For by 1535 Sadler was a familiar figure at the court as well as about Cromwell's household. Fitzwilliam once remarked that Sadler was on a shuttle between Cromwell's London offices and the king's palace.[9] John Whalley mentioned casually that Sadler often stood near the king deep in talk.[10] Richard Layton, the same man who played such a key role in the dissolution of the monasteries, wrote to Cromwell asking that Sadler stop the king from writing on behalf of any of the royal chaplains in consequence of an office pursued by Layton himself. If

---

[1] *L & P*, VII, 1,340.

[2] *L & P*, IX, 160. Rice was Sadler's close friend (*ibid.* p. 466).

[3] *Ibid.* p. 905, Sir William to Thomas Wriothesley, 30 Nov. 1535.

[4] See the treatment of patronage within the general framework of the secretaryship in ch. 4 below and in ch. 9.

[5] See especially the treatment of the Sadler–Lisle correspondence in ch. 4 below.

[6] *L & P*, VIII, 653.

[7] *L & P*, VII, 601 and 761 (3), for the clerkship of the hanaper and the protonotary's post, discussed in detail in ch. 8.

[8] Westminster Abbey Muniment Room, Register 2, fo. 297, 15 May 1534. I owe this reference to Miss Helen Miller's generosity.

[9] PRO, SP 1/99, fos. 28–9, Sir William Fitzwilliam to Thomas Cromwell, undated.

[10] *L & P*, IX, 799, 10 Nov. 1535.

Ralph would oblige him in this, Layton remarked, he would surely succeed in his own suit![1] For reasons of his own, perhaps not unrelated to what we have already said about Sadler from time to time having the signet in his own hands, Layton never doubted the efficacy of Sadler's intervention.[2]

That odd request of October 1535 highlights another phase in Sadler's changing relationship to Cromwell and the king. We know from the funeral monument at Standon that Henry VIII 'conceavyng a good opynyon of hym as a manne meete to serve hym, took hym from lord Crumwelle, above the twentie sixt yere of his raigne, unto his service...'.[3] The obvious reference is to the fact that Ralph Sadler became a groom of the chamber about that time. But something more is also implied. While Whalley could describe Sadler as 'Cromwelles manne' in November 1535, that was only a half-truth. Eustache Chapuys, the Imperial ambassador, came nearer the exact nature of Sadler's relationship to Cromwell at that time. He cited him as one 'que fait toutes les ambassades entre le roy et luy', as the go-between connecting the king and his minister.[4] That does not seem at all errant, recalling that in the sixteenth century the term 'ambassador' meant little beyond 'anybody sent by another' (*quicunque ab alio missus*).[5] By 1535 Ralph Sadler had indeed become Cromwell's representative at court, dependent as ever on Cromwell but in the process of moving beyond that allegiance to the green and white livery of Henry VIII.

[1] *Ibid.* p. 632, Oct. 1535. Layton was one of the chief agents in the making of the *comperta* and the *valor* of 1535. Robert Shorton was the dean of Stoke, described in *articulo mortis* 12 Oct. 1535 (*L & P*, IX, 621), and dead 17 Oct. 1535 (*ibid.* p. 640).

[2] My own interpretation of the secretaryship of state rests on the basic work done by Evans and Elton, as well as on conversations with Dr Richard Barnett of Wake Forest University, North Carolina, who has investigated the household of Lord Burghley, and Dr Alan Smith of Glasgow University, who is completing a book on Sir Michael Hickes, the Cecilian patronage manager. I owe special thanks to them for their kindness in sharing information while we were working at the Institute of Historical Research, London.

[3] *SSP*, II, 618.

[4] PRO, PRO 31/18/3, no. 1, 25 Feb. 1536, Eustache Chapuys to Charles V. Chapuys wrote of his efforts to get news of Catherine of Aragon. Cromwell sent answer by Sadler 'que fait toutes les ambassades entre le roy et luy'. For Chapuys and his reliability as a diplomat see Garrett Mattingly, *Renaissance Diplomacy* (London: Jonathan Cape, 1955), pp. 243–6.

[5] B. Behrens, 'Treatises on the Ambassador Written in the Fifteenth and Early Sixteenth Century', *EHR*, LI (Oct. 1936), 619.

3

BETWEEN CROMWELL AND
THE CROWN

> My poore state...I onlie remitt to your lordshypp as to him that hath
> hitherto from the yeres of discressyon nurrisshed broughte up and
> admyryd me to the degree where I trust your lordshypp wyl not leve
> me until I be well settled.   RALPH SADLER to Thomas Cromwell

Sadler's place in the king's chamber has an interest beyond that of
marking a stage in his personal advance as a courtier and politician. In
the context of Cromwell's struggle to dominate Henrician politics it
provides an example of the texture of Tudor government, one facet of
which was noted by Sir John Neale in his account of Leicester's bid for
power under Elizabeth:

> In the Privy Chamber next to her Majesty's person, the most part are his
> creatures (as he calleth them)—that is, such as acknowledge their being in
> that place from him; and the rest he so over-ruleth that...nothing can pass
> but by his admission...[1]

The packing of the chamber was a stratagem in effecting a ruling faction
in Henry VIII's time no less than in that of his daughter. Although no
scholar has as yet dissected the Henrician political scene with the skill of
Neale's Elizabethan studies, a glance at the privy chamber lists of the
1530s places Sadler in a probable setting: he was a part of Cromwell's
design to crowd out the men ruled by Gardiner and Norfolk.[2]

The first mention of Sadler's advance came from Lord Lisle's gossipy
factor John Husee, who mentioned the appointment as a recent one in
July 1536.[3] There also exists evidence which implies that Sadler's
promotion came before 12 May 1536, at which time his name first
appears listed with the gentlemen of the chamber.[4] Two months earlier
Gostwick noted Sadler as a 'groom of the chambre'.[5] It is possible,

---

[1] *Essays in Elizabethan History*, pp. 72–3, quoting the *Secret Memoirs of Robert Dudley*, p. 52.
[2] *L & P*, x, 834 (2); xiv, i, 2 and ii, 572.
[3] *L & P*, xi, 31, 5 July 1536, John Husee to Lord Lisle, Sir Arthur Plantagenet.
[4] *L & P*, x, 834 (2).   [5] *L & P*, xi, 117.

however, that the change in livery was effected as early as 11 January 1536. On that day Sadler reported to the king in his chamber, in order to discuss some details of the funeral of Catherine of Aragon, while at the same time hoping to expedite some of Cromwell's business. Informing Cromwell of the interview, Sadler wrote:

The kinges highnes fyrst appoynted me to cum to him at Mass tyme to rede the same (Cromwell's memo)[1] unto hys grace, at whych tyme when I came he saied he wolde take a tyme of more leysor, commaunding me to tarrie until the evenyng when...he sholde have best leysor...and I doute lest hys grace wyll cause me to tarrie veray late whereof I thoughte good to signifie thys unto you and also to send all the lettres that be stamped[2] by thys berar. I thinke also hit wolbe herde to gett any billes signed at thys tyme seeyng that I have missed to have them done at Masse tyme. I shal nevertheles do the best I can albeit as you knowe his grace is alwaies lothe to signe. I deliveryd your locke unto hys grace and opened all the gines of the same whych hys grace lyketh marvellouslie well and hertelie thankyd you for the same...[3]

The wording of this letter suggests the ease of access to the king enjoyed by Sadler. It also may be understood to imply that he lived at court and was already installed about the privy chamber. He certainly knew the royal habits well enough to note the king's dislike for writing with something more than normal candour. Yet it is also clear that Sadler was still very much Cromwell's agent. The simple matter of fact is that he did his best to distract the king with gifts from Cromwell while also hurrying along bits of work Cromwell wished expedited. The other side of that coin is also revealed in a letter: Sadler used his position to delay business urgently pressed by Lord Lisle, who needed a licence to leave Calais in order to make his pleas in person.[4]

Sadler had the king's ear. Nobody was startled to see him in close conversation with Henry. Even his chance remark might alarm a minor official such as Thomas Cotton.[5] That poor man had sent a chain of gold

---

[1] Although it is not stated, Cromwell wrote the 'memoryall'.

[2] Letters signed by stamp constituted signed bills authorising the signet clerks to issue formal signet warrants.

[3] PRO, SP 1/101, fos. 57–8, Ralph Sadler to Thomas Cromwell, 11 Jan. 1536.

[4] PRO, SP 1/105, fos. 13–14, John Husee to Lord Lisle, undated; they were deceived in believing that Sadler promoted their bill.

[5] Thomas Cotton was comptroller of the household of the duke of Richmond, a friend of Cromwell and later an agent of Sadler.

to the mint for an assay soon after the death of the duke of Richmond, Henry VIII's bastard son.[1] Gostwick, who was Cotton's superior, protested the result of the evaluation.[2] He believed the chain to be of some worth, since the king himself reported it cost some five or six hundred pounds, according to Ralph Sadler. But the mint had it down for forty shillings. And Sadler's chance remark disturbed Gostwick.[3] Apart from the very sobering impact Sadler's gossip might have on functionaries, it is difficult to measure his influence. Surely he was in no way able to influence the king by virtue of his own standing.[4] Yet he was able to make his presence felt in many matters, the more so as Cromwell became lord privy seal in 1536, thereby virtually monopolizing the patronage machinery since he retained the secretaryship.

The fragility of Sadler's own grasp on power, however, remained unmistakable. Certain letters of 1536 and 1537, while showing his slowly shifting relationship with Cromwell, demonstrate that he was a slender reed when faced with the wind of the king's wrath. Valuable he might be to Cromwell, venturing on occasion to warn his patron about the king's moods, as when he told him of Henry VIII's anger over the secretary's failure to appear at an appointed time. When Cromwell alleged Michaelmas as a holiday,[5] the king raged that it was not so high a day as to warrant the lord privy seal not keeping 'hys daie' with his sovereign. Sadler urged Cromwell to 'look to the kinges pleasure'.[6] But in most cases his tone was servile, if not fawning, especially when he had to report adversities or reversals suffered in the course of unfolding some complex scheme touching state affairs.[7]

Far more valuable than such reports and letters in attempting to assess Sadler's progress towards emancipation is the record of hurdles not cleared. The summer of 1537 is instructive in that regard, since a sequence of largely fortuitous events took place which threatened to halt Sadler's steady climb and virtually to destroy his position so labori-

---

[1] See *DNB*, article 'Henry Fitzroy, Duke of Richmond'.

[2] *L & P*, xi, 174, 28 July 1536.

[3] PRO, SP 1/105, fos. 183-4.

[4] This statement disregards minor offices in the chancery of no importance in political matters.

[5] The feast of St Michael the Archangel began the Michaelmas court terms and also marked an accounting period in exchequer and in chancery affairs.

[6] Great Britain, Public Record Office, *The State Papers of Henry VIII*, 11 vols. (London, 1830-52), i, 461.

[7] *L & P*, xi, 1,124; xii, 821 and 827; xii, ii, 1,336, and appendix, no. 44; xiii, i, 1,875; xiii, ii, 178; xiv, i, 236 and 529; xiv, ii, appendix, no. 20—a small selection of the relevant material.

ously built on expanding work in affairs of the court, administration and diplomacy.[1]

The year had started well for Sadler. His position with Cromwell was firmly established. His work in everyday routines of government rested on a pair of minor offices in chancery. A major change in his experience was shaping up, as he was selected for an important embassy in Scotland, a move that began his lifelong expertise in things Scottish. Despite all of these good omens, his utter dependence on Cromwell remained the vital fact of his life.

The first hint that he had incurred the king's displeasure, with possibly disastrous consequences, came from Sir John Russell.[2] On 11 July 1537 Russell wrote to Cromwell, telling the secretary of the king's wish that he accompany his grace on a hunting expedition despite the reported illness of William Bolde, one of Cromwell's men.[3] While Cromwell was to stay away from the queen's entourage at court, where Jane Seymour was lying in expectation of a son, there was business to be done, and the hunt was as good a place to do it as any. Russell also noted that he had made an excuse for Sadler, who had been away from court above the three days allowed him as a mourner for the late earl of Northumberland.[4] Mentioning Sadler's fear of appearing so shortly after he had been with Bolde, who seemed mortally ill, was not enough, however. The king was persuaded that Sadler's real reason for being away was other than the alleged one. Henry had in fact accused Ralph of reneging in 'his bounden dutie' to appear, wryly remarking that Northumberland was long since dead and buried. Hence a written excuse, either from Sadler's own hand or, better still, from Cromwell, would be required to right matters.[5]

Since we hear no more of that affair, we may assume that Sadler cleared himself to the king's satisfaction. A short while later, however, similar difficulties arose. One of Sadler's men had returned from London ill at ease. Knowing that the city was plague-wracked, Sadler thought it best not to attend the king, though his man might be 'sicke of nothynge but an ague'. He would not presume any 'medicall skille',

---

[1] See chs. 5, 6 and 8 for diplomacy and administrative affairs.
[2] Comptroller of the household and a privy councillor; he rose to a peerage as earl of Bedford.
[3] Bolde was so identified in the letter quoted.
[4] Sir Henry Percy, the sixth earl of Northumberland. Sadler had earlier served Cromwell in the actions that wrecked the family in the wake of the Pilgrimage of Grace.
[5] PRO, SP 1/122, fos. 227–8, 11 July 1537.

33

he wrote to Cromwell, but would await the outcome of his man's sickness. Meanwhile, he would look for orders from the court, knowing too well that Henry VIII 'lovys not that anie manne shold breke hys daie wyth hys grace'. He had taken the precaution of asking a courtier friend, Thomas Heneage, to make an official excuse. But he remained anxious, despite the reasonableness of his case. He in fact feared the revival of the royal displeasure so recently stilled:

And yet peradventure hys grace wil thinke the same to be fayned to thintent I wolde procure a longer daie. But I had lever hys grace thoughte so thanne I shold do so, for it wolde become me ful ill to lye or fayne to hys maiestie. To nighte or to morrow I truste to see the certaintie of my mannes disease and then if it be non otherwise thanne I take it I wyl ymedyately repayre to the courte.[1]

Nothing more is heard of this incident.

But the terrible consequences of the plague that raged in London in 1537 continued to dog Sadler's heels, threatening his career. As summer faded into early autumn the feel of death gripped the weary capital tightly. The king moved the court and his expectant queen beyond the perimeter of contagion, the courtiers and politicians, including Sadler, following along gladly.[2] Then, in October, Sadler's fortunes encountered a tremendous blow. A servant in his household came back from London in a feverish condition. After lying in at Sadler's quarters within the court for a time, he had gone off to lodgings maintained by his master outside the palace confines. Sadler promptly reported the matter to Cromwell, mentioning at the same time that the king had been informed through Sir Francis Bryan.[3] Henry had sent word back to the effect that Sadler was to stay well away from the palace. The king did not appear angry or resentful toward Sadler. On the contrary, construing Bryan's report, Sadler found that 'the kinge tenderyth the helthe of me and the reste of my poore familie at home and hath advysyd me not to repayre to my wyfe forasmoche as she ys grete wyth childe...'[4] Henry advised Sadler to avoid his home, and to go instead to a house in Hackney, where none was known to have died of the plague, except William Bolde.

---

[1] PRO, SP 1/127, fos. 205–6, Ralph Sadler to Thomas Cromwell, undated.

[2] Smith, *Tudor Prelates and Politics*, p. 196.

[3] Bryan was a very trusted agent of Henry VIII, with service reaching well back into the Wolsey years.

[4] They were at Lesnes, Sadler's farm in Kent.

Despite the encouraging nature of the royal suggestion, Sadler was downcast. He complained bitterly to Cromwell of the malign fate that seemed to pursue him:

Syr I assure your lordshypp thys chance hath broughte me into a grete perplexitie. But I canne ascribe it to no othre thinge than my mal fortune. And if I shold eftsoons be compelled to be so long from the courte as I was latelie,[1] oneless your lordshypp be good lorde to me it wolde muche hinder me. Wherefore I can no more whether I be absent or present but repone my hole truste and hope in the kinge and your lordshypp as knowith our Lorde... Your lordshyppes old servaunte and dailie bedysman. At Hamptoncourte.[2]

Banished from the court! Through no fault of his own, Sadler faced prospects of disaster. Prolonged absence from the source of power and patronage was often fatal to the rising young man interested in a career in politics or about the person of the ruler.

Luckily for Sadler, Cromwell moved with alacrity and attempted to reassure his friend and valued agent. Although his own letter to Sadler on this occasion has not survived, we do have what appears to be Sadler's reply, in which it is clear that he suspected some 'imputed faulte' damaging to his career was on the king's mind. Dropping the courtier's mask, Sadler expressed his anguish and his anger over the imputed sin of non-attendance on his lord. While recognising that in the past the king had forgiven some very real errors on his part, Sadler also bitterly rehearsed the facts of the case: 'hys maiestie sholde allege for an example thereof my departyng at thys time...whyche I did not without recourse to hys graces warraunte and most dred commaundment signified unto me from Mr Bryan by the mouthe of my fellowe Jenyns'. He clearly felt himself to be the victim of an injustice. To prove his point, he proposed to send to Cromwell Bryan's letter, which he had thoughtfully saved, in the hope that it would be vindication enough. Plagued by fears about the health of his family and that of his servants about him, Sadler was at the same time helpless in the face of adversity, able to trust only to 'God who has the relief of supplicantes' in his hands. Even more unsettling was the prospect that his career was on the verge of ruin: 'My absens from the courte wyl so moche hindre me that I shal nevar be able to recovre...' In a mist of theologically

---

[1] Bolde's death is mentioned in *L & P*, xii, ii, 821.
[2] PRO, SP 1/125, fo. 116, 3 Oct. 1537.

coloured language, itself apposite on the lips of a careerist serving an English king more nearly *rex et sacerdos* than any of the past generations, Sadler placed himself in the hands of Cromwell, a nearer patron than God and one for whom 'he nevar had more nede of' than at that moment.[1]

Exactly how Cromwell directed his efforts in Sadler's behalf is unfortunately not known. But only a week after he wrote the begging letter just quoted Sadler was back at court, busily drafting a letter announcing the birth of Jane Seymour's long-awaited son.[2] Since the young prince was delivered on 12 October in 1537, Ralph's period of watchful waiting was really a short one. Yet we cannot dismiss the suspicion that he still laboured beneath some cloud of uncertainty. He alone of the grooms was absent from the christening ceremony.[3] Be that as it may, we can be sure that Cromwell was unwilling to see his agent go under, although he could not immediately satisfy Sadler's desire for a complete restoration. Indeed, so keenly did Sadler feel the threat to his career that after his return to court he wrote despairingly to his patron:

I am oute of harte and hope to attayn any thynges of the kenges highnes here of late who withyn thys laste fortnite hath usyd hys liberalitie to divers whiche have deservyd no bettar than I. My poore state consyderyd I have asmoche nede as any that is towardes hys grace, the relief wherof I onlie remitt to your lordshypp as to hym that hath hitherto from the yeres of discressyon nurisshed broughte up and admyryd me to the degree where I truste your lordshypp wyl not leve me untyl I be well settled.[4]

We can ask for no more striking proof of Sadler's dependence on Cromwell at a time when he was already directly in the king's service. Nor could we expect Sadler to put his case more cunningly. Conscious of the fact that he had reached a crossroad of his life, Sadler played carefully on Cromwell's sense of loyalty to a faithful agent as well as upon Cromwell's interest in maintaining members of his affinity about the king.

Subsequent evidence bears out Sadler's view of the mutuality of interest binding him and his more powerful patron. We soon see Sadler's hand at work in the framing of state papers.[5] His name is

---

[1] PRO, SP 1/125, fos. 123–4, 4 Oct. 1537.   [2] BM Cotton MSS. Nero x, i, fo. 34a.
[3] *L & P*, XII, ii, 911.   [4] PRO, SP 1/127, fos. 250–1, Oct. 1534.
[5] See Elton, *Tudor Revolution in Government*, pp. 237 ff., as well as PRO, SP 1/119, fos. 105–8, a council memo in Ralph's hand; see also BM Cotton MSS. Cleopatra E v, fo. 371.

entered in a list of men Cromwell thought worthy enough to be held 'in the kinges moste benigne remembraunce' on more than one occasion in 1538. We have a good example of that in the New Year's gift list of 1539, at which time Sadler received a silver cup from the king, giving a gold signet 'wyth a draft therein' in return.[1] By 1539 his precedence in privy chamber lists was high enough to cause him to be ranked with Russell, Heneage, Sir Anthony Browne and Sir Francis Bryan, men among the most favoured commoners.[2]

Nor were other signs of the king's grace wanting. On a great day of state, the reception held for Anne of Cleves, Sadler rode in the parade, mounted on a black charger specially caparisoned for the event, his rider made splendid by virtue of the long gold chain hung about his neck.[3] Then in 1539–40 Sadler was once again sent to Scotland on an important diplomatic mission. Onerous as such service might be, it was a mark of high honour and a special show of royal confidence.[4]

The restoration of Sadler's fortunes can be seen from yet another perspective. He continued to work closely with Cromwell in the king's business. When so highly favoured a jouster and reveller as Richard Cromwell found it difficult to gain the king's ear, the reason was put bluntly: no audience was necessary, since the king's pleasure was to communicate his wishes through his faithful servant Ralph Sadler.[5] Even great Norfolk admitted to seeing Sadler busy about Cromwell's work of countering the duke's machinations.[6] Enough of the chief minister's business passed through Sadler to insure Cromwell's continued maintenance of his trusted friend.[7]

That fact is best illustrated by a consideration of Sadler's role in Cromwell's handling of foreign affairs, which came to occupy the most critical place in Cromwell's ministry toward the end. Sadler's letters of the period 1538–40 are a veritable index to his patron's diplomatic worries. There we meet details of the intrigues of foreign agents in Scotland,[8] of news secretly conveyed out of Flanders touching

[1] *L & P*, xiii, i, 1, 187, 878–9. For further evidence see the list of new year's gifts exchanged in 1538: Folger Shakespeare Library, Miscellaneous MSS. Z. d. 11, m. 4r and m. 5v.

[2] *L & P*, xiv, i, 2.   [3] *Ibid.* ii, 572.

[4] See ch. 5 for these missions.

[5] *L & P*, xiii, i, 1,006, Richard Cromwell to Thomas Cromwell, 15 May 1538.

[6] *L & P*, xiii, i, 1,375, 14 July 1538.

[7] *L & P*, addenda, i, ii, 1,404, Lady Elizabeth Carew to Thomas Cromwell, undated.

[8] *L & P*, xiii, ii, 178, 24 Aug. 1538.

Wriothesley's mission to France[1] and of the growing resentment of Charles V over English policy.[2] These letters were usually written at the express command of Henry VIII.[3] Hence it would be wide of the mark to see in them signs of initiative. But it would be equally wrong to deny that Sadler's reports had an effect on Cromwell's policy, since that policy was often an image of the king's mind as viewed by Cromwell through the reflecting medium of Sadler's thoughts. Inasmuch as Sadler's very choice of words coloured decisions and attitudes about crucial matters, he was indeed a main cog in the Cromwellian machinery.

That involvement in foreign affairs may well have had a decisive influence on Sadler's career in yet another way. Looking back over the years after Wolsey's death, it is obvious that during that time Sadler systematically gained experience in every sort of work related to the administration of Tudor government. To a fair knowledge of chancery affairs about the notary's office and the hanaper had been added familiarity with the secretariat, especially with the signet office and matters of patronage. From the very beginning, Sadler had some insight into the handling of financial matters and routine legal administration. There is a sense, then, in which the long season of apprenticeship in domestic affairs led naturally into the realm of foreign policy and high politics. A sixteenth-century secretary without diplomatic experience was a contradiction in terms.

It is in that sense that Sadler, approaching his thirty-third birthday early in 1540, may truly be styled Master by his correspondents. His experience fitted him for further advancement. His circle of friends included future bishops, among them Edmund Bonner and Roland Lee; important financial agents, Vaughan and John Baker being good examples; and future secretaries of state, especially Wriothesley and William Paget. On the threshold of a new decade, therefore, well might Sadler ponder the wisdom of another friend, Sir Edward Seymour, to whom this saying is credited: 'There are but three thinges to rase a man to observacyon. 1. Some peculyar sufficiencies; 2. Some

---

[1] *L & P*, xiv, i, 236, undated, bearing a contemporary endorsement Anno XXX.

[2] PRO, SP 1/144, fos. 116–17, 16 March 1539, where Henry asked Cromwell to recall that 'diligence passes sense'.

[3] BM Cotton MSS. Titus B1, i, fo. 269, Cromwell to Henry VIII, 14 March 1539: 'the poyntes signified to me by Mastre Sadleyeres lettres writ on your graces behaulfe'; see also *L & P*, xiv, ii, appendix, no. 20, Ralph Sadler to Thomas Cromwell: 'now that I have declared the king's pleasure'.

particular exploites; 3. An especiall friende.'[1] Of the first two of these we have given evidence. And of the third, there can be no doubt, a fact which was soon to be revealed as the special strength and weakness of Sadler's position.

The 1530s had been Cromwell's decade. As never before, he had set his stamp on every action of the government. His influence was evident in every state paper of the time. Despite Pollard's claim that Henry VIII was the great political genius of the age in England,[2] Dr Elton has had little difficulty showing that Cromwell was in reality the author of the very complex changes in government that distinguish the epoch of the Reformation.[3] In fact Cromwell did more than alter institutions; there is a very real truth at stake in seeing him as the artificer of the stage and the actors moving upon it during the years 1532–40. It is for that reason, which we may restate by saying that his household supplied the state with a corps of bureaucrats, that his fall was to create a political crisis which remained unresolved right up until the day of Henry VIII's death, a crisis in which the live Cromwellians were the men best placed to wind up affairs, just as Cromwell himself was the man 'to wind up Wolsey's complicated political bankruptcy' in the 1530s.[4] With this proviso: that the Cromwellians survive their master.

Cromwell had excited great opposition in the course of creating the basis of a bureaucratic monarchy.[5] Hence any little failure of his policy gave heart to his enemies, who always looked to supplant him about the king. To that extent it is true to say that Cromwell had failed to transform the most vital institution of all, the monarchy itself, which was still quite personal. Allowing for the existence of important enemies of a very powerful kind, Gardiner and Norfolk for example, was thus all the more important for the success of Cromwell's policies. It was exactly in that regard that Cromwell's failure was most patent. While it is true that early in 1539 he had managed to secure Gardiner's

---

[1] BM Sloan MSS. 1523, fo. 40b. This manuscript consists of two treatises bound together and paged continuously, although the first concerns agriculture and the second contains characters of Henrician statesmen which either served as a basis for remarks in Lloyd's *States-men* or were copied from that work. The hand of the manuscript is late Stuart.

[2] *Henry VIII*, pp. 306–7.

[3] *Tudor Revolution in Government*, throughout; this is also the view taken by Dom David, Knowles, 'Elton's *England Under the Tudors*, a review', *CHJ*, XII (1956), 93.

[4] Garrett Mattingly, *Catherine of Aragon* (Boston: Little, Brown and Co., 1941), p. 314.

[5] For this interpretation of Cromwell's ministry see Elton, *The Tudor Constitution* (Cambridge University Press, 1960), esp. pp. 131–3. See also the symposium in *Past & Present*, July 1963.

effective banishment from both court and council, thus nullifying 'wily Winchester',[1] it was also true that certain foreign policy reverses plagued his efforts to contain the men hostile to his ministry.

Even the exclusion of Gardiner from public business for a time could not mask the fact that the bitter feeling against Cromwell spilled over into parliament.[2] In 1539 Norfolk and his cohorts made a determined bid to secure conservative support in the Commons with marked success. The fact that the Six Articles became the law of the land inspired in some Protestants a shrewd suspicion that Cromwell's day was at an end, although they were guilty of selling short Cromwell's resourcefulness.[3] Aware that his grip on power was threatened, Cromwell attempted to control the leadership of the Commons, the arena in which he was most valuable to his sovereign, to that end securing the election of his two chief agents, Wriothesley and Sadler, perhaps with an eye to repeating the strategy of 1529. The former sat for Hampshire, where Cromwell intervened strongly in the election.[4] The latter was returned by a constituency not identifiable now, almost certainly by virtue of the same pressure that saw Wriothesley elected.[5] As a sign of reassurance to his supporters, he did stay the execution of the Six Articles.

These manoeuvres, however, would be of great significance only in the event of Cromwell's solving the foreign policy puzzles then before him. In 1539 he thought it imperative that an alliance be made with some Protestant dynasty, as a counterweight to the recently concluded Habsburg–Valois peace, an amity which was a clear danger to England's security. A cross-channel invasion sponsored by Rome was a distinct possibility, while the Scots fished in waters troubled by the aftermath of the Pilgrimage of Grace. The Borders were still not pacified.[6] Thus

[1] Kenneth Pickthorn, *Early Tudor Government*, 2 vols. (Cambridge University Press, 1934), II, 422.

[2] For this parliament see Pollard, 'Council, Star Chamber and Privy Council under the Tudors Part III, The Privy Council', *EHR*, xxxviii (1923), 46.

[3] See *L & P*, xv, 411, 414, 425, 429, 485.

[4] Elton, *The Tudor Constitution*, p. 292, where a letter from John Kingsmill to Thomas Wriothesley appears, dated 1 April 1539, concerning the struggle for seats.

[5] There are incomplete returns for most sixteenth century parliaments in PRO, C 218/1, Petty Bag Office of Chancery. The best composite lists are those kept by the History of Parliament Trust Staff, Tavistock Square, London. Miss Helen Miller, at the time Dr Bindoff's assistant (1960), made these available to me in mimeographed form. For the evidence touching Sadler's seat in 1539 see *S.P.* II, 623–4. On at least one subsequent occasion his return was ordered by the government: see Nicholas Pocock, *Troubles Connected with the Prayer Book* (London: Camden Society, 1884), p. 77.

[6] Pollard, *EHR*, xxxviii, 46.

England was neither strong nor secure.[1] It seemed an open question 'whether the country would be invaded by France or Spain'.[2] Accordingly, Sadler, who was once more in Scotland, shared Cromwell's concern, warning his master that the imperial threat was very great indeed, while France and James V seemed about to launch an invasion.[3]

It was against that background that Cromwell negotiated the supreme folly of his career in marrying Henry VIII to Anne of Cleves, setting the seal finally to the abandonment of Wolsey's policy of an imperial alliance and preparing the occasion of his own downfall. His miscalculation was stupendous. The king's aversion to Anne was complete. Since Henry was nowhere more easily touched than in his sensitivity about his marriages, it was not unsuspected that he turned for advice to men hostile to Cromwell.[4] Early in 1540 Norfolk was back at court again. Gardiner and Tunstal were once more at the council board. By February, as Pollard noted so rightly, tension was acute. England was at sixes and sevens once again.[5] Signs ominous to the Cromwellians appeared in every quarter. Friar Robert Barnes, a Lutheran partisan named to preach at court during Lent, was replaced by the king, who himself selected Gardiner for the task.[6] So shaken was Cromwell by a succession of events, that he had to abase himself before the bishop of Winchester. When Henry exiled Anne of Cleves from the court, those who knew the portents looked for the gleam of the axe.[7]

Then there took place one of those spectacular oscillations of fortune such as Wolsey had hoped for in vain. Cromwell's best hold on the king's confidence had always been his mastery of Parliament. He now bargained on that strength, using the prospect of his management of the Commons in order to retain Henry's favour. While Parliament was sitting, Cromwell struck at his enemies. A scant few days after his humiliating interview with Gardiner, he routed Norfolk, attacking the duke in council over the propriety of his management of the customs.[8]

---

[1] Froude, *History of England*, III, 343–95, an opinion also held by Pollard, Fisher and Elton.

[2] Fisher, *Political History of England*, V, 431.

[3] *L & P*, XIV, i, 529, 16 March 1539. For a more detailed discussion of Sadler's diplomacy see chapters below.

[4] *SP*, I, 699–702 and *L & P*, XVI, 1,426, 7 Dec. 1541: the former is from Browne and Sadler to Council in London, while the latter is from M. Marillac to Francis I.

[5] Pollard, *Henry VIII*, pp. 297–9.　　[6] Muller, *Stephen Gardiner and the Tudor Reaction*, p. 85.

[7] Merriman, *Life and Letters of Thomas Cromwell*, I, 288–90.

[8] Elton, 'Informing for Profit: A Sidelight on Tudor Methods of Law-Enforcement', *CHJ*, XI (1954), 154.

It once again seemed plain to all that Henry's dismay about the reforming activities of Barnes and Latimer was less important than the
king's need for the minister who coped with Parliament better than any
other: 'Cromwell's chief distinction lay in the management of parliament.'[1] If Cromwell and his agents, especially Wriothesley and Sadler,
were to be effective in the difficult task of bending the Commons to
the royal will, they stood in need of some sign of the king's grace. What
better proof of their power could there have been than their ability to
put to flight the conservatives?[2]

If further demonstration of Cromwell's revived fortunes was necessary, it was quickly given. In order to more effectively control the king's
business Cromwell sponsored a change in the secretaryship of state that
put Wriothesley and Sadler in the office jointly, each of them being
styled principal secretary in his own right.[3] In order to advance his own
programme while at the same time protecting his flanks, Cromwell
advanced his two most loyal agents in a way that will soon be explained
more fully. Suffice it to say at this point that their new role was marked
by a display of the pomp so loved by the king and so easily understood
by the courtiers and politicians then nipping at Cromwell's heels.
Cromwell was granted an earldom. After the patents were read by the
two secretaries, royal orders knighting the Cromwellians were presented, the king himself dubbing Sadler and Wriothesley.[4]

The urgency that gave rise to the pageantry was not forgotten. Sadler
moved immediately in behalf of his patron. He played a key role in
easing the plight of Hugh Latimer, the staunch Cromwellian.[5] He also
took an active part in efforts then made to undermine Henry VIII's
trust in those of the Gardiner–Norfolk coalition. Both within and
without Parliament his voice spoke with new authority.[6]

The tide of the Cromwellian reaction of April 1540 ebbed even more
rapidly than it rose, however, as the king's basic fidelity to a conservative religious settlement and his dislike of Anne of Cleves lasted longer
than did the Parliament. In a sense Cromwell's very efficiency worked

[1] Dorothy Gladish, *The Tudor Privy Council* (Retford: The Retford, Gainsborough and
Workshop *Times* Press, 1915), p. 22.
[2] Fisher, *Political History of England*, v, 422. [3] *SP*, II, 623–4.
[4] See ch. 4 for a fuller treatment of this episode.
[5] *SP*, I, 627, Ralph Sadler to Thomas Cromwell, undated. Sampson was arrested 17 May 1540;
see also *L & P*, xv, 719.
[6] Merriman, *Life and Letters of Thomas Cromwell*, II, no. 343.

against him. As soon as he got from Parliament what the king wished it was prorogued *sine die*, thus playing out Cromwell's hand. While it was sitting Lord Audley, who was then chancellor of England, ventured the remark that even the chancery was reduced in importance owing to Cromwell's genius and power. Norfolk himself cringed before the upstart earl of Essex.[1] But once the members went home, waspish resentments built to a fever pitch claimed their due. It was then commonplace at court that either Cromwell or the opposition must perish.[2] With Wriothesley playing the role once held by Gardiner in 1529, history seemed to repeat itself. Gardiner seized the initiative, luring the king at his weakest point, somewhat cynically, introducing to Henry Catherine Howard, possessed of enough beauty and charm to italicise Cromwell's blunder in the Cleves fiasco.[3]

The storm broke on 10 June. Cromwell was degraded by Norfolk in Star Chamber in the presence of many councillors. Immediately after his arrest, he was put in the Tower, while out on the streets a few lamented his fall while more rejoiced, 'specially suche as either had bene religious men or favoured religious persones...Othres who newe nothynge but trewth by hym...hertelie praied for hym.'[4] Cromwell's mounting spirits, spurred by low birth and great success, had been downed by Gardiner.[5] Badly in need of friends, Cromwell found himself deserted by the hard but pliable henchmen who were omnipresent during the days of power and profit. Only Sadler stood by to offer aid and comfort.[6]

---

[1] Gladish, *The Tudor Privy Council*, p. 25.

[2] *L & P*, xv, 442, 485, 486, 498, 541, 719, 736, 737 and 767.

[3] *L & P*, xvi, 578; see also *Original Letters Relative to the English Reformation, 1531–1558*, ed. Hastings Robinson, 2 vols. (London: Parker Society, 1846–7), I, 200, Richard Hilles to Henry Bullinger, undated.

[4] Hall, *Chronicles*, p. 838. For contemporary opinions of Cromwell see Lord Herbert's *Life of King Henry VIII*, pp. 521 ff. The poet Michael Drayton wrote a long poem about Thomas Cromwell. Entitled *The Legend of Great Cromwell* (London: Felix Kyngston, 1607), the poem deals at some length with Cromwell's fall and also with the problem of rehabilitating him as the 'great'st man of England'. It is worth noting that the poem was dedicated to Drayton's patron Sir Walter Aston, who was Sadler's heir at Standon through Thomas Sadler's daughter Gertrude.

[5] Both quotes are from a play once erroneously attributed to Shakespeare: *The True Chronicle Historie of the Whole Life and Death of Thomas Lord Cromwell* (London: Thomas Luodham, 1613) pp. 3 and 29. The play rests entirely on the account of Cromwell given by John Foxe, *The Acts and Monuments of John Foxe*, ed. Stephan Reed Cattely, 8 vols. (London: Seeley and Burnside, 1837–41), v, 362–404. For a criticism of the play, Foxe as a source, the problem of authorship and related matters see Felix Emanuel Shelling, *The English Chronicle Play* (New York: Macmillan, 1902), pp. 215–18.

[6] *Acts and Monuments*, v, 404–7.

From the Tower, Cromwell wrote to the king, begging some show of mercy. One after another, old friends declined to take the letter to Henry VIII, 'whereof when none durst take the carriage upon him, Sir Ralph Sadler went unto the king to understand his pleasure, whether he would permit him to bring the letter or not'. Obtaining permission, Sadler then read the letter three times, 'inasmoche as the king seemed to be moved therewith'.[1] Such is the account of Foxe, who stands alone among writers close to the events in question in giving some account of the trial to which Sadler was put. The king could hardly have missed the qualities of loyalty and courage then displayed by the one man willing to risk the royal ire in behalf of Cromwell, one who had for so many years dispensed royal graces to those about him in a way reminiscent of Wolsey.

The gravity and meaning of Sadler's actions were caught by a Jacobean dramatist in an interesting play once wrongly placed in the Shakespeare canon. There, Cromwell charged Sadler:

> Sir Ralph Sadler, pray a word with you
> You were my man, and all that you possesse
> Came by this meanes, to requite all this,
> Will you take this letter here of me,
> And give it with your owne handes to the Kinge?

To which Sadler answered:

> I kiss your hand, and never will I rest,
> Ere to the Kinge this be delivered.[2]

Thus did Sadler return the trust and favour so generously bestowed by Cromwell, playing the role of 'one frende in store' in a way not unlike that attempted by Cromwell eleven years before. But where the poet supplied a last minute reprieve, unfortunately delivered moments after the fall of the executioner's axe, our contemporary source shows Sadler performing no such mission.[3]

The exigencies of drama aside, the play reflected well the parallelism of the situations of 1529 and 1540. Where Cromwell's entire career

---

[1] *Acts and Monuments*, v, 404.   [2] *The True Chronicle Historie...*, pp. 46–7.

[3] *Ibid.* p. 49. For the whole matter of the letters begging clemency see Merriman, *Life and Letters of Thomas Cromwell*, II, nos. 349 and 350, esp. the note to no. 350. He identifies the bearer of the first letter as Sadler and the second as Vaughan. An anonymous tract entitled *The Life of Thomas Lord Cromwell* (London: J. Roberts, 1715) treats of the matter of letters begging clemency but mentions that *none* would dare carry the letters (p. 32).

before 1529 was inextricably linked with Wolsey's, Sadler's before 1540 cannot be separated from that of his own great patron. As we have already observed, even after entering the royal service, Sadler remained Cromwell's man in all things. It is therefore not difficult to understand why Sir Ralph Sadler came to be Cromwell's heir in things political, ready to carry forward the work of administration in a way commensurate with the designs of his master, having in mind perhaps the political testament which our playwright provided for him:

> Flatter not fortune, neither frowne upon her,
> Gape not for state, yet loose no sparke of honour.
> Ambition, like the plague, see thou eschew it.
> I die for treason, man, and never knew it.[1]

Whether or not Sir Ralph Sadler was suited for the tasks that he fell heir to, we must now examine.

---

[1] *The True Chronicle Historie...*, pp. 47–8. See also Elton, 'Thomas Cromwell's decline and fall', *CHJ*, x (1951), 150–85, for supporting arguments.

4

MASTER SECRETARY

...Therefore the prince's assurance must be his confidence in the secretary, and the secretary's life his trust in his prince.

ROBERT CECIL

Cromwell's rise and fall equally provided opportunities for Sir Ralph Sadler, since the politics of the 1540s were in large measure determined by Cromwell's successes and failures. So was the direction of Sir Ralph Sadler's subsequent career. His very existence at the centre of power and intrigue was a consequence of the Cromwellian revolution, although it was merely a significant coincidence that his rise was marked by the dispersion of the monks of Waltham abbey, the last of the great houses to be dissolved, which fell almost on the very day of Sadler's promotion to the secretary's office.[1]

The date and circumstances of Sadler's advance to the secretaryship are somewhat obscure. The secretary was then appointed by word of mouth or household warrant.[2] In any case, no enrolment was made in chancery. It is therefore worth noting that Charles Wriothesley, a cousin of Sadler's co-secretary and an astute chronicler of Henry VIII's last years, reported that Sadler and Wriothesley were promoted in April 1540.[3] He also recorded the knighting of both men. But his account supplies no precise date for the ceremonies, while certain state papers leave the point in doubt, especially a letter from Cromwell to Sadler, dated 7 April 1540, addressed to 'Mr Secretarie' but omitting the title of knighthood.[4] Another document states clearly that Sadler's

[1] Hughes, *History of the Reformation in England*, I, 327.

[2] The original warrant is in PRO, SP 1/158, fos. 153–6, undated. A copy is in the British Museum, but also without date (Stowe MSS. 141, fo. 78). The warrant is printed in *SP*, II, 623–4.

[3] *A Chronicle of England during the Reigns of the Tudors from 1485 to 1559*, ed. W. H. Douglas, 2 vols. (London: Camden Society, 1875–86), I, 115. This work is of great value for the years 1540–59.

[4] Evans, *The Principal Secretary of State*, p. 34, claimed that the promotion and knighthood came together. There are some notices to the effect that Sadler was knighted before April 1540: BM Arundel MSS, 97, fo. 170b, 21 Jan. 1539 (not in a contemporary hand) and PRO, E 210/ D 10497, 16 Nov. 1538 (not in a contemporary hand). See also Cromwell's salutation: BM Royal MSS. 7C xvi, fo. 149, in which he hails Sadler as secretary of state but makes no mention of knighthood. Cromwell was very careful in his form of address, never omitting honours and titles of rank. Here, however, 'mastre', traditional usage in addressing a knight, is ambiguous.

initiation into that order was performed on 18 April. On that day the recently created secretaries heard Cromwell's new dignity of rank read out, as he became Earl of Essex and Lord Chamberlain. Immediately after Cromwell's installation the two secretaries were 'made knightes and paid their fees...'.[1] Each of them was invested with an annuity adequate to the burdens of the office.[2]

Apart from any constitutional significance inherent in the division of the office between Wriothesley and Sadler, Pollard and Dr Hughes were quick to see the political significance of that step. The new secretaries were, after all, Cromwell's men, his satellites, appointed on the very eve of their master's downfall.[3] Hence, politically, the move seemed to have some relationship to the efforts made by Cromwell to sustain his influence in the king's council, to advance his policies and opinions. But this also adumbrates the essential novelty of Cromwell in the constitutional equation of the day. He had been a secretary and minister who was neither a servant incapable of pursuing an independent line of action nor a functionary carrying on the business of government in the king's name. While he never uttered the phrase *ego et meus rex* as had Wolsey, he seemed at times to follow policies and goals of his own choosing, using whatever means came to hand and often creating new ones.

The new secretaries of state were apparently means towards Cromwell's ends, although this view has not gone unchallenged. Indeed, until very recently, an opposite point of view prevailed. The king, according to the once standard interpretation of the division of 1540, realised that Cromwell's political power threatened the balance of the monarchical constitution, reluctantly admitting that an independent minister was a luxury he could no longer afford. His experiences with Wolsey and Cromwell had more than convinced him of that truth. It was Henry who had suggested to Cromwell that the secretaryship be divided, in order to increase the efficiency of a much burdened office, while at the same time diminishing the power of its incumbent. Furthermore, Henry knew that Sadler and Wriothesley would eventually come to rest on opposite sides of the political fence. Hence, he could use the one

---

[1] BM Harleian MSS. 6,074, fos. 57b–58a.

[2] PRO, E 315/235, fo. 31b, an enrolment of the annuity dated 25 Sept. 1540 'pro supportatione onerum offici'.

[3] Pollard, *Henry VIII*, p. 394; Hughes, *History of the Reformation in England*, II, 9.

47

to balance the other; Henry VIII was the master-craftsman of the constitution in 1540.[1]

This elaborate and attractive thesis must be scrutinised closely, if we are to understand Sadler's part in the political life of the 1540s. If Henry VIII really feared that Cromwell was making a party in the state, why did he not appoint men of an entirely opposite faction to the divided office? It was no secret that Sadler was warm in his support of the policy of reform, the policy Henry was on the verge of disavowing when he let the conservatives tear at Cromwell's heels.[2] Furthermore, it seems quixotic to maintain that Henry intended to reduce the influence of the secretaryship, since he allowed each of the two new incumbents to exercise the full powers of that office. Finally, it was the case that both Wriothesley and Sadler were equally Cromwell's debtors. In the light of these facts Henry's actions were calculated to increase the supposed danger arising from the Cromwellians, unless we suppose that the shrewd and powerful king posited by this thesis was ignorant of Sadler's views or ignored what he knew to be true. The king knew of the high regard in which Sadler and Wriothesley held one another.[3]

These facts demand a quite different interpretation of the events of April 1540, one put forward by in part Dr Elton, and one which accords better with the known facts. The initiative came from Cromwell's administration, in which political matters and the routine of government were far more important than any supposed constitutional innovation. The move was in effect a brilliant stratagem in Cromwell's struggle to remain alive.

Cromwell had made the secretaryship the centre of administration. By controlling the writing processes of the state and by shrewdly manipulating finance, Cromwell had achieved temporal power in excess of that enjoyed by Wolsey. Through the financial machinery he controlled the pace of the government's movement; through the secretarial office he controlled the flow of political favour. The secretary of state had full power over the signet office, a fact that enabled him to

[1] Evans, *The Principal Secretary of State*, pp. 33–4.
[2] *Ibid.* p. 36.
[3] See below for the powers of the secretaries and the friendship existing between them. Pollard, *Henry VIII*, p. 402, saw their survival as the result of a rapid change of front, for which problem see ch. 7 below.

stop or start the entire network of patronage, dependent as political grace was on the application of the seals. It was the secretary who stood nearest the Crown in such matters. He secured the royal assent to every petition or bill; he dammed the flood of benevolence.[1] While it was true that Cromwell also held the privy seal, he could ill afford to let the signet slip through his fingers. Yet he needed to be divested of the routine work connected with the secretaryship and the signet, if he was to succeed in remaking his policies in a way satisfactory to the king.[2]

In that dilemma nothing seemed more natural to Cromwell than a division of the office between two men who together knew every phase of his own business and that of the secretaryship. They would control the office for him. For a number of years before 1540 Wriothesley had been his personal agent at the signet and the privy seal. Sadler had been his representative at Court.[3] Their combined efforts would actually improve Cromwell's hold on power. One of his chief difficulties had always been his inability to remain with the king in order to curb his critics and at the same time attend to the press of affairs. Now, one of the secretaries could attend the king, faithfully representing his patron's point of view. The other could remain in London, keeping a watch on the operation of the sealing process and the horde of politicians drawn to the centre of government like flies to sugar. Sadler and Wriothesley would work in tandem; they would be the eyes and ears of a remote but omnipotent minister.

Sadler's labours in the 1530s lend some colour of truth to this construction of the innovation of 1540. But what of Wriothesley? While his career is not our real concern, the interpretation of Sadler's advance here advocated demands that we know exactly how Sadler's partner rose to the secretaryship in 1540. In the absence of any study of his early career, we must ourselves offer some evidence for the case made above.

The only volume of papers dealing solely with Wriothesley now preserved in the Public Record Office amply supports our contention.[4] It fully demonstrates his role in Cromwell's household and at the signet and privy seal during the 1530s, while Sadler busied himself with the

---

[1] Elton, *CHJ*, XI, 155.

[2] Elton, *The Tudor Revolution in Government*, pp. 298–315.

[3] *Ibid.* pp. 312 ff.

[4] PRO, SP 7/1, a volume of some eighty letters which has never been carefully studied for the light it throws on either Wriothesley or patronage and political factions.

loftier matters of diplomacy and court intrigue.[1] These letters show Wriothesley's vigilance in matters touching the seals and patronage. Those avid for favour knew to whom to turn. One correspondent promised to pay 'as goode a geldyng as you ever rode' for his favour in a suit.[2] Another offered to share a part of one thousand marks sterling in return for passage of a privy seal bill.[3] John Orforde flatly promised twenty marks for Wriothesley's help in speeding an already favoured request.[4] William Passhe sent an 'amblyng nagge' for a favour done.[5] Richard Palmer, a member of the Calais garrison, urged that Wriothesley intervene on his behalf with Cromwell, assuring him the present 'recompense for your paynes...'.[6] More than a score of similar letters could be adduced to show the nature and power of Wriothesley's position: in Tudor England payment and power went together.[7] It is therefore worth noticing that other Cromwellians were anxious to secure aid from Wriothesley, including William Paget and his own agent[8] as well as William Petre, both soon to be secretaries of state subsequent to Sadler and Wriothesley.[9] Even Sadler had been a suitor to his friend 'to do for me lyke my frende as I have alwaies founde you and as ye shal alwaies finde me'.[10] On occasion, Sadler's own servants, operating from a vantage point much further down the line of power and influence, had recourse to their master's good offices in order to obtain favours from Wriothesley.[11]

In the course of this service to Cromwell both Sadler and Wriothesley became members of the royal household.[12] Their work advanced their sovereign's interest as well as their patron's. The harmony of their own working relationship is suggested by the fact that a single document speeding some suit or bit of state business might bear the signatures of both men.[13] Thus the promotions of 1540 merely gave official sanction to an already well-established working arrangement.[14] Such was Cromwell's accomplishment, according to Dr Elton.[15] Even Wriothesley's subsequent desertion does not lessen the force of the argument.

---

[1] See chh. 7–9 below. [2] PRO, SP 7/1, no. 5.
[3] *Ibid.* no. 7. [4] *Ibid.* no. 13. [5] *Ibid.* no. 17. [6] *Ibid.* no. 27.
[7] *Ibid.* nos. 1–4, 8, 10, 16, 29, 37, 41, 45, 47, 49, 51, 54, 64, 65 and 73.
[8] *Ibid.* no. 14. [9] *Ibid.* nos. 21–3. [10] *Ibid.* no. 40. [11] *Ibid.* no. 51.
[12] *Ibid.* no. 65. [13] PRO, SP 1/99, fo. 117 and 101, fos. 57–8.
[14] This interpretation is similar to that of Elton, obviously, but reflects the work of the author on a basic problem from a perspective different from that employed by Dr Elton.
[15] Elton, *The Tudor Revolution in Government*, pp. 312 ff.

Sadler came to the secretaryship at a time when the power of the office had increased markedly. His place was a far cry from that once held by the clerk of the wardrobe under Edward II, a man who knew the king's business, knew what was *secretum* simply because he was close to the king.[1] Slowly but steadily the secretary's power grew as he functioned in the interstices of offices in varying stages of transition. During the course of the centuries the subordinate officers of the household had shouldered aside the ancient aristocracy of royal servants, a trend given new impetus by the pronounced revival of household government under the Yorkist and early Tudor kings. The movement was especially prominent under Henry VIII, perhaps for no other reason than the notable fact of the competence of Pace, Gardiner and Cromwell. Such men would have elevated the power of any office in an age during which men made the offices they filled.[2]

Yet, paradoxically, one might speak of Sadler's post as barely emerged from its childhood. It had none of the dignity of the great state offices that had 'gone out of court' in the thrifty times of Edward I. Even a Cecil or Cromwell felt the pinch in that regard, which may well help account for their pursuit of the privy seal or the treasurer's staff. Cromwell had added to the dignity of the secretaryship in 1539, when he obtained from Henry VIII a new set of household ordinances elevating the prestige of the secretary of state, a personal triumph that did not survive his own surrender of the post. When Sadler and Wriothesley shared the office, it was immediately returned to the second rank of precedence, well below that enjoyed by the ancient and noble positions at Court.[3] Nevertheless, mere household office had its compensations, not the least of which was the ceaseless contact afforded Sadler with the king.

A secretary's advance could not be halted by a ceremonial setback. A wide variety of duties insured that Sadler and his partner must be powerful ministers of the ambulant king. These fell into five more or less distinct categories. The most important of course was the custody and application of the seal. Then, there was the complex of functions

---

[1] Tout, *Chapters*, I, 30.

[2] Brewer, *The Reign of Henry VIII*, I, 68. See also the pioneer effort by J. Otway-Ruthven, *The King's Secretary in the Fifteenth Century* (Cambridge University Press, 1939), *passim*.

[3] Evans, *The Principal Secretary of State*, pp. 1–4; Elton, *The Tudor Revolution in Government*, pp. 124 ff. and *The Tudor Constitution*, pp. 120–1, for discussion of the ordinance.

determined by the fact that the secretaries were the recognised channel of communication between the Crown and the subject. *Ex officio* the secretaries were important parliamentarians. Again, the office was emerging as the focal point of the nascent diplomatic service. Finally, the secretaries played a major role in matters of domestic security, chiefly because they were always members of the small number of councillors appointed to inquire into treasons and heresies. Thus the secretary of state was expected to attain competence in every aspect of administration related to what we should call foreign and domestic affairs. His powers were effectively limited only by the disposition of the king's will.[1]

The royal favour fell for the most part on men of marked ability. But even the ablest of them, a Robert Cecil for example, was dismayed by the burdens and responsibilities that were the secretary's:

All officers and counsellours of princes have a prescribed authority by patent, by custom, or by oath, the secretary only excepted, but to the secretary, out of the confidence and a singular affection, there is a liberty to negotiation at discretion at home and abroad...Therefore the prince's assurance must be his confidence in the secretary, and the secretary's life his trust in his prince.[2]

Sadler's handling of these complex responsibilities needs attention in two ways: on the evidence supplied by Sadler's tenure of office substantiating the five-part division of labour; secondly, and more impor-

[1] No treatise on the office survives from the Henrician era. My general statement of secretarial burdens is a composite gathered from my own reading of Sadler's papers, from several Elizabethan treatises and from the literature of administrative history. The chief Tudor writings are BM Yelverton MSS. CLXII, 'A Treatise of the Office of Counsellour and Principall Secretaire to Her Maiestie, Composed by R.B.' That is doubtless the work of Robert Beale, the brother-in-law of Sir Nicholas Wotten, who expected to be appointed secretary in 1593. This tract is printed in full in Conyers Read, *Mr. Secretary Walsingham and the Policy of Queen Elizabeth*, 3 vols. (Oxford: Clarendon Press, 1925), I, 424–39. The other great Tudor treatise is Nicholas Faunt's 'Discourse Touching the Office of Principall Secretary of Estate that now is *et cetera*', in Oxford, Bodleian Library, Tanner MSS. 80, fos. 91–4, printed by Charles Hughes in *EHR*, xx (1905), 499–508. Other manuscripts that throw light on the subject are BM Add. MSS. 35818, 'The Signet Register of Sir Ralph Sadler' and 35840, 'The Letter Book of Roger Ascham, Latin Secretary'. Also of use are BM Stowe MSS. 162, 'Walsingham's Table Book' and Harleian MSS. 6085, 'Walsingham's Official Journal'.

[2] *The Harleian Miscellany*, ed. William Oldys, 8 vols. (London: 1744–6), II, 265. Although the comparative study of European administrative history is in its infancy it can be stated that in most states the secretary was viewed as the most intimate of the royal counsellors. For the best modern treatment of the problem with a critical review of the bibliography see Fritz Hartung and Roland Mousnier, 'Quelques problemes concernant la monarchie absolue', *Relazioni* (Florence, Italy: 10th International Congress of the Historical Sciences, 1955), IV, 3–55. For England and its relationship to continental developments see Gerald A. Aylmer, *The King's Servants* (London: Routledge and Kegan Paul, 1961), pp. 439–53.

tant, a dynamic account of Sadler's tenancy. This latter objective will necessitate an extended treatment of diplomatic and political questions which will be reserved for subsequent chapters. Here we can deal only with the formal aspects of his work during the period 1540–3.

Sadler's role as a parliamentary leader *ex officio* cannot be too clearly demonstrated due to the paucity of Henrician parliamentary sources. That he was an active member of Commons, however, can be established. Although Sadler retained the Cromwellian privilege of attending the Lords from time to time, his main role was in the lower House. The king took special notice of his and Wriothesley's service there, while allowing them to attend the Lords on special occasions. If the king or the speaker of the Commons was to be in the House of Lords, both secretaries could appear there without any breach of privilege. They might also be summoned to the upper House to supply information of a technical sort. In much the same way, of course, they gave special help to the Commons in legislative work. But the normal situation was for each of the secretaries to sit for a week in each house alternately.[1] Yet, we must be careful about attributing this or that action to Sadler in his secretarial capacity. He wore two hats. As a councillor he was part of the corps of men who maintained the Crown's corner on the initiative. That alone would account for the part taken by Sadler in the direction of debate and the expediting of bills. We do have an occasional glimpse of Sadler doing just that.[2]

As one of the king's agents in Parliament Sadler was required to speak effectively in behalf of the Crown in all matters touching the

[1] Sir Thomas Smith, *De republica anglorum*, ed. L. Alston (Cambridge University Press, 1906), p. 51. The question of writs of assistance is discussed by E. R. Adair and F. M. Evans, 'Writs of Assistance, 1558–1700', *EHR*, XXXVI (1921), 356–72. An examination of the writs in PRO, C 218/1 reveals that the secretaries did receive formal writs. The authors of the article erred, however, in asserting that Sir Thomas Smith spoke in a session of the Lords in 1549 (p. 360). Sir John Neale advises me that the discussion of the Book of Common Prayer on 14 Dec. 1549 was not a session but a colloquy in which members of both houses could freely participate. The earliest Tudor writ comes in 1545, when Paget and Petre were called: C 218/1, no. 3.

[2] The expansion of the secretary's role in Parliament is best studied in Elton, 'The Evolution of a Tudor Statute', *EHR*, LXIV (1949), 174–97; 'Parliamentary Drafts, 1529–1540', *BIHR*, XXV (1952), 117–32 and his 'A Further Note on Parliamentary Drafts in the Reign of Henry VIII', *BIHR*, XXVII (1954), 198–200. The discussion began with Wallace Notestein, 'The Winning of the Initiative by the House of Commons', *Proceedings of the British Academy*, XI (1926), 125–76. Neale throws much light on this matter in his books about Elizabethan parliaments. For Sadler see John Strype, *Annals of the Reformation and the Establishment of Religion*, 4 vols. in 7 parts (Oxford: Clarendon Press, 1824), I, i, 99, where he is mentioned as a frequent transmitter of bills from one house to another.

royal prerogative and other monarchical affairs. Although none of the scant records of Henrician Parliaments records a speech delivered by Sadler, we can obtain a fair idea of his style as a speaker from several Elizabethan addresses that have survived. It is clear from these sources that Sadler was a vigorous and polished speaker and debater. He was at his best in treating issues of a highly controversial nature, a feature of his oratory that caused Sir William Petyt, the seventeenth-century parliamentarian and Williamite antiquarian, to style Sadler a 'fearless defender of the right'. Petyt also noted that Sir Ralph excelled in the delivery of 'dangerous speeches', truly the mark of a great Commons' man.[1]

Perhaps the most vital task assigned to the secretary of state, far more important than the parliamentary duties about which we are so scantily informed, was that of caring for the signet which was in Sadler's keeping, although he rarely applied the seal in person. In actual practice bills were presented to the secretary and were then shown by him to the king. If Sadler favoured a petition or bill, he attempted to influence the king's opinion of the matter therein presented.[2] Once the royal assent was gained, Sadler would then send such bills to the signet office, where one of the four clerks ordinarily drafted a formal warrant authorising the privy seal clerks to send their own warrant to chancery. Before a signet warrant went forward, however, the clerks submitted their draft to the secretary for his approval and counter-signature. Only then could the seal be applied to legalise the bill. This sequence of events illustrates perfectly the nature of the vast influence and power exercised by the secretary of state. From the great bulk of correspondence and suits daily presented, Sadler and Wriothesley had to select those for immediate presentation. It was therefore almost impossible for any action to go forward without their favour, although more powerful patrons could be sought in an effort to force the secretary to act. Even then, given the utter dependence of the signet clerks on the secretaries, given the need for their counter-signing all warrants, the timing of crucial suits dictated that all but the incautious or the mighty mollify the king's secretary.[3]

[1] Petyt's remark is preserved in the margin of a copy of Sadler's speeches now with the parliamentary collections of Inner Temple Library, Petyt MSS. 535/4, fos. 289a–295b. Council speeches are recorded in 535/4, fos. 282a–289a.

[2] In actual practice petitions and bills for the signet were distinguished, if at all, by a step in the process of sealing, apparently, since a petition become a bill by virtue of the secretary counter-signing the draft of an approved petition.

[3] See Evans, *The Principal Secretary of State*, pp. 155 ff.

The operation of the system during Sadler's tenure of office can be studied, due chiefly to the accident of survival that has made his signet register for the period 1540–2 the earliest extant document of its kind. Preserved among the Hardwicke Papers in the British Museum, the document truly has singular interest to our story in particular and to Tudor scholars in general.[1]

Sadler kept the book in order to comply with the direct order given him when he took office.[2] That order in turn was based on a reform sanctioned by a statute drafted by Cromwell, who no doubt realised the value of recording the affairs of the signet office. The secretaries were thus enjoined to keep a record of everything passing their seal, each of them to keep a separate register or docket book. Each of them was also to have complete freedom of access to the record kept by his fellow secretary. Further, they were to keep a tabulation of all signet warrants sent to other departments of state and of all warrants authorising action on private petitions. Thus, every gift or grant or other writing that eventually had to pass the great seal had first to go through the secretary's hands.[3]

Sadler and Wriothesley stood to benefit directly from this evidence of Cromwell's struggle to increase his power. Although they might wish to consult one of the law officers of the Crown touching some suit or another, the real initiative in the whole process of meeting the demands of patronage rested with them. They kept their clerks well supplied with precedent books as a means of tightening their own hold. Since Sadler rarely entrusted the signet to anybody but one of his own most trusted agents, his control was virtually complete. Hence the tempo of politics often depended on the temper of the secretary of state.[4]

This power is amply illustrated by the contents of Sadler's register. Bills and petitions sent forward at the king's order were always allowed to pass the signet without the exaction of the traditional fees and were always so entered (*nihil quia per regem*). Sadler took advantage of this himself on a number of occasions when a perpetuity was at issue, for which the charges were considerable.[5] But an even larger number of

---

[1] BM Add. MSS. 33818 (also listed as Hardwicke MSS. 470), covering the period Apr. 1540–Dec. 1542.

[2] BM Stowe MSS. 141, fo. 78. [3] *SR*, III, 542, 27 Henry VIII c. 11.

[4] Edward Chamberlayne, *Angliae Notitia*, 2 vols. (London: T.N. 1679), II, 11. See also Evans. *The Principal Secretary of State*, pp. 195–7.

[5] The difference between warrants and perpetuities was one of value and not the term of years involved. Ordinary grants of all kinds cost 6s. 8d. Perpetuities cost 60s.

gratis entries were made in behalf of various third parties patronised by Sadler by the waiving of fees.[1] That Wriothesley carried on a similar practice may be inferred from the existence of a unique entry in Sadler's register recording the gift of a prebend's post in Durham cathedral without charge. It was noted that this was business in Wriothesley's register done 'at mi lorde of Duresmes suite'. Wriothesley's transactions were always summarised in Sadler's register, thus providing confirmation of the common nature of his own practice.[2]

There were still other ways in which the signet was an expression of Sadler's influence. There is bound into the register kept by Sadler a single foreign page signed by Sadler and sealed with *his* signet ring.[3] It is a unique record of what Sadler wished to do at a particular time. At first glance it seems to be a mere list of names in Sadler's hand. But more careful examination proves that it is a list of things to be remembered, the only one of its kind found for Sadler's tenure of office. Here is a partial transcription of its contents:

Mense Junii anno regni Henrici Octavi xxxiij. A gifte of a certain tenemente in London to Mr Hobbye,[4] a wardshypp to Mr Cofferer,[5] a gifte in fee simple to Mr Bryan.[6] A denizen for Mr John Tyler Frenchemanne, an indenture to Mr John Semeondes, a wardshypp to Elizabeth Edwardes. The endowement of Rochestre, the erectyon of Rochestre. A speciall lyvery to Lutterall, the like to Humphrey Swynnerton. A forfait to John Belsonn, and indenture to John Chytlynge. A presentacyon for Lelylow. A goode lease to Frances Knollys gentilmanne pencyoner.[7] A commission to Clarenciaulx. A fyne lease to John Wennyworthe knt. The kepyng of a lunatycke to John Peers. An exchange of landes for Syr Thomas Seymour. A graunte of a fayre to the towne of Gyllyngham. A denizen to be made of Hugh Ryall Scott. An office for mi frende Rychard Lyngham.

Only six items listed passed the signet in June. The grants for Peckham

---

[1] Prominent names were Lord Audley, Sir John Dudley, Sir Richard Lee, Sir Edward North, Lord Cromwell and Sir Richard Cromwell. Most *gratis* issues happened for reasons now lost, but several were issued by virtue of specified suits: e.g. 'at the suite of Mr Burnes', 'at Master Laygmets suite' and 'upon Stowaldes suite'.

[2] BM Add. MSS. 35818, fo. 68.

[3] *Ibid.* fo. 39a. When page numbers were inserted in a later hand pagination was continuous. Sadler's signet contained a small classical head, possibly that of Caesar, rather deeply set; it measured $\frac{1}{2}$ in. in length and about $\frac{1}{4}$ in. in width.

[4] Sir Philip Hobby, a very prominent courtier and official.

[5] Sir Edward Pechham received a wardship that month: see BM Add. MSS. 45716, fo. 21.

[6] Certainly Sir Francis Bryan, an old friend and Hackney man.

[7] Knollys received a lease at the time: BM Add. MSS. 45716, fo. 6b.

and Knollys passed in July.[1] Without this knowledge, it might have been possible to construe the list as an account of things that had to be done, either by direct royal order or for some other adequate reason. But the inclusion of such personal qualifications as 'goode lease' and 'mi frende' suggest another conclusion. The paper represents a number of favours Sadler wished to expedite, either for reasons of his own or because of the inherent worth of the petition from those suitors quite unknown to Sadler. Further light is thrown on the secretary's sphere of influence when one considers the avenues of patronage encompassed by the list: lunatics, wards, offices, denizenships and grants of land, all easily within Sadler's grasp.

These facts relate directly to another aspect of Sadler's work as secretary of state. He was the chief link between the king and the nation. Here the evidence of the signet register is equally illuminating. It shows beyond a doubt that Wriothesley handled more signet business than did Sadler. Perhaps that was due to Sadler's frequent and prolonged absences related to Scottish diplomacy.[2] Whatever the reason, Wriothesley soon was established as a more effective go-between with Henry VIII's subjects than Sadler.

Sadler, however, was far from ineffective. A brief sampling of documents from the register illustrates the point completely. The town of Shrewsbury begged Sir Ralph's aid in their request for a new charter.[3] Suitors within the jurisdiction of the Court for offences committed within 'the verge' were referred to Sadler.[4] Other subjects, even so powerful a man as Cromwell,[5] asked the secretary's help in expediting some legal matters involving a private suit, despite the fact that such suits were always to be channelled through the common law courts or the masters of requests.[6] One such suitor, no doubt a very cautious man and a learned one, addressed the secretary in petitions written in Latin, French and English, to better obtain the necessary 'supportation'.[7] Constantly busy with a hundred-and-one such routine

---

[1] See p. 56, nn. 5 and 7. Perhaps some items listed by Sadler passed Wriothesley's signet.

[2] Sadler's register rarely showed a large number of entries, even when both secretaries were at court together.

[3] *L & P*, xvII, 285 (10).   [4] *L & P*, xv, 1,027 (7).

[5] BM Royal MSS. 7C xvi, fo. 149, Thomas Cromwell to Ralph Sadler, undated.

[6] Read, *Mr Secretary Walsingham*, I, 424.

[7] BM Royal MSS. 7C xvi, fo. 152a, 3 Apr. 1540, the sons of John Heron to Ralph Sadler.

matters, the secretary found little relief when he inclined toward the court itself.[1]

He was expected to be available as a link between the king and the council. Sadler was specifically charged with writing to the council on a variety of subjects touching the court, the country and the continent. The matter at hand might be a letter to Lord Lisle and Southwell concerning the fortifications at Berwick.[2] Orders in council had to be drafted for such a minor thing as the arrest of a disturber of the peace on the Scottish borders.[3] Or perhaps Sir Edward Seymour wished authority to try a man for treason under conditions of martial law.[4] The same commander also wrote to Wriothesley, begging him to move Sadler in order to expedite the shipment of needed supplies.[5] If the king's commissioners for the forced loan visited Hertfordshire, as they did in 1542, they confessed that without Sadler's help they would surely fail to raise the required sum from the local gentry.[6] Councillors away from London plagued the secretary for the latest political news.[7] On some occasions, especially when gossip and politics were inextricably linked, Sadler replied at length; a good example in his telling the duke of Norfolk about Henry VIII's passionate unhappiness with Anne of Cleves.[8] This summary statement can easily be supplemented by any consideration of the council registers themselves.[9]

Another activity of the secretary involved the internal security of England. His role was twofold. There was the ordinary process of gathering information from the shires. Sadler also attended to the more demanding business of sifting the wheat from the chaff in matters of heresy and treason.[10] These were often indissolubly linked and were an important concern of Sadler and Wriothesley, but they can best be understood in a different context, hence discussion of such issues will be pursued separately. Both ordinary matters of security and the special cases of heresy and treason might have military aspects and the secretary

[1] See ch. 8 below for a discussion of place and profit.
[2] *L & P*, XVII, 399, 13 Dec. 1542.
[3] *Ibid.* 1,251 (29), 30 Dec. 1542.
[4] *Ibid.* appendix A, no. 9, 9 May 1542.
[5] BM Add. MSS. 32648, fo. 162, 29 Nov. 1542.
[6] PRO, SP 1/170, fo. 122, Sir Anthony Browne to Sadler, 13 May 1542.
[7] *L & P*, XVI, 932, William Paget to Thomas Wriothesley, 27 June 1541.
[8] *L & P*, XV, 883, 13 June 1540, in Sadler's hand.
[9] *L & P*, XVI–XVIII, esp. the summaries of Privy Council actions.
[10] See ch. 7 for the Catherine Howard investigation.

had to be prepared to follow such details carefully.[1] Especially important in this regard was the constant preoccupation with the recruitment
of troops whenever war threatened.[2] Furthermore, the most difficult
logistical problems often crossed Sadler's desk.[3] The secretary was also
expected to keep the council informed of the progress of the war efforts
under way, if such there were.[4] The routine security of the court fell
within his purview.[5] In connection with all of these areas of security,
Sadler might on occasion apprehend suspects or cause them to be
apprehended.[6] Although surviving evidence in this area is ambiguous,
it appears that the secretary had powers of arrest. On record there is a
case in which Sadler personally committed a man to the Marshalsea.[7]
When any matter took a dramatic turn, such as the occasion of Lord
Leonard Grey's alleged betrayal of England in Ireland, Sadler busily
surveyed the entire Grey correspondence.[8] All in all, even where the
documents are thin, it is fair to state that security matters were vital in
the daily work of Sadler's secretariat.

No matter what importance we attribute to any of the roles already
treated, late Tudor tracts dealing with the secretaryship of state make it
clear that diplomacy was the special province of the secretary. Nicholas
Faunt pointed to that fact intentionally, in the course of complaining
about the variety and uncertainty of the secretary's labours.[9] He illustrated his point by stating that while domestic correspondence was
'consuming', by virtue of sheer volume, foreign letters required
infinitely more care, since such matters touched the friends of the
sovereign in a direct and personal fashion.[10] The secretary laboured under
a mountain of intelligence reports, ciphers, dispatches from resident
ambassadors, negotiations and other 'bookes peculiar to forraine
services'.[11]

---

[1] No study of this problem exists for the Tudor era.

[2] *L & P*, XVII, 1,192, Ralph Sadler to Sir Thomas Seymour, 12 Dec. 1542, requiring him to
recruit landsknechts in the Nurnberg district.

[3] *Ibid.* p. 903, Privy Council to Commissioners at York, 4 Oct. 1542, draft in Sadler's hand;
and 925 (2), same to the same, 8 Oct. 1542.

[4] *Ibid.* p. 764, 10 Sept. 1542; for other military matters see 776, 886 (2), 889 (2) and 1,141.

[5] *L & P*, XV, 1,027 (1).

[6] Sir Harris Nicholas, *Proceedings and Ordinances of the Privy Council in England*, 7 vols. (London:
1837), VII, 10. (Hereafter cited as *Proceedings and Ordinances*.)

[7] *Ibid.* p. 11. The power of arrest was mentioned by Beale: 'and if the secretarie commit anie
manne of hymselfe, let his manne kepe a note of it...' (Read, *Mr Secretary Walsingham*, I, 426).

[8] *Proceedings and Ordinances*, VII, 96–101. Grey's was a courtesy title.

[9] Hughes, 'Faunt's Discourse', p. 500.   [10] *Ibid.* p. 501.   [11] *Ibid.* pp. 502–3.

To do all this, Sadler had to keep a staff or expert clerks about, among them a loyal 'inwarde manne' or confidential clerk, without whom the mountain of work could not be accomplished. Beale and Faunt agreed on that point, while the former went a little further in his discussion of the problem. According to Beale, the secretary ought to keep a set of files or cabinets for every category of papers entrusted to his care. A circumspect agent was to look to the ordering of the entire system of record keeping. To insure that these files were well stocked, a good secretary had to retain the services of trustworthy and gentlemanly 'spies' in every major European city and at the chief courts of the continent. The best use of their services depended on the secretary's own mastery of geography, a relatively new and sometimes occult science. Know your Ortelius! That was Beale's advice. Beyond that, the secretary must be a good linguist, a close student of history, a master of Christian doctrine and a man well informed about religion in general.[1] Such was the recipe for secretarial success.

All of this added together was enough to make the office difficult, if not impossible. Yet, upon mature consideration, another problem faced Sadler as an incumbent, a problem of special interest in any effort to understand the Scottish diplomacy of Sir Ralph Sadler. Constitutionally, the secretary was nothing more than the executor of such policies made by the king and the council. He was not charged with the design of policy, although a Cromwell or a Cecil did just that. In fact, initiative and responsibility in foreign affairs was badly split. A good secretary of state might suffer for the failure of a policy conceived by others, with lines of implementation also externally directed.[2]

Sadler provides a good example of this trouble of the Tudor system. I say this for an obvious reason. In his own time Sadler was known primarily as a diplomat skilled in the execution of difficult instructions, while never enjoying the reputation of being a great statesman of an innovatory sort. His greatest qualities were those of the good diplomatic administrator: loyal subordination and the ability to serve an exacting and often impatiently capricious master. This raises the capital question of his tenure of the secretarial office: who really was responsible for the failure of English diplomacy in Scotland in the 1540s?

[1] Read, *Mr Secretary Walsingham*, I, 427–33. Ortelius was a famous Dutch cosmographer.
[2] Evans, *The Principal Secretary of State*, pp. 320–1.

Before any answer to that question can be had, another must first be attempted. Did Sadler have the basic qualities obviously required of any successful holder of the office he inherited from Cromwell in 1540?

It was a commonplace of the sixteenth century that secretaries of state be university men. Indeed, Beale and Faunt seem to be describing sages and scholars, not secretaries, in their commentaries on the office and its holders.[1] Richard Pace, diplomat and early Tudor secretary, sang the praises of the tough, classical education then available as a necessity for success in secretarial work.[2] Laymen of Pace's talent were required to bring the same learning to their tasks brought by clerics like Ruthal, men proverbially at the top of the heap of late medieval education.[3] When Sadler was appointed in 1540 it was necessary that his clerks and assistants be university educated. '...Well-travelled and well-read men...who had attended the universities' were the companions of the secretary, his own qualifications being taken for granted.[4]

Here again a search of the records reveals to what a marked degree Sadler was his master's man. Like Cromwell he had not the benefits of either Cambridge or Oxford. Sadler and his patron were the only Tudor secretaries who were not university men.[5] They learned their craft by other paths, largely by the practice derived in serving Wolsey in the one case and Cromwell in the other. There is no shred of evidence proving Sadler went to any school, and the temptation to identify Ralph with the 'Mastre Sadler' who accompanied Cromwell's son Gregory to Cambridge must be resisted. That Sadler was a tutor at Jesus College.[6] Apparently Ralph Sadler lacked even the schooling in

---

[1] See the references given on p. 52, n. 1.

[2] Brewer, *The Reign of Henry VIII*, I, 68–9, quoting Pace's treatise *De fructu* which faults the nobility on that account.

[3] Evans, *The Principal Secretary of State*, pp. 28–9.   [4] *Ibid.* p. 161.

[5] Every secretary between 1485 and 1533 was *doctor legum*; most were clerics. Cromwell was neither. The same was true with regard to Sadler. Apart from Cromwell and Sadler, every Tudor secretary of state was a university man.

[6] PRO, SP 1/50, fo. 208; 1/57, fo. 3 and 1/58, fos. 152–3, a series of undated letters from John Chekynge to Thomas Cromwell. These relate the progress made by Gregory Cromwell, son of Thomas Cromwell, as well as other boys called 'Crumwelles scholares'. All were enrolled at Jesus College, Cambridge, where mention is made of Mr Gifforde and Mr Sadler. But Sadler's given name was Nicholas in so far as one can make any inferences from the letters. But the Gifford at Jesus College with Gregory was Nicholas Gifforde. It is unlikely, however, that this confusion will warrant the guess that Ralph Sadler was the Sadler at Cambridge. *L & P*, v, 15 and 359, demonstrate that there was a Nicholas Sadler at Jesus in a tutorial capacity in Cromwell's service. We must assume that it was to him that SP 1/57, fo. 3 refers. Ralph Sadler's name does not

the law that came to Cromwell in Gray's Inn, since his admission in 1561 argues something other than a late aspiration for the law.[1]

Yet Sadler was well educated. He was a good linguist. His competence in Latin has already been discussed. To that we must add at least a rudimentary knowledge of Greek, although the graecisms sprinkled throughout his work do not enable us to claim him for the exquisitely trained Grecians of his day. All that we can say is that youthful jottings and some references to the lack of such talent in others stamps him as a man interested, and perhaps *mediocriter doctus*, in that tongue.[2] His knowledge of French was excellent, conversation in that language being necessary for his work in Scotland and in the council.[3] In his native tongue it would be no exaggeration to say he was an adept writer. Despite the fact of his being described as a man 'sobre in discourse', his letters are crisp, witty and always to the point.[4] Apart from these

occur in the list of Cambridge men in John Venn and J. A. Venn, *Alumni Cantabrigienses*, 4 vols. (Cambridge University Press, 1932–7) or in Mary Bateson, *Cambridge Grace Books: Book B, 1488–1544* (Cambridge University Press, 1907) or in C. H. Cooper and T. Cooper, *Athenae Cantabrigienses*, 2 vols. (Cambridge University Press, 1858–61). All of Sadler's sons attended Peterhouse and are listed by the Venns. No evidence that he attended Oxford was known to Anthony A. Wood, *Athenae Oxonienses*, 2 vols. (Oxford University Press, 1692), s.n. 'Sir Ralph Sadler', where Wood expressed the view that our knight was not a university man. Under what circumstances Sadler was educated must therefore remain one of the unsolved problems of the study here presented.

[1] Cromwell's admission to Gray's Inn in 1524 is recorded in the common register: *Register of Admissions to Gray's Inn, 1521–1889*, ed. Joseph Foster (London: Hansard, 1890), p. 4. Sadler gained admission in 1561, at the age of 54 (p. 29). It is hardly likely that he read law at that age, since the Inns of Court were fashionable addresses for government men in London, especially for men with business at the nearby chancery offices. For all matters of legal education see William Sears Holdsworth, *A History of the English Law*, 14 vols. (London: Methuen, 1910–64), II, 484–512.

[2] *SSP*, throughout. He used a Greek tag for a motto on his livery. Latinisms, especially tags from the *New Testament*, about in his writing. Early evidence of an interest in Greek literature appears in *marginalia* in PRO, SP 1/83, fos. 209–10, definitely in Sadler's hand and giving classical authors and muses in random jottings.

[3] His letters are full of French tags. More vital is the fact that in his Scottish embassies he talked often with Mary of Lorraine, who knew no English. He also summarised French chapel sermons, preached before the Queen of Scots. When he was secretary of state with Wriothesley he had charge of the French correspondence: PRO, SP 1/211, fo. 91*b*, undated, Paget to Sir William Petre.

[4] Sadler's style drew the comments of a number of writers: Fuller considered his prose to be lucid and polished (*Worthies*, II, 41); Foxe, *Acts and Monuments*, VI, 71–2, quoted Gardiner to the effect that Sadler's discourse was sober and discreet; Lloyd, in his *States-men and Worthies*, pp. 61–2, spoke of Sadler in terms of highest praise both as soldier and man of culture: 'King Henry understood two things: 1. A Man: 2. A Dish of Meat; and was seldom deceived in either: for a Man, none more compleat than Sir Ralph, who was at once an exquisite writer and a most valiant and experienced soldier; qualifications that seldome meet (so great is the distance between the Sword and the Pen, the Coat of Mail and the Gown) yet divided this man and his time...' Elsewhere he linked 'Discipline and Intelligence' as the two 'incomparable qualities' possessed by Sadler.

attainments, Sir Ralph Sadler was especially fond of the reading of history, even to the extent of patronising Clio in the 1540s in the person of the translator and historian Peter Ashton.[1] His vivid interest in religious doctrine can easily be illustrated from a number of examples: two will suffice. He frequently lectured friends on the meaning of the Vulgate.[2] And until he was an old man his opinion in matters of doctrine was often solicited. In such matters he was held one of the 'best judges of policie and discretion' by the Puritan strategist Thomas Norton.[3]

What eludes us is this: how did Sadler come by that education so amply displayed in his Henrician and Elizabethan career? Since we know that he was not a university student, we must fall back on a reasonable assumption. Perhaps the fundamentals came to him in a petty school in Warwickshire or London. Perhaps he was simply another in a long list of Tudor men of wit and learning privately educated in the household of his patron, building on petty school foundations or other training.[4] We can say without fear of contradiction that he was qualified, by whatever means, for the post he inherited in 1540, if learning could qualify him.

Even more important to the successful secretary than the *sine qua non* of a sound education, however gained, was what may be called the ideal of efficiency. The secretary had to be an efficient organiser. Unfortunately it is hard to give any picture at all of Sadler's organisation of the routine work of the secretariat. No great ledger books and journals, no treaty books and precedent books from his tenure have

---

[1] Sadler's taste for historical writing led him to sponsor Peter Ashton's translation of Petrus Jovius, *Turcicarum rerum commentarius*, printed as *A Shorte Treatise upon the Turkes Chronicle compyled by Jovius Bychop of Lucerne* (London: Edward Whitechurch, 1546). See esp. pp. 2–11, the 'Epistle Dedicatorie', where Sadler's taste for Clio is discussed and much praised.

[2] For his habit of spelling out portions of the Latin gospels see *SSP*, I, 31.

[3] Throughout his life he was consulted on matters of doctrine of political significance. In that connection see the following: Hatfield House, Salisbury MSS. 159, fos. 107–8, 24 Aug. 1573, where we learn from Sadler that the dean of St Paul's asked his opinion on a difficult point in a tract deemed seditious; Inner Temple Library, Petyt MSS. 538/38, fo. 65 a, Thomas Norton to Whitgift, 20 Oct. 1572, advertising that Sadler gave advice to 'Precisians', since he was one of the 'best judges of policie and discretion' in religious matters. Earlier, Sadler read and translated a number of theological tracts for Cromwell: see PRO, SP 6, *passim*.

[4] For the scope of grammar and petty school education and curricula see P. S. Allen, 'A Sixteenth Century School', *EHR*, x (1895), 738–44. See also Foster Watson, *The English Grammar Schools to 1660* (Cambridge University Press, 1908); J. H. Hexter, 'The Education of the Aristocracy in the Renaissance', *Journal of Modern History*, XXIII (1950), 1–20; W. T. Baldwin, *William Shakespeare's Small Latine and lesse Greeke*, 2 vols. (Oxford University Press, 1944), as well as the bibliography in Baldwin's book.

survived. That such were kept cannot be doubted. Otherwise, the office was not manageable.[1] The only concrete reference to the mechanics of Sadler's performance in office is not flattering to the image of efficiency already posited. On 27 November 1545 Sir William Paget wrote to Sir William Petre, his co-secretary, requesting that a certain letter of Francis I's secretary relevant to peace negotiations then being led by Paget be sent him at once. Petre was instructed to refer the matter to Sadler, who had handled French affairs at the time of the original royal correspondence. If Sadler had no specific knowledge of its place in the files, Petre was to search about in the former secretary's quarters at court for a key to a house in Cannon Row, where Sadler had apparently maintained his secretarial staff.[2] A week passed without any reply. Sadler did not turn up the required letter, causing Paget to write somewhat in anger, noting with disgust the inefficiency of both Sadler and Petre.[3] While the episode cannot be ignored, it also cannot be taken to mean that Sadler was generally derelict in his duty. The most likely explanation of the loss of Paget's paper is the simple one which sees Sadler carrying off his horde of state papers in 1543, when he vacated the office in Paget's favour. Even Paget followed that custom of the time.[4]

No doubt Sadler's 'inwarde manne' might have been the culprit in the above incident. Many clerks had his confidence during the years of his government service, though none was more important than Gregory Raylton. Raylton was the agent who more than any other was responsible for helping Sadler in secretarial work in the 1540s. He was in fact Sadler's chief clerk, with a special grasp of the diplomatic affairs that figure so largely in Sir Ralph's career from 1537–47. He knew the details of every negotiation conducted by Sadler.[5] He was an expert in the handling of the numerous ciphers employed *vis à vis* Scottish affairs.[6] Both Sadler's avid affection for him and the long years of continuous service given by Gregory Raylton testify to the clerk's

[1] This was the point made so well by Faunt and Beale. See the works listed on p. 52, n. 1.
[2] PRO, SP 1/121, fo. 91*b*, 27 Nov. 1545.
[3] *L & P*, xx, ii, 919, 2 Dec. 1545.
[4] The Paget papers not in the PRO or other public depositories are at Plas Newydd.
[5] Sadler described Raylton as the man 'who hath in a manar hoolie and doinge of all mi thynges under me these fyve yeres, wherein he showeth me both honestie and diligence...' (PRO, SP 1/200, fo. 129, Ralph Sadler to William Paget, 1 May 1545).
[6] *SSP*, ii, 482.

merit.[1] But the best evidence of that is the way in which Raylton advanced in government service, of course under Sadler's patronage.[2]

Even Raylton's expert help could not, however, lessen the great weight under which the secretary groaned. The comings and goings of rival ambassadors had to be noted carefully. Their doings provided the background of the various instructions given to English agents, whose credences and instructions were at least drafted, if not designed, by Sadler and his co-secretary. Although we know that all such drafts went to the king for ultimate approval,[3] it nevertheless was true that Henry's course was influenced by the drafter of any vital state paper. The secretary was formally charged with reading and digesting the documents prepared by Englishmen throughout Europe and the shires as well as the correspondence of aliens.[4] Thus Sadler's endorsement is found on the backs of dispatches relevant to the prince of Salerno,[5] an imperial invasion of Gueldres,[6] the revolution in Cleves in favour of Francis I,[7] some reports on the conditions in Italian and French commerce[8] and the state of French military preparedness.[9]

Scottish problems occupied a large place in Sadler's diplomatic service and that work must be treated at length elsewhere in this account. But here it can be said that his state papers in that regard are voluminous, as are the scores of letters, reports and intelligence surveys issuing out of Scotland in Sadler's hand or that of one of his staff. From 1542 on the major share of his energy was spent in Scottish affairs and the related problem of the Border.[10] In all matters touching the 'Soote

[1] *Ibid.* pp. 417, 441 and 482.

[2] Paget's clerk was the Flemish signet clerk Nicacius Yetswert. Somerset's chief secretary was Sir John Thynne, founder of the present line of the Bath marquisate. Raylton's family retained some connection with government until well into the Caroline era.

[3] *L & P*, xv, 468–9.

[4] *Ibid.* p. 735, Henry VIII to Edward Wotten, June 1540, a draft in Sadler's hand. Henry VIII was not as energetic in the '40s as he was when Wolsey led his ministers. The very fact that important bills were authorised by stamp, with Sadler among those privileged to use the stamp, can be construed as a sign of the king's waning power. But the stamp was also used in the 1530s: see PRO, SP 4, *passim*.

[5] BM Royal MSS. 7C xvi, fo. 149.

[6] BM Cotton MSS. Vitelius B xxi, fo. 201, Ralph Sadler to Edward Wotton, ambassador to the emperor, undated.

[7] BM Cotton MSS. Galba B x, fo. 113, extracts from a newsletter from Antwerp in Sadler's hand.

[8] *L & P*, xvi, 174, 18 Oct. 1540, Henry VIII to John Wallop, draft in Sadler's hand.

[9] *Ibid.* xvii, 25, 80, 246 (2), 435 (2) and 889 (2).

[10] *Ibid.* xvi, 434 and 499; xvii, 764, 776, 851 (2), 886 (2), 903 (2), 925 (2), 1,244–5, all written by Sadler.

Scottes' his long experience transformed Sir Ralph into a leading expert whose opinion was more than that of a mere administrator of diplomacy. He took a hand in the formulating of Henrician Scottish policy in the '40s.[1] Yet the council was not dependent on him in such matters. Far from it. Scottish diplomacy was often treated by the council in his absence, even when it was easily possible for him to attend a sitting. Of the more than four hundred sessions examined in the period from 1542 to 1547, a quarter dealt with Scottish affairs.

Sadler attended only half of these.[2] Part of that was no duobt due to the lack of specialisation in the council as an advisory body, although the generally deficient state of our knowledge of the council at this time, hopefully to be supplied by Dr Elton's labours, makes even that statement somewhat hazardous.

This same difficulty exists in making a precise estimate of Sadler's transactions with foreign representatives in London. When he met some ambassador for a business talk or even for mere gossip, was he acting for the council or as an independant royal agent? Marillac and Chapuys considered Sadler to be less hospitable to the Catholic powers than was Wriothesley, thus intimating that the secretaries obviously influenced the course of negotiations, while also expressing their own conviction that religion was the prime factor in English factionalism.[3] Whatever the truth of their reading of the situation, and we will do well to guard against any superficial reading of the factionalism of the 1540s, recalling that Bishop Thirlby rejoiced upon hearing of Cardinal Beaton's murder[4] and equally noting Paget's friendship with the Protestants of Sadler's kind in halting persecution of English dissenters,[5] the quality of secretarial initiative is hard to read. Paget, for all his protection of dissenters, laboured mightily for an imperial alliance, advising Henry to side with French reformers and German reactionaries, advice in which Sadler and Vaughan, both Protestants, concurred.[6]

The heart of the matter seems to lie in recognition of the distrust of simple and clear-cut patterns of political action engendered in secre-

[1] *HP*, I, 59, Privy Council to deputy warden *vice* Sir William Eure, 7 Jan. 1541. See also *HP*, I, 243, Sir Edward Seymour to Thomas Wriothesley, 29 Nov. 1542.
[2] This is based on a survey of *Proceedings and Ordinances*, VII and *APC*, I.
[3] *L & P*, XVII, appendix B, no. 13, 16 Apr. 1542.
[4] *Ibid.* XXI, i, 1,070, where Thirlby's delight appear in the postscript.
[5] Every writer of any note from Pollard to Hughes made this point.
[6] *L & P*, XXI, 1,420.

taries of Sadler's generation by the hazards of such simplicity. A good case in point is the imperial alliance resumed in 1543. After Sadler had freed himself of the stigma of the Cleves fiasco, largely by sitting on the board hearing Henry VIII's petition for an annulment,[1] he came to favour a renewal of Wolsey's old pro-imperial policy.[2] He had all along the way kept abreast of both German affairs and the increased tempo of French agitation in Scotland.[3] The logic of the situation was compelling, very much so to even the staunchest Protestant in religion: England needed Charles V, with all that implied for the fate of the Schmalkaldic League, in order to avoid the threat of war on two fronts, across the channel and in the north. Much to Chapuys' surprise, therefore, who was at first so upset to learn that Sadler had replaced the more reliable Wriothesley in the Anglo-imperial negotiations, Sadler proved sympathetic to Charles V late in 1542 and early 1543.[4] It is hardly to claim too much to say that the great treaty of mutual aid of 1543 was the work of strange diplomatic bed-fellows, at least on the English side: Gardiner and Sadler.[5] Chapuys was both amazed and delighted that all went off so well, since the infirmity of his own analysis of English factions was plain to see in the labours that led to the treaty.[6] Before the signing of that solemn accord, Sadler rushed to Edinburgh, to help cement a pro-Catholic German alliance by courting Scottish Protestants against the family of the cardinal of Lorraine![7]

Any truly balanced judgement of Sadler's worth as a secretary and diplomat must wait therefore on an evaluation of his Scottish missions. The work begun there in 1537 and ended, for a time at least, in 1545 was in a real sense the making and the undoing of a Tudor secretary. General considerations must, if we are to understand Sadler's loss of the secretaryship early in 1543, give place to a detailed study of Sir Ralph Sadler in Scotland. Only after that is done can we turn back gainfully to matters that will enable us to strike the balance of his place in the Tudor political scene of the post-Cromwellian years.

[1] *Ibid.* xv, 883.
[2] PRO, SP 1/168, fos. 150–4, Earl of Hertford to Ralph Sadler, 15 Dec. 1541.
[3] See chh. 7–9 below.   [4] *L & P*, xvii, appendix B, no. 13.
[5] *Ibid.* p. 320; *SP*, ix, 23/a.
[6] *L & P*, xvii, 329, Bishop Gardiner to Ralph Sadler and others, 17 May 1542.
[7] Hughes, *History of the Reformation in England*, ii, 16.

THE HIGH ROAD TO SCOTLAND

*Anothre bruit they made, that all my men were monks, and that I had
them out of the abbeys in England...*

SIR RALPH SADLER to Thomas Cromwell

One of the keys to success in Henrician government was affinity.
Another, and just as vital, was the achievement of balanced training in
the various aspects of administration. A third was experience in diplomacy. Most early Tudor politicians of consequence, and certainly every
secretary of state, except Cromwell, stood squarely on the tripod of
connection, administrative skill and diplomacy. Sadler's affinity and the
chance it provided him to learn the ways of the administration are now
known. It remains to be demonstrated that Cromwell's patronage involved Sadler in the efforts to solve the diplomatic crisis engendered by
the Reformation in England, to explore the details of Ralph's travels
on the High Road to Scotland in the 1530s, since Scotland was to be his
main preoccupation in the '40s. Thus the next two chapters have as
their objective the provision of an adequate understanding of England's
diplomatic predicament to the extent that Sir Ralph's career was in-
separable from that predicament. The main stress falls naturally on his
efforts to bring off a marriage alliance between his king and the Scots,
the vicarious wooing of the future queen of Scots on behalf of Edward,
prince of Wales and then king Edward VI. Inevitably, the major share
of the story must focus on the rougher, famous 'English wooing' that
so embittered Anglo-Scottish relations for centuries and that has to this
day provided the occasion for a broad stream of historical and pseudo-
historical justificatory pieces.

In 1536 the key to England's safety lay in the gift of Scotland. English
independence in the years following the break with Rome was by no
means assured. That she might become a French satellite or an imperial
appanage was easily conceivable. Henry VIII had inherited a policy of
peace from his father; he had complicated that testament by his love for
war. He had inherited friendship with Scotland, an amity symbolised by

the marriage of his sister Margaret Tudor to James IV. He wrecked that peace and amity at Flodden and again at Solway Moss. The hoped for marriage in the second generation never took place.[1]

Unhappily for English security the obstacles to a peace anchored in the bed of state were of the first magnitude. The nobility along the border on both sides tended toward bellicosity and irresponsibility. If either kingdom experienced internal unrest, that discord was played upon and skilfully tuned to resonance by the aggressive border folk who did their best to influence both kings and councils. There was also the papacy, to which Scotland had from time out of mind given loyal and willing aid. That devotion to the Holy See tended in the sixteenth century toward a pro-French policy on the part of the Scottish council, a fact Henry VIII could never for a moment safely ignore. Finally, there was the Scottish king himself, James V, who had shaken off his long minority in 1528. In 1536 he was twenty-three years old and of a mind to marry. His eye had fallen on the daughter of Francis I, thereby deciding a great deal of Anglo-Scottish history for a century and more. From all of the offered princesses of Europe, James picked a woman from the one house most anathema to his English neighbours.[2]

The choice of a Valois marriage committed Scotland to France more openly than ever before. During the long minority that followed the death of James IV at Flodden Field in 1512, the young heir had been tossed about between competing factions in a bitter struggle over the regency. James V had finally come to rest squarely in the arms of James Beaton, the archbishop of St Andrews. Already possessed of little reason to love his uncle Henry VIII, that canny and reforming Harry who was, after all, his father's slayer, James succumbed to the clerical influence easily.[3] As

---

[1] For a careful analysis of early Tudor attempts at marital diplomacy in Scotland see A. N. Millar, 'Scotland Described for Queen Magdalene: A Curious Volume', *ScHR*, 1 (Oct. 1903), 27–39. After Pavia, the French promised to forego a Scottish marriage in return for English aid against Charles V.

[2] For the internal machinations of the long minority of James V see the *DNB* articles on the king himself, Henry Stuart, Archibald Douglas and James Beaton. The best survey of Scotland in the international arena is that found in William Croft Dickinson, *Scotland from the earliest time to 1603* (London: Thomas Nelson and Sons, 1961), vol. 1 of *A New History of Scotland*. Of the older works, Fisher, *A History of Europe from the earliest times to 1713* (London: Eyre & Spottiswoode, 1957 impression), pp. 525 ff. is more judicious than Froude's pages in *History*, II, 343–95, and those of P. Hume Brown, *The History of Scotland*, 3 vols. (Cambridge University Press, 1911), I, ch. 12 *passim*. The recent survey by Gaston Zeller, *Histoire des relations internationales* (Paris: Hachette, 1953), II, 110–13, is useful.

[3] Margaret Tudor, the dowager, was of course Henry VIII's sister and the mother of James V.

he matured, the great ecclesiastics of the realm retained their hold over the king's mind. And, alarmed as they were over the reforms taking place in the Church in England, the leading clergymen in Scotland insulated the young ruler from every suggestion that he emulate his schismatic uncle. They often reminded him that Henry was also a heretic and, what was worst of all, Scotland's scourge and enemy.[1] That their words had some effect cannot be doubted, for the vote to marry in France was all that Rome could have hoped for.[2]

If an English diplomat, weary of the troubles brewing in the north, turned his gaze across the rough waters of the channel, the signs were even less encouraging. The pope seemed to want only a temporal arm to drag Henry VIII back into the fold. Spain, despite the death of Catherine of Aragon, stood able and apparently willing to support the prayerful fulminations of the Roman *curia* with ships and men. Paul III did not lack allies in France, and Wolsey's policy of a French league against the Empire, formulated in the utter despair consequent on the Battle of Pavia, tottered on the edge of the abyss of wrecked English dreams.

The sole ray of light was derived from the fact that birds of a feather sometimes failed to flock together. Francis, the Most Christian King, cherished Milan more than the chest brimming with pater nosters promised by Paul III. The memory of Pavia still rankled in his breast.[3] He was easy to divert from the aims of the Holy See, especially as new occasions arose on every side to expose old wounds scraped raw and rubbed rough with shame. In 1536 he finally rejected the counsel of the papal surgeon, deciding to bleed his Spanish enemy instead of the English one. He began the treatment by hurling his armies across the Piedmont.[4] Much to the pope's despair, Charles V would rather be treating than treated. He responded with alacrity to the violation of the Treaty of Cambrai by invading France. Henry VIII and his counsellors looked on in glee, while Paul III fumed. With the Turk poised on the Danube and a reasonable facsimile busily dissolving monasteries in England, Rome looked on in horror while Christendom's two mightiest princes fought each other over a duchy in northern Italy.

[1] Fisher, *The Political History of England*, v, 454–5.
[2] *Ibid.* p. 455.
[3] Pollard, *Henry VIII*, p. 281.
[4] A. J. Grant, *A History of Europe, 1494–1610* (London: Methuen, 1957), pp. 145–6.

The breathing spell provided by Francis I and Charles V did not suffice, however, to keep Henry's troubles from reaching a climax in 1536–7. The king's agents in Europe informed him that James V had sailed for France, amidst speculation that the king of Scots 'would marrie with the Fraunche kinge...'.[1] English spirits, already faltering because of the Lincolnshire rising, could not have been more downcast.[2] James V's move was correctly construed as proof that Francis I wished to pursue an aggressive policy *vis à vis* England. Since the northern shires were in the grip of a popular revolutionary movement, the Pilgrimage of Grace, at just that time, and the prestige of the government was very low, the French news seemed to portend disaster.[3] Henry and his ministers were not men paralysed by fear, as the correspondence of the time shows, yet there was little they could do but sit and watch the unfolding of danger heaped upon danger.[4]

The rebellion of the Catholics in the northern counties spurred on papal plots laid in Rome, Toledo, Paris and Edinburgh. At Rome the Spanish ambassador Dr Pedro Ortiz grasped the seriousness of England's situation and urged the empress to take heart, noting also that 'Renaldo Polo' had arrived at Rome from Venice. Pole, of course, was the cousin of the English king and had gained Paul III's favour. What mischief might come of that conjunction, Ortiz sighed. It was clear for all the world to see: Henry VIII could rule neither his family nor his country! Ortiz's fertile mind schemed and decided to urge a course of action to strike Henry where he was weakest. A bull of deposition ought to be published by none other than the king's cousin. Copies would be smuggled to the pilgrims in the northern parts of England, in the hope that a general uprising might ensue.[5]

While Ortiz intrigued at Rome, Sir John Wallop, the English resident in Paris, looked on helplessly as Wolsey's alliance with the French disintegrated. Others observed the same thing with relish. Bishop Faenze, the papal notary and *nuncio*, wrote to Rome in joyous terms about the sad state in which the English found themselves.[6] On

---

[1] *SP*, v, 60–1, Sir Archibald Douglas to Thomas Cromwell, 30 Sept. 1536. Douglas was the sixth earl of Angus as well as the former husband of Margaret Tudor. His divorce from the Dowager cheated him of the regency spoils and turned him into an English agent.

[2] *L & P*, xi, 780, 826, 843 and 947.   [3] *SP*, v, 59–60.

[4] *L & P*, xi, 1,124; for the full text see *SP*, i, 510.

[5] *L & P*, xi, 1,160.

[6] Faenza's correspondent was Monseigneur Ambrogio, a papal secretary.

26 November 1536 he happily announced the Franco-Scottish *paren-tado*, modestly adding that his own efforts to stir hatred of the English prospered.[1] In fact Faenza had managed to quiet any qualms of conscience Francis I felt about breaking his English treaties, his 'little obligation' signed by the long dead Wolsey. Francis I, Faenza wrote, would now shed blood for the church. Nor did that exhaust the bounties wrought by God: James of Scotland announced his readiness to join with his new father-in-law against his old uncle. The best means ever devised for bringing a schismatic to reason were an army of 40,000 billmen, some artillery and a great *flotta*. Faenza also thought of a bull of deposition as a way of forestalling any English attempt to buy a countering alliance on the continent, suggesting that Pole might be made a cardinal in order to lend prestige to the Holy Father's efforts in behalf of the faith.[2]

Two days after Faenza's serpentine remarks were uttered his hopes and England's fears were realised. James V and Magdalene were betrothed, Faenza standing by quoting what Wallop had been rash enough to say aloud: Paul III was on the way to give England to the first taker! James also aided the papal efforts by his obvious effrontery to all Englishmen at the Valois court, thus playing into the hands of Cardinal du Bellay, the driving force behind French hatred of everything English.[3] The last part of Faenza's account was especially ominous. James could be counted on for another reason: his conscience was in the hands of a young churchman, the abbot of Arbroath, David Beaton, a member of a family publicly sworn to secure Scotland for the papal cause.[4]

The churchmen were having their day: Ortiz in Rome; Faenza and du Bellay in Paris; the Beatons, James and David, in Edinburgh and Paris; all scheming to make Henry do out of necessity what he refused to consider doing from motives of faith, hope and charity. Christmas in England was gloomy. The system of Wolsey was shattered beyond repair, and Cromwell's assiduously cultivated friendship with James V,

[1] A *parentado* is a special case of precontract *in nuptiis pro verbis de futuro*. The documents hailed by Faenza are printed in Teulet, *Papiers*, I, 122–34; for earlier negotiations see pp. 109–22.

[2] Transcripts of the originals are in PRO, PRO 31/9, fos. 65a–b. For help in reading and transcribing the Italian letters cited here and below I am indebted to Dr Francesco Gianelli of the university of Pisa.

[3] *L & P*, XI, 1,183. See also PRO, PRO 31/9, fos. 66a–67b.

[4] David Beaton was the nephew and heir-apparent of James, archbishop of St Andrews.

so necessary alike by virtue of the facts of geography and politics, breathed faintly, if at all.[1] Those facts, coupled with the failure of Henry to win a French princess as a third wife upon the death of Jane Seymour, made English spirits droop still more.[2] Events in Europe seemed to be impelled by some evil genius hostile toward England, while on the ground at home a rebellion of major proportions flourished in the counties tied by religious preferences and agrarian conservatism to the old order. Even the death of the Valois queen of Scots could not allay English fears, for James found another French girl to his liking, this time a princess of the Guise family.[3] Such were the facts of diplomatic life early in 1537.

Recalled by necessity to the troubles on the frontier and in the northern counties, Henry had to eschew an adventurous foreign policy, which in practice meant turning the other cheek to James V. He at once decided to abandon the cultivation of friction along the line of the Cheviot Hills. He might think bloody deeds, but the hand went from scabbard to quill by instinct and by the advice of his chief minister Thomas Cromwell. Rome was busy advertising chrism and the duties of annointment, which Henry seemed to have forgotten. Therefore, Cromwell reasoned, the well-oiled tongue of his own agent Ralph Sadler might serve to supply balm for the wounds inflicted on English pride and ambition.

The Scots themselves provided the immediate occasion for England's first gesture at conciliation. Margaret Tudor's three marriages had been a cause of consternation to her son James and the Scottish council. In the past she had often caused discontent between Henry VIII and his nephew, the more so since her divorce from Angus, her second husband and a pensioner of the English king, hence an English agent. Her third husband, the handsome and young Henry Stuart, a man a dozen years her junior, she rushed to wed as quickly as possible after shedding Angus, determined to 'look no moe' to her brother's will in marital matters.[4] Stuart was a devoted follower of the French lead and of the

---

[1] *L & P*, XI, 1,194. [2] Merriman, *The Life and Letters of Thomas Cromwell*, I, 156–8.

[3] See *L & P*, XII, ii, 829 and 1,201. For the events following the death of Magdalene on 7 July 1537 leading to the Guise marriage see Marquerite Woods (ed.), *The Balcarres Papers, 1537–1548* (Edinburgh: Constable, 1923), pp. viii–ix.

[4] On the question of Margaret Tudor's power in Scotland, her break with Angus and her infatuation with Henry Stuart, see Michael Glennie, *King Harry's Sister* (New York: Roy Publishers, n.d.), pp. 175–81, esp. p. 181, where her words are quoted.

clerical party; he was an insistent advocate of Francis I and the Valois policy in Scotland.[1]

Stuart's rise had been spectacular. Immediately after his marriage to Margaret he was created Lord Methuen and then was called upon to take over the functions of the lord treasurer. Shortly, he tightened his hold in government by also assuming the burdens of the chancellorship during the minority of his step-son. Powerful, handsome and young, he had just realised his ambitions when he began to tire of the aged dowager of Scotland. His attitude toward Margaret was less than gallant, even condescending, as his appetite for power was fulfilled. He was, in brief, a blessing for English diplomacy. For Margaret, jaded though she might be, remembered her birth; she was a Tudor and as such she turned to her brother Henry, crying out about her birth rights and the marriage agreements that had sent her to Scotland and which she now wished England to enforce.[2] Froude's ingenious theory which held that a sympathetic nerve in Henry was struck by his sister's marital disasters may recommend itself to some.[3] But the conclusion is hard to avoid that the decision to send Ralph Sadler northward fitted well with Henry VIII's own needs: by acting to secure justice for Margaret, Henry would hopefully be a stroke up in the new game of conciliation.

No time was lost. Although the details of Sadler's trip are lost to us, since no formal instructions seem to have been issued, at least none survive, it is clear from his letters that Ralph was on the way north by the middle of January or a little thereafter.[4] Taking into account that York was the half-way house of the four hundred mile journey between London and Edinburgh, and recalling that it was difficult to make any more than twenty-five miles a day under ordinary conditions, we may assume that Sadler left London about 15 January.[5] He wrote to Cromwell from York on the Great North Road on the 23rd of the month. His journey was delayed as much by the necessity of a safe-conduct, difficult to secure because of the turbulent state of the border, as it was by the bad roads.

What Sadler witnessed while moving northward troubled him. The

---

[1] *L & P*, IV, i, 166–7.
[2] BM Cotton MSS. Caligula B II, fo. 5, Margaret Tudor to duke of Norfolk, undated.
[3] Froude, *History*, III, 385.   [4] *Ibid.* p. 387.
[5] Ephraim Lipson, *An Introduction to the Economic History of England*, 3 vols. (London: Longmans, 1920), I, 211.

shires about Lincoln buzzed with rebellion. Rumour was enthroned on every side. The bandit element thirsted for a new rising, and passing post-riders told him of the sad state of affairs in the furthest reaches of the kingdom. The popular fear that Norfolk was on the way with a hanging commission in his pouch shook the people and made for new outbreaks of wild discontent. Sadler told Cromwell that the people were thoroughly upset and frightened by damnable sedition-mongers led by local gentry. The common folk would remain loyal only if royal forces arrived on the scene before the rebel hordes, since most men were of a mind to preserve their property and would run with the rebels to do so, if need be.[1]

The first exposure to the realities of England far from the safety of the verge of court sobered Sadler and made him fear both for his own and England's safety, to say nothing about the success of his complex mission. He was to arrange for the pacification of the most turbulent of the English Border dynasties, especially the Percies, since it was obvious that negotiations with Scotland were fruitless unless the frontier could be kept in order. For that purpose, he carried with him a credence to Sir Thomas Clifford, the captain of Berwick, ordering the arrest of the Percies, who were to be sent in custody to Grimsby, from whence they would be taken to London.[2]

After doing that much, Sadler sent word to Cromwell via Clifford's chaplain—such was the diplomatic pouch of the day—in which his fears of further violence were clearly expressed. While the area between York and Newcastle was more peaceful than wind-blown rumour had it, with the exception of the inevitable *latrones* who roamed the countryside hoping to profit from the miseries inflicted on their neighbours, that between Durham and Cleveland was very doubtful and disordered. Bills and scrolls against Norfolk's coming north were up on the church doors. At Darlington Sadler had been attacked by villagers, a sure sign that men were reluctant to credit even the king's ambassadors. What was worse, even safe-conducts from the Scots were of no avail with Henry's own subjects: he was wary of going on without local guarantees of safe-conduct. Meanwhile, he was far from idle.

[1] *L&P*, xii, i, 200; *SP*, i, 526–8. The editor of *SSP* printed no documents relating to the mission of 1537. That Sadler was in London on the 15th is established by PRO, SP 1/114, fo. 113 b, John Husee to Lord Lisle, 15 Jan. 1537, where a talk on that day with Sadler is cited.

[2] *L & P*, xii, i, 225, undated instructions to Sir Anthony Browne.

There were defences at Newcastle to inspect; Clifford had to be further instructed in the Percies' arrest and the apprehension of the other leaders of the rebels.[1]

Sadler's long letter from Newcastle helps bring the entire mission into focus. In addition to observing the true state of the northern shires and arranging the capture of the Percies, Sadler was to report on military affairs and related matters upon which clarification was needed before an intelligent policy could be formulated.[2] Evidently the council at home realised that no agreement with Scotland was meaningful while the north was in an uproar.[3] Cromwell relied on Sadler to supply the deficiencies.

The main tasks of the mission lay in Edinburgh, and as soon as conditions allowed him to do so Sadler hurried there. His sense of urgency was fed by rumours out of Scotland, although he thought it 'no gospull' that Margaret had taken a nun's habit.[4] Upon his arrival in Edinburgh, Sadler went directly to the old queen, delivering his royal letters from her brother. After reading them, Margaret got down to cases, as we know from her replies to Henry VIII's letters. She showed Sadler the true state of her marriage with Methuen, complaining that the council there would not render justice in her suits. Thus she admitted that she had to fall back on her brother, while at the same time emphasising the mutuality of interest that linked her to him. Once the French queen arrived in Scotland, Valois influence would be so buttressed as to make any effective action in her behalf and, by implication, in Henry's, impossible. She was determined to play a good game with the few cards she held.[5]

The limitation placed upon her action was clearly not of her own choosing, however. Her letters made it abundantly clear that she knew from Sadler in unambiguous terms that neither Henry nor Cromwell was of a mind to let her interfere with their desire to conciliate James V. Her own scheme to flee to England was discounted on the grounds that

[1] *SP*, I, 529, Ralph Sadler to Thomas Cromwell, 28 Jan. 1537.

[2] Henry's long range plans to ruin the Percies are fully treated in Howard Pease, *The Lord Wardens of the Marches of England and Scotland* (London: Constable, 1913), pp. 21 and 199; Rachael Reid, *The King's Council in the North* (London: Longmans, 1921), pp. 117, 132–4; Gaillard T. Lapsley, 'The Problem of the North', *AHR* (1900), v, 440–66; Sturge, *Cuthbert Tunstal*, pp. 154–5; M. H. Dodds and Ruth Dodds, *The Pilgrimage of Grace and the Exeter Conspiracy*, 2 vols. (Cambridge University Press, 1915), II, 104 ff. See also *L & P*, XII, i, 369, Henry VIII to Norfolk, undated, where the king calls Percy 'the lock, key, and mover' of the Pilgrimage of Grace.

[3] BM Cotton MSS. Caligula B II, fo. 344a.

[4] PRO, SP 1/115, fos. 136a–137b, Thomas Clifford to Thomas Cromwell, 30 Jan. 1537.

[5] BM Cotton MSS. Caligula B II, fo. 346.

unilateral action would not be tolerated in London, whatever the Scots might think. Sadler let her know that Cromwell was adamant on that score.

It was Sadler's job, therefore, to make the old queen as happy as was consistent with his instructions. How he was to do so is not a matter of record. But it could hardly have escaped him that Margaret's situation fitted England's needs well. If James could be turned against his step-father, who after all represented the French interest, it might well drive a wedge between him and his French father-in-law, and that was the purpose of English diplomacy in 1537. The way to do it, of course, was to rehearse the matter with the king of Scots himself. For whatever Sadler had learned in Edinburgh could be of use only if James could be compelled to take some action in his mother's suit against Methuen before the French princess arrived at Leith.

This reconstruction is made probable in the absence of conclusive documents by one fact alone. No sooner had Sadler returned to London from the first trip than he was on his way to France. Of this French leg of what was to become a three-legged mission, little more than its purpose remains clear. From Sadler's instructions we may state the intent of the trip: he was to hurry to Paris, there to inform James V of his mother's plight. Henry assumed that his nephew was now honour-bound to obey the terms of the original contract by which Margaret had been sent to Edinburgh. Redress of her real and imagined grievances rested on a contractual basis. Hence Sadler was to feign that he believed James to be in ignorance of the entire scandal of Methuen's conduct, including the well-known fact that Stuart had usurped his wife's marriage portion. While he could not presume too much on the state of the royal ignorance, Sadler was gently to inform James that queen Margaret was poorly used by the Scottish council. He was to appeal to the king's sense of knightly virtue and to his magnanimity. Sadler was to beware lest he anger or grieve the king of Scots. In fact, Henry VIII reminded his envoy that he had been chosen for his proven qualities of 'wisdome and grete fidelitie' and because he could 'sett furthe and with siche dexteritie conduit negotyacyons that he coulde gentilie perswade the sayde kinge...'.[1]

---

[1] *L & P*, xii, i, 540, undated instructions for Ralph Sadler. The contents make it obvious that these instructions formed part of the effort to utilise the data gathered in Edinburgh.

So instructed, Sadler set sail for France on 28 March in 1537. The short but perilous passage from Dover to Boulogne was doubly so by virtue of tricky seas in the early springtime. After a whole day on the water, Sadler was put ashore near Boulogne and quickly made his way to Amiens, where he talked with Stephen Gardiner, who immediately sent off to Montmorency, the grand master of the French court, in order to gain permission for Sadler to visit Francis I's guest James V. Gardiner was in France as a part of the same complex diplomacy that caused Sadler to be there. He told Sadler that his own part was to prevent Pole's hawking of the bull of deposition within France.[1]

Apparently no answer was forthcoming from the grand master, at least none is on record and further circumstances of Sadler's movements make it seem likely that he grew impatient at the delay and set out for Paris via Montreuil, a bit of initiative that served him well. For it was while on that road, not far from Abbeville, that a lucky accident of the war raging between Francis and Charles forced Sadler to take a detour. In the course of observing the armies in the field Sadler heard a rumour that James had already left Paris for Rouen, hopeful of catching the first good breeze in order to take his bride back to Scotland. Sadler did an about face and headed for the coast again in the hope of intercepting James and executing his commission. That he was able to do, although no very precise record of their talk has survived.[2] After delivering his message, Sadler went back to England by way of Calais, picking up what news he could from other English agents along the way.[3] He was back in London by 15 April, or at least it seems so, since the annuity granted him on the 14th looks suspiciously like a reward for the completion of his mission.[4] Furthermore, John Husee, Lord Lisle's London factor, mentioned seeing Sadler about that date, apparently in the vicinity of Westminster.[5]

Meanwhile, Margaret, the object of everybody's concern, in one

---

[1] Winchester was also charged with trapping Pole (see *SP*, v, 72–3).

[2] *L & P*, xii, i, 760. Two items testify to the circumstances of the interview, while implying conflicting dates: Sir H. B. Paul (ed.), *Compota thesauri regum Scotorum* (Edinburgh: HMSO, 1907), vi, 21, gives 1 Apr. 1537. But a rather perplexing note in Paris, Bibliothèque National, Trésor des Chartres J. 965, Ier paquet, fo. 84, an account of James V's schedule after leaving Paris for Rouen, gives the date as 15 Apr. 1537. The letter is not a contemporary document.

[3] PRO, SP 1/118, fo. 12a, Sir Thomas Palmer to Thomas Cromwell, 6 Apr. 1537, a letter that apparently supports a date *c.* 1 Apr. for the interview noted above.

[4] *L & P*, xii, i, 1,103 (13).

[5] PRO, SP 3/5, fo. 21a, Husee to Lord Lisle, 15 Apr. 1537.

way or another, was entirely uninformed about the efforts made in her cause. She complained bitterly that she was being ignored, not knowing that what she had anxiously communicated to Sadler was already being considered in France.[1] Her whining letters to the duke of Norfolk, begging compassion, can only underscore the fact that in 1537 Margaret Tudor was an aged and foggy-minded woman.[2] But she erred in supposing that her sad state had been forgotten.

There had already been taken concrete steps to improve her position. James V had written to his council, urging them to do her justice.[3] Even the accident of the king of Scot's being in France was overcome by the dispatch with which Cromwell and his agent acted, although English failure to inform Margaret of events can hardly be excused or passed off as skilful work. True, Henry had other things to do, to which might be added the fact that he always found it tedious and painful to write anything in his own hand.[4] He was not especially anxious to communicate with his sister, or anybody else, for that matter.[5] Anyone familiar with his small, square, cramped hand will readily understand his reluctance to write.[6] All things considered, however, it was more than likely the slow pace at which diplomacy moved, blown by the wind or sloshing along muddy roads on horseback, which caused the greatest delays and thereby increased Margaret's anxieties.

The same letters in which the Tudor princess voices her discontent throw some further light on the complexities of Sadler's mission in 1537. When James and his French bride docked at Leith late in May 1537 Henry Ray, the Berwick pursuivant, was on hand.[7] Mingling freely in the crowd at the quay, Ray had found himself face to face with John Crayn, an old English soldier of fortune lately of the retinue of Magdalene of France. He was still an Englishman, however, and was moved to tell Ray an amazing tale of misprison of treason. Near the north-eastern coastal town of Scarborough, where the French had put in for provisions, a dozen villagers had gone to meet James V, begging

---

[1] *SP*, v, 74–5.
[2] BM Cotton MSS. Caligula B II, fos. 5–12; PRO, SP 1/117, fo. 273 *a*.
[3] *L & P*, XII, i, 1,028.   [4] *L & P*, III, i, 1.
[5] *Ibid.* p. 1,424.
[6] Elton, *The Tudor Revolution in Government*, p. 68.
[7] *SP*, v, 79–80. The pursuivants were officers below heralds in the Herald's College, an organisation of some antiquity chartered anew and reinvigorated by Henry VIII as part of his programme of public display and spectacle as instruments of royal power.

him to invade England and so forever end the scandals suffered by the faithful. The same thing had happened at other provisioning places, according to Crayn. In fact, James had vowed to break a spear on an English breast within the year. Ray was urged to pass this news to Sadler, whom he had met at Rouen.

Ray was himself a man of some discrimination and trust and was already familiar with the major outlines of Sadler's three-legged mission; he also was thoroughly conversant with Scottish affairs by virtue of his job.[1] He gave full credit to Crayn's story, although the duke of Norfolk, to whom the tale was also told, counted it a fantasy of Crayn's devising, assuring Cromwell that Crayn was victimised by his own overactive imagination. Norfolk communicated the same view to Sadler in a discussion had between the two, claiming that Crayn's sailing for France before he could be questioned by the duke's agents thoroughly discredited the whole episode.[2]

Both Sadler, who had just been sent northward again, and Cromwell were alarmed, however. If the tale had even a grain of truth, in so far as the report of the king's attitude was concerned, then Sadler had been on a fool's errand all along. Although no instructions for the third and final leg of Sadler's mission survive, since the documents so described by various editors are demonstrably not related to any mission of 1537,[3] it is possible to reconstruct this last phase of the mission, partly from Norfolk's letters relating to Crayn and partly from other evidence.

Sadler had obviously been sent to Scotland again in the summer of 1537 for two reasons. First of all, he was to help end the lingering unrest occasioned by the northern uprisings of the pilgrims. Secondly, he was to settle, in so far as that was possible, all matters relating to Margaret Tudor. It is clear that Sadler visited the old dowager, offering her money to tide her over the period of necessity which had grown out of

---

[1] *SP*, v, p. 75.

[2] PRO, SP 1/120, fos. 237–40. This letter helps to date the second trip to Scotland, since it was dated 31 May 1537. A document of 21 May 1537, a deposition given by Sir William Bulmer touching the rebellion in Lincolnshire, makes note of Sadler's presence (PRO, E 36/120, fos. 87–91). For Crayn's reputation see Dodds and Dodds, *The Pilgrimage of Grace and the Exeter Conspiracy*, II, 254–6.

[3] *L & P*, XII, i, 1,313, places this document in 1537. The error was then 'corrected' by Gairdner, who assigned it to 1539. Commenting on the error in *SP*, v, 81, n. 1, Froude, *History*, III, 384, also challenged the *SP* date of 1541. The crucial fact in establishing the true date is that the document makes mention of the *published* bull of deposition and excommunication. Such a bull was issued 30 Aug. 1535 but was not published until 17 Dec. 1538 (see Hughes, *History of the Reformation in England*, I, 200, n. 2). Burnet, *History*, IV, 318–31, published the bull.

her marital problems.[1] At the same time, letters from Henry VIII were finally delivered to her.

Other things in Edinburgh demanded Sadler's attention. The completion of all arrangements for safeguarding the border was urgent.[2] Ralph reported to Cromwell on that problem, providing the memoranda needed by the council, if it was to act intelligently in those matters.[3] He was also evidently empowered to conciliate James V on the border skirmishes, since it is clear that he offered a general exchange of prisoners and rebels. If the Scots would surrender all religious rebels, Henry would agree to extradite all fugitives from the courts presided over by the march wardens. Both sides were to give an earnest for their good intentions for the future in that way.[4]

The talks between Sadler and James completed the mission of 1537. Between January and June, Ralph had been to Scotland twice and to France once. In the immediate train of these visits Margaret had secured her divorce from Lord Methuen, although its publication had been delayed.[5] That was certainly a major accomplishment for England's limping diplomacy, since the francophile lost his high offices as a consequence, thus putting a crimp in Franco-Scottish relations. Furthermore, James V was now more charitably disposed toward his English uncle, with Margaret pledged to do all in her power to maintain that disposition. Sadler himself had established his diplomatic talents firmly in James's mind, a fact which was readily admitted by Margaret Tudor.[6]

On a narrow view of the subject, these were the only real achievements. Yet we cannot afford to lose sight of the larger English gambit of the day, which entailed moves requiring skilled players who would be requited accordingly.[7] English hands had laid hold of the fabric of Franco-Scottish amity at the point of a small tear with every intention of splitting the cloth in two. Sadler's missions were a part of the series of movements designed to offset the threat posed by the *parentado* of 1536. In order to secure England against border diversions, James V's intentions had to be fully grasped, with Crayn's tale always in the fore-

---

[1] *L & P*, xii, ii, 55, Margaret to Henry VIII, 7 June 1537.   [2] *Ibid.* p. 203.

[3] PRO, SP 1/119, fos. 105–8, in Sadler's hand. See Elton, *The Tudor Revolution in Government*, p. 237, n. 1, for a different view.

[4] Dodds and Dodds, *The Pilgrimage of Grace and the Exeter Conspiracy*, ii, 246–8.

[5] *L & P*, xii, ii, 616.   [6] *Ibid.* p. 55.

[7] Lord Herbert of Cherbury, *The Life and Reign of King Henry the Eighth* (London: Andrew Clark, 1672), pp. 492–3.

ground of English thought on that subject.[1] Much remained to be done, starting with the retrenchment of the border garrisons along the lines of Sadler's memoranda. One consequence of Ralph's mission can possibly be seen in Norfolk's being named to be Shrewsbury's replacement as commander in the north.[2]

Sadler's efforts had some effect at home also. The reformers led by Cromwell were daily being vilified in the council and in the country at large.[3] Domestic unrest in the northern shires tended to promote the urgency of the border skirmishes and their allied Scottish problem. Thus the two Scottish trips served to help Henry VIII and his minister Cromwell place those matters in context, an important thing to recall when we remember that for many writers the Pilgrimage of Grace looms as much the greatest crisis of Henry's reign.[4] Sadler's negotiations with James lessened for a time the immediacy of the threat in the far-flung counties along the border and about York. A measure of relief was gained.

At home the mission had its impact upon Sadler in a more personal way. His employment in Scotland in 1537 determined the subsequent development of Ralph Sadler's career. He was to gain fame on the Great North Road to Edinburgh as one of the principal architects of the early efforts to unite the kingdoms of England and Scotland into a greater Britain. He had begun to earn Sir William Cordell's description of him as England's greatest expert on things Scottish.[5]

Sadler had hardly shaken the dust of the Great North Road from his boots in the summer of 1537 before he found himself once more immersed in Scottish affairs. All that his earlier work had settled could be apprehended as a promise that in the future Border problems would be solved through the work of commissioners closely connected with various councils and *ad hoc* bodies composed of men familiar with the problems of the North. The main aim of English policy, to induce a split between James V and the Valois power, was barely under consideration; its fruition would require both time and skilled diplomacy, a period of wooing the Scots of unpredictable duration and intensity.

---

[1] *L & P*, XII, ii, 422, 431, 479 and 555.
[2] Dodds and Dodds, *The Pilgrimage of Grace and the Exeter Conspiracy*, II, 229.
[3] *L & P*, XI, 705, 828 and 874.
[4] Reid, *The King's Council in the North*, p. 121.
[5] *HMC Report on the MSS. of George Allen Finch*, I, 7.

Although it was unknown to Sadler at the time, his future and that of English policy in Scotland were inextricably linked.

In 1538 Sadler began to deal with things Scottish again, taking up the labours that caused Maitland to innocently remark that 'Sadler knew his Scotland'.[1] A number of papers related to northern problems, in Sadler's hand, survive to testify in this concern.[2] But aside from a very cryptic entry in an account book belonging to David Beaton, we have no evidence that Sadler saw Scotland in 1538.[3] The possibility that he went there on some diplomatic business cannot be ruled out, for there is an account of a conversation had between him and Norfolk at Berwick in 1538, a talk in which matters of great moment were discussed, including the temper of Scottish affairs:

Mi lord I beleve thabbot of Arbroth[4]...is goyng into Fraunce to know what helpe his Maiestie shal have aswell of the Frenshe kinge as of the bisshop of Rome, if he wyl breke with us, without whose helpe I beleve he wyl not breke with us.

Some say in Scotlande that he wyl goe from Fraunce unto Rome. Some say he wyl be at a metyng that shalbe betwene thempror oder menne and the Frenshe kinge. Wheresoever he shal come I thynke he wulde provoke all the hurt he can agaynst thys realme, for England hath no greter enemye to his powre. The younge Quene is all a papiste and the olde Quene[5] not muche lesse, as I am informed by Sadlair, wherof I am sorrye.[6]

Unless Sadler was relating impressions based on his personal estimate of the situation in Edinburgh, and that would accord well enough with Beaton's mention of Sadler noted above, Norfolk's comments lose their impact. That is the total of our evidence for a 'mission' in 1538.

Whatever the truth of the matter of Norfolk's letter may be, Ralph Sadler certainly was slated to visit Scotland in 1539 on some urgent business. We can surmise from a rather elaborate correspondence that the trip intended for Sadler was actually made by somebody else.[7] But

[1] Frederic William Maitland, 'The Anglican Settlement and the Scottish Reformation', *Cambridge Modern History*, ed. A. W. Ward and others, 14 vols. (New York: Macmillan, 1903–34), II, 574.

[2] BM Cotton MSS. Caligula B VII, fos. 248a, 250a–251b and 242a–245a.

[3] Paul, *Compota thesauri regum Scotorum*, VI, 22.

[4] See the *DNB* article on Beaton.

[5] Respectively, Mary of Lorraine and Margaret Tudor.

[6] BM Cotton MSS. Caligula B VII, fos. 228b–229a, Norfolk to Thomas Cromwell, 29 March 1538.

[7] Probably the Lancaster Herald.

the concise instructions prepared by Cromwell were the subject of an inquiry by Sadler in April 1539 in a letter implying that he was hard-pressed to leave as scheduled.[1] Furthermore, the originals of the instructions were made by Cromwell with Sadler's name as head of the embassy.[2] As late as 15 April Sadler anticipated that he would shortly be leaving London for an extended trip, his departure being delayed solely by his wife's illness.[3] What started as a delay, however, became a postponement. A letter dated 28 May 1539 shows clearly that Sadler finally had to surrender the mission to another, regretfully noting that he had to remain with his wife, who was thought to be *in articulo mortis*.[4]

The evidence just traced has a point. In consideration of that data it is impossible for us to agree with Froude, who was misled by the instructions, themselves undated,[5] and by the fine oration delivered by a herald but drawn up for Sadler by Cromwell,[6] into supposing that Ralph's promotion to the secretaryship in 1540 resulted from his success in Scotland in 1539.[7] In fact, we cannot even be confident that the instructions assumed to be for the mission of April 1539 were actually not drawn up for another occasion.[8] All that we know positively is that *some* papers drawn up for Sadler were entrusted to another man who performed the embassy in question.

There were other missions to accomplish in which Sadler did have a hand. The best authority for his diplomacy in 1540 is the body of dispatches Sadler drafted while in Scotland on a mission ostensibly the

[1] PRO, SP 1/150, fo. 136, Ralph Sadler to Thomas Cromwell, Apr. 1539.

[2] BM Cotton MSS. Nero B vi, fo. 5, Thomas Cromwell to Henry VIII, 23 Apr. 1539.

[3] PRO, SP 1/150, fo. 135, Ralph Sadler to Thomas Soulemont, 15 Apr. 1539; see also SP 1/151, fos. 247–8, Sadler to Cromwell.

[4] *L & P*, xiv, i, 1,034.

[5] These were first printed in *SSP*, i, 50–6 (1541). *SP*, v, 81–9, assigned them to 1537. *L & P*, xii, i, 1,313, put them in the same year provisionally, until Gairdner finally decided that they belonged to 1539 (*ibid.* xiv, i, 771, enclosure 2).

[6] Foxe, *Acts and Monuments*, v, 103, a summary of which is in *L & P*, xiv, i, 773.

[7] Froude, *History*, iii, 392.

[8] The originals of the documents in question are in BM Cotton MSS. Caligula B i, fos. 52–70. Gairdner, dealing with the purely domestic facts of the document proved 1537 a false date (*L & P*, xiv, i, 771, note at the foot of the page). Paul Van Dyke, 'The Mission of Cardinal Pole to enforce the Bull of Deposition against Henry VIII', *EHR*, xxxvii (1922), 422–3, showed that Pole's mission fell in the middle of Dec. 1538. That leaves only 1539 (Gairdner) and 1541 (*SP*) in contention. Since my evidence rules out 1539 as the date of Sadler's embassy, we have to admit that either Gairdner's case or that made in *SP* answers well enough to the demands of the internal evidence without proving illuminating as to the course of Sadler's career or English diplomacy in 1539.

outcome of a common theft.[1] Late in 1539 Henry VIII's warden of the East March, Sir Robert Bowes,[2] apparently allowed an agent of his to loot the letters of a French agent bound for Edinburgh but shipwrecked on the English coast below Berwick.[3] The rewards of perfidy were greater, perhaps, than was hoped for. The stolen sack contained a letter from David Beaton, who had recently been named to the cardinalate, addressed to Lord Andrew Oliphant, vicar of Fowles and Innertig, the cardinal's Roman agent.[4]

Beaton's missive supplied a summary of a detailed correspondence in which two points loom large. The cardinal was determined to oppose any English meddling with the Kirk and he was prepared to risk body and soul 'pro conservacione libertatis ecclesiasticae'.[5] His means to that end were to be an assertion of the dignity of his office outstripping even Wolsey's claims. He was pledged to carry James V over into the papal camp, boasting that James would do great service to the 'siege apostolick, and obedience thereof, and maintenance of the faith Catholick in this realme of Scottlande...'.[6] In return, the pope had promised Beaton a legateship endowed with extraordinary faculties beyond those usually ascribed to legates, especially in temporal matters.[7] Henry VIII, so often plagued by the powers of a legate of his own making, was now faced with a churchman prophetically staking his life on the success of an anti-English union with Paul III.[8]

The English reacted quickly to the news garnered from the purloined letter. Feigning that all knowledge of the Beaton correspondence arose from the accident of the shipwreck, a plausible sophistry, and that if Brunston, Beaton's messenger, had not been so vicitimised England would have remained ignorant of a vile plot, Henry and his advisers decided to send Sadler to Edinburgh in order to lodge a complaint against the cardinal, a situation plainly revealed in Sadler's detailed instructions.[9]

[1] See the introduction to *HP* for notes on the sources for this mission.
[2] Pease, *The Lord Wardens of the Marches*, p. 199.
[3] *Ibid.* p. 188. The French agent was the laird of Brunston. John Horley committed the theft for Bowes.
[4] *SSP*, I, 13–17, 10 Dec. 1539.   [5] *Ibid.* p. 14.   [6] *Ibid.* p. 15.
[7] *Ibid.* p. 17: 'iuxta dispositionem juris communis ut patet de officio legati'.
[8] Van Dyke, *EHR*, xxxvii, p. 423, quoting a MS. in the Vatican Library, which fully illustrates the power enjoyed by Beaton over the king: 'et hunc novum creatum cardinalem scotum virum magni faciendum et multae authoritatis in illis partibus'.
[9] *SSP*, I, 3–13.

James was to be placated with a gift of six fine geldings, Henry pandering to his nephew's known weakness for good horses.[1] Ostensibly, the mission was to deal with nothing more serious than some minor border unrest.[2] Once the pleasantries were over with, however, Sadler was to gain an interview with the king in secret, well out of Beaton's hearing.[3] Then Sadler was to open things of importance, chief among them the letters taken by Bowes. The main pleas were to be simple ones, namely that 'undre colour of sarving the kinge...he... laboreth to bring into his owne handes the whole spirituall jurisdiction and under the same colour also the temporall'. If James refused to lend credence to these reports against his adviser, Sadler was as a last resort to play his unfairly gained ace: he carried with him Beaton's autograph letter.

It was obviously Cromwell's (and the king's) view that Beaton's misfortune had provided England with a chance to gain the upper hand. After dealing with the cardinal, Sadler was instructed to find a convenient time to talk about the reformation of religion under way in England, broadly hinting at its introduction into Scotland. Here Sadler was asked to carry off a task fraught with grave risks. He was to admonish James, in Henry's name, on a very sore point. James V was a Scottish David, that is to say, he raised and fleeced sheep. Sadler was to suggest that such work was unkingly. The raising and fleecing of monasteries was to be praised as a more fitting and profitable occupation for the king of Scots. James, after all, ought 'to easilie establish his estate in such wise as he should be able to lyve like a king, and yet meddle not with sheep'.[4] Sadler, for his part, was to deliver his speech with his eyes searching James's countenance, continuing with his suggestion only if the Scot remained calm, for the most daring prodding was yet to come. James was in effect to be urged to choose between English amity and pulling down religious houses, on the one hand, and the French alliance *pro papa* on the other. It was to be made clear that James could not keep Henry's friendship while exploiting the French connection and seeking some advantage with the emperor. Sadler was to urge that James be a Scottish Solomon, choosing and dividing

[1] For the horses and their late arrival see *SSP*, I, 21, 23, 39–40; also BM Royal MSS. 18 B vi, fos. 72*a* and 73*b*, Sir Thomas Wharton to Henry VIII, undated.
[2] BM Royal MSS. 18 B vi, fos. 72*a* and 81*a*, Wharton to James V.
[3] *SSP*, I, 5.   [4] *Ibid.* p. 8.

wisely, surrendering whatever pastoral impulse led him to emulate king David.[1]

The carrot and the stick were to be used together. Sadler was also to uncover to James the mysteries of the English succession, showing how the whole dynasty rested, ultimately, on the slender body of the infant prince of Wales. Might not a premature death in the Tudor line cause Henry to recognise the princely merits and virtues of the king of Scots; James was, after all, half a Tudor! Clearly, the merits of the bastard daughter of Catherine of Aragon or those of the love-child born to Anne Boleyn were merely congruent while Henry's nephews were condign, a distinction that might not escape the theologically minded king of Scots.[2]

James was not to be given time to brood over the substance teasingly exhibited by Sadler. His attention was to be distracted by talk of minor border problems and the like. But he was to be encouraged to ponder the issues in his chamber, while Sadler went off to talk with Mary of Guise and the Tudor dowager. Such were the instructions given to Sadler on the eve of his trip to Edinburgh, in the dead of winter of the year 1540.[3]

On 11 February Sadler was at Newcastle, with Sir Thomas Wharton. There he was handed certain letters which foretold that James was likely to be an inhospitable host. Reports of the king's ill-will toward England were rife and were an evil omen for the success of his delicate work.[4] From Newcastle Sadler went to Skaithley, near Alnwick, where he rested while awaiting the arrival of his safe-conduct, which the Berwick pursuivant had gone to fetch.[5] The arrangements for his entry into Scotland were unaccountably delayed, another bad sign; so Sadler cooled his heels on the frontier.[6] He had ample time to consider that James did not seem at all disposed to receive an English emissary, since he was not allowed to enter Edinburgh until 17 February.[7]

[1] BM Royal MSS. 18 B vi, fo. 82b, 26 Jan. 1540, James V to Charles V.

[2] Edward VI, Jane Seymour's son, had *meritum de condigno* no doubt.

[3] BM Royal MSS. 18 B vi, fo. 87b, James V to Henry VIII, 28 Feb. 1540, mentions 27 Jan 1540 as the date of the credences given to Sadler.

[4] PRO, SP 1/157, fo. 164, Ralph Sadler to Robert Holgate and others, undated.

[5] Paul, *Compota thesauri regum Scotorum*, vii, 289.

[6] *Idem.*

[7] *SSP*, i, 17–46, Sadler to Henry VIII, 22 Feb. 1540. The letter mentions that Sadler arrived on a Tuesday. In 1540 (O.S. 1539) the following February dates were Tuesdays: 3, 10, 17 and 24. Within the chronology established in the text the 17th appears the most likely date of arrival.

Immediately upon his entry there, Sadler entered into a series of talks with James V, several members of the council of state, among them the famed poet David Lindsay, and the two queens. He also spoke with David Beaton. Although Sadler's reports of these talks cover some sixty folios, apart from the insight they afford into Scottish anti-clericalism, there is little that can be gleaned from them not available in a summary of the letters prepared by Wriothesley for Henry VIII. The digest of Sadler's mission is therefore offered in its entirety, thus underlining the view of the proceedings available in London:[1]

Sadlair arryved at Edinburgh the xviith of thys monthe and the next day in the mornyng the Kinge sent Rothsay to congratulate hym on hys comyng, declaryng that he and the others that should cum from the kynges maiestie hys uncle were ryght dere unto hym, and howe that the Kynge hand made commaundements to the custodyan of the towre to see hym furnysshed with all thynges mete and convenyent to hym.

The next day he had audience with the Kynge, beyng conveyed to the courte by Syr Walter Ogelby, Captayn Bertyk and Lynsley and Rothsay.

Aftur commendacyons on the Kynges Maiesties behaulfe, he demaunded most hertely agayn of his graces helth. And when Mastre Sadlair had answered that God be thanked hys maiestie was helthful and merrie, he replied I am hertely glad therof. And soo he read the Kinges lettres.

And when Mr Sadleyr had declared the furst parts of hys instrucyons touchynge the kind doinges towardes his maiesties, by my trewth saieth the Kinge of Scottes, and whatsoever I may doe in the worlde as a prynce may doe withyn hys honour to plese hys maiestie and for the continuance of the peace and amyte betwene us I shalbe sure to doe yt to the uttermost of my powre. And for noe man alyve shal I doe that thynge that may tend to the breache of my worde and promys made to hys grace. For whyle I lyve I shal surelie byde by the same. And, saieth he, I truste hys grace wyl doe syk lyke, where yt was answered that he myght be assured of that et cetera. On my soule, saieth he, I nevar douted it and whyl I lyve...I wyl not fayle hym and whatsoever he pleseth I can doe for hym noe man alyve shalbe gladder to doe yt thanne I. And that hys grace shalbe sure of whyl I lyve, whyche he utteryd moste hertely. He gave Mr Sadleyr hertie thankes for hys presens not yet sene and saied that yt shulde be grete plesure to hym yf he had anie commodyte in hys realme.

He then appoynted anothre more secret audience the next daye for the othre matyers of importance thenne not in anie parte touched.

[1] BM Cotton MSS. Caligula B vii, fos. 100*a*–*b*, undated and unsigned; a large folio sheet in Wriothesley's hand.

The next daye Mr Sadleyr was broughte fyrst into the Chapul where he salutyd the Quene who declared herselfe muche bounden for the remembraunce, gyvyng humble thankes wyth promyses to do what she culde wyth all her powre to entertayn and encrese thamyte desyryng hym to make her ryght humble commedacyons agin to the Kinges maiestie.

Soo he was coveyed to the Kinge. And upon the request to kepe the matyers secrete he answered: whatsoever, saieth he, you wyl tell me on the Kinge my uncles parte whych hys grace wyl have secrete, let me have the blame yf ever you here anie more of yt.

Whanne he had harde the matyer of the Cardinall, he saied ther were twoo lawes, the spirituall and the temporall. Thone pertayned to the Popes holynes and the spiritualitie, thothre to kinges and even the mene temporallyte. And hereappon he discoursyd appon the powre of the kyrkemenne et cetera, complaynyng nonetheless yn fine that yf the Cardinall had offendyd he shulde be punyshed.

Touchyng the shepe, he answered he had none, and wyth abbeyes he wulde not meddle but by waye of reformacyon, trustynge that theryn he shulde not displese the Kinges Maiestie. He saied he had a gud olde manne in Fraunce to hys fathre whych wulde not see hym mustre, but saieth he I shal seke nothynge of anie manne but love and frendsyp and holde my worde and be behest and for noe manne lyvyng shal I theryn stayn my honour.

He wysheth that hys soule nevar cum in heven yf he ever sayd he wulde eithre helpe Frensshe kynge or Empror agaynst the kinges maiestie.

In the course of the conversation Sadler allowed himself to test James by making several harangues against monks and the Cardinal Beaton. He had touched a sore spot in the Scottish king, who stoutly defended both his monks and his cardinal. It seems likely that Sadler had misread the mood of James, although he took pleasure in recalling his words for Henry VIII:

Syr quoth I, it may plese your grace to considur that God called you to be a kinge and hath put the sword into your handes for the punisshment and reformacyon of the transgressors of the lawes. And thynkes your grace, that yf the mynysters of the lawes wythyn the realme, for that they noe your grace taketh no regarde thereof, shal not doe their dutie as that your pepul in their defaulte shal perysh for the lacke of dutye?[1]

Or again, speaking of the monks, Sadler's venomous contention:

Syr... they are a kind of unprofytabul pepul, that lyvyd idly appon the sweat and labours of the poor, and their fyrst foundacyons founded appon popery

[1] *SSP*, I, 27.

and mannes constitutyons; and yet doth none of them observe the ground and rules of theyr professyons; for they, in theyr fyrst entries in religion, profess chastyte, wilfull poverty, and obedience. And, if yt please your grace, as to the fyrst, that is chastity, I dare be bold to say, that unless your monks be more holie in Scotland than ours were in England, there reigneth nowhere more carnality, incontinency, buggery, sodomy and lechery, and othre abominations, than is used in cloysters, among monks, channons, nuns, friers, whyche culde nevar appere, so long as the Kinges Maiestie, your uncle, commyted hys trust to bishops and clergy and theyr visitations,[1] as your grace does now; for those visitors alwaies cloaked their vices and abuses, because they wulde not have theyr own appere. And for obedience, I thynke surely they are obedient in heart to theyr captain and chief, the bishop of Rome; but I trow they be not without bulles under lead, whereby they wyl be exeemed[2] from theyr obedience... Ye must do as Christ saieth, *Omnis plantatio quam non plantavit pater meus caelestis eradicabitur.*[3]

Even the great pleasure James anticipated having with the geldings had not eased his displeasure with Sadler's remarks, especially those on the subject of his pastoral activities.[4] What is puzzling in the light of the critical state of England's position, is that Henry should have expected any favourable reaction, which is even more difficult to comprehend when one understands that the Scottish council, with which Sadler had to deal also in these matters, was dominated by clergymen and presided over by Beaton himself. No wonder that Beaton found it easy to undermine Sadler's credit with James V! Even less wonderful is Sadler's notice of the fact that James acted as if he feared Beaton's displeasure, excusing the cardinal's every fault somewhat nervously. Denunciations and plans for church reform met with a stony reception on every side.

It is hard to escape the conclusion that Sadler had been sent on a fool's errand, and that not for the last time, as we shall see. While James staunchly defended his minister, Sadler's orders required him to produce from his pocket 'the copis of the device made for the reformacyon of the Churche in Canterburye and Yorke'. That investment in temerity paid scant dividends. James cut Sadler off in mid-sentence, refusing to

---

[1] Sadler's picture seems to agree well enough with that given in the much debated Cromwellian *comperta* which he doubtless knew well.

[2] The copyist apparently misread 'exempted'.

[3] *SSP*, I, 30–1.

[4] James lied when he denied the charge (*SSP*, I, 29). That he raised sheep and sold the wool is proved by *The Exchequer Rolls of Scotland*, ed. George P. McNeill (Edinburgh: The General Register House, 1897), pp. 172, 189, 289, 290, 296, 359 and 741.

hear of any such plans. For his own part, Sadler could do no more than sadly confess that 'James had no wyl to take more thereof...The next advertysement of my proceedynges here, I thynke I shall bring to your maiestie miselfe; for I understand it that the Kinge here intendeth to dispatche me awaie shortly...'[1]

No attempt was made to conceal the displeasure of the Scots, although a certain diplomatic amiability was preserved in royal letters sent to Henry VIII on 28 February, in which it was alleged that James was pleased by his uncle's care for 'our well beyng'.[2] The English were not deceived, however, and they realised from Sadler's accounts that the mission had failed of its purpose.

The most interesting confirmation of this view comes in a letter from Sadler to Cromwell, who was badly in need of a victory in the diplomatic arena, if the bitter thrusts of his enemies at home were to be turned aside. Sadler admitted that he had failed, yet his failure was not puzzling to him. Wherever he went in Scotland, he told Cromwell, the 'Scottes were well geven to the verity of Christes word and doctrine'. The nobility gave no lead in the direction of reformation; Sadler believed that they were lacking in the requisite skills, thus forcing James to rely on clerical advisers, the only capable ministers of state, while the people were well disposed toward true religion.

Politics in Scotland were thus the key to England's dilemma. There was nobody like Cromwell to lead the way. The popular willingness to act seemed omnipresent, a fact that haunted Sadler as he wistfully remarked to his master and friend: 'that the kinge of Scottes had one suche councillor and servaunte as the kinges maiestie hath of you...'. With warmth and just a touch of flattery, Sadler exposed the impossibility of his accomplishing his mission. England had little to hope for in Scotland until a leader appeared on the scene. Diplomats might contrive to alter the course of events; but they could not invent a leader for the Scots! In the absence of such a man as Knox, whose great career was then not beyond its earliest stages, Beaton and his party would continue to rule all. The king was little more than the cardinal's dupe. Given these facts, the 'Christian partie' lacked spirit, lacking leadership, while the anti-English and papal party was animated by the brilliant cardinal.

[1] *SSP*, I, 44–5.
[2] BM Royal MSS. 13B VI, fo. 87a, a contemporary copy in Latin and English.

The chilling sum of Sadler's mission was this: English hopes were stymied; further conversation was useless.

Cromwell's agent and friend knew full well the burden of his cheerless letter, and he thus conspired to end on an amusing note, hoping to distract the harried minister with a few trifles. In Edinburgh tales of barbarism were rife, in so far as Ralph Sadler was concerned. He ate meat during prescribed fast periods; he was an 'evill fishman'. But in truth he ate only white meats, which, being pure, could give no offence, he remarked. Then, to illustrate his reputation at the court of James V, which had a totally Roman and hence a Latin orientation, Sadler played the Grecian for Cromwell's benefit:

Anothre bruit they made, that all my men were monks, and that I had them out of the abbeys in England, and now they were serving men. I gave a badge, a Greek word on my mens coats,[1] which is '*mono anakti douleuo*'; the Latin whereof is, *soli regi servio; a rege tantum pendeo; ex regis ministerio unus;* and such other may be interpreted of the same.[2] Now, the bishops here have interpreted my word to be, as they call it, *monachulus*, which they say, is in English, a little monk, as a diminutive of *monachus*; and they affirmed for a verity that meaning. Whereappon they bruited that all my men are monks. But it appereth that they are no good Grecians.[3] And now the effects of my words are known, and they be laughed at for their learned interpretations. Thus I do trouble you with some trifles to recreate you with all your great affairs.[4]

Sadler's ending was more symbolic than he knew, for throughout the 1540s the party sympathetic to the revived Greek learning of Erasmus and its implications for reform made no headway in Scotland. And so Sadler, heavy-hearted, made his way back to London to attend to the mundane business of collecting travel expenses while the sands ran out for Cromwell.[5]

The mission of 1540 was perhaps conceived in desperation by Thomas Cromwell as part of his doomed effort to retain control of the council

[1] The statute made by Henry VII entitled *De retentionibus illicitis* was not still in effect; Sadler and many others were licensed to give liveries (see *SR*, II, 521).
[2] The implication of this pedantic letter is that Sadler knew Greek but that Cromwell did not.
[3] Greek scholars at Cambridge were patronised by Cromwell. In the 1540s several of them were prominent: e.g. Roger Shore, Roger Ascham and John Cheke.
[4] This and the preceding quotations are in *SSP*, I, 46–9. The Greek transliteration into English is mine.
[5] BM Arundel MSS. 97, fos. 145–6; Cotton MSS. appendix xxviii, fo. 128b; PRO, SP 1/161, fos. 147a–147b. All are accounts filed by John Gostwick, treasurer of the court of first fruits and tenths. Each entry lists a payment made to Sadler for expenses incurred during the 1540 mission.

and the machinery of state. For Sadler, even the failure of that mission could not mask his advance in both Cromwell's and the king's favour. Shortly after his return from Edinburgh, he was named principal secretary of state.[1] His apprenticeship, which had been marred by the circumstances of Wolsey's great fall, was at an end. Ironically, his dependence on Cromwell was terminated not by his own proportions as a minister of the king but by the execution of his patron and ally a scant three months after Sadler became a knight. Between the beginning and the end of Ralph's initiation into the mysteries of English politics there had occurred the two most egregious examples of the power of the Crown: the legal murder of Cromwell and the banishment and subsequent death of Wolsey. Such were the auspices under which Ralph Sadler emerged from obscurity to play a part in politics as a pluralist administrator and the government's Scottish expert.

[1] See ch. 4 above.

6

THE ENGLISH WOOING OF
SCOTLAND IN 1543

Scotland is a court and a kingdom as full of welters and uncertainties
as the moon of changes...   TOBY MATHEW to Lord Burghley

It has been our contention in treating Sadler's early Scottish missions
that Anglo-Scottish problems stemmed from the major difficulties encountered by England in settling her policies with regard to the Habsburgs and the Valois. Viewed in that light Sadler's work was in no sense
peripheral; it stood at the head of the list of vital diplomatic tasks left
unsolved at the death of Thomas Cromwell. If Scotland seemed a poor
and shabby place, whose scattered inhabitants were beggarly and dis-
honest to a degree that caused English imaginations to boggle, it was
nevertheless of vital concern to all Englishmen. The fact that Scots
roamed freely across the northern frontier escaped nobody's notice; the
fact that many Scots spoke French impressed Henry VIII and his council.
That so wretched and rustic a people as the Scots should naturally
hunger after Valois gold might pass for an axiom. But that French
money meant French politics could hardly be viewed with equanimity
by Sadler and his fellow councillors.[1]

The English government was compelled to see Scotland in the light
of Reformation politics. Like Henry VII, who had formulated the basis
of Scottish policy in 1502, Henry VIII, for different reasons, felt constrained to secure a perpetual peace.[2] His peace, hopefully, would also
rest on a marriage alliance, on a renewal of the English wooing which
sent Margaret Tudor to James IV.[3] In that way both Henries hoped to
exclude the reinvigoration of the 'auld alliance' between France and
Scotland that had for three centuries menaced England's northern

---

[1] Sir Thomas More, *Utopia* (London: Everyman, 1952), p. 96: 'Therefore the Scots are to be
kept in readiness to be let loose upon England on every occasion.'

[2] *Foedera*, XII, 793. The Treaty of Berwick in 1529 was one such Henrician attempt. Another
was the treaty signed in London 11 May 1534 as a part of Cromwell's peace offensive (*Foedera*,
XIV, 529).

[3] *Ibid.* p. 787.

boundary. Nothing was more natural for Henry VIII than to anticipate what would happen if the Scottish royal line should fail. Thus, the idea of unifying the island by a marital union was the obvious implication of the old dream of a united Britain and the French threat as well.[1] The collapse of the scheme of Henry VII in 1512–13, with the renewal of Anglo-French and Anglo-Scottish hostilities, a breakdown only partly the fault of Henry VIII's martial ardour, since other personalities and impersonal troubles of a commercial sort also played a part, made the pursuit of such a policy more difficult.[2] But by 1540, with the Valois marriage an accomplished fact and the Guise marriage that followed also part of the record, whatever chance for success existed had to be seized.

The alternating current of Anglo-Scottish relations in the years from Flodden to Solway Moss flowed from two basic generative forces. At one pole stood Henry VIII's assertion that he was the rightful suzerain of Scotland, deriving the claim from the troubled days of John Balliol and Edward I.[3] By Henry's standards, the peace of 1502 had revealed serious contradictions in Scottish policy, especially the French status as guarantor of Scottish independence. Henry believed the French guarantee to constitute an admission on James IV's part that English claims were good. In the wake of Flodden, Scotland more than ever appeared as the cockpit in which English and French ambitions would be fought over and vindicated.

At the other pole of the field of force there were arrayed the great powers of the incipient counter-reform led by Paul III. For that reason Henry VIII had passed the 1530s trying to salve old wounds as a means of making a Valois alliance to complement that made by Wolsey after the great imperial victory at Pavia. Driven by logic and necessity into courting Francis I, English politicians, led by their king, were obliged to allow Scottish grievances a fair hearing. Only gradually did it become clear to those in power in London that Francis I was playing a shrewd and risky game, exploiting England's domestic strife and her foreign policy problems in such a way as to strengthen his own hold on Scotland. Thus Henry was more than ever bound to conciliate James V,

[1] John D. Mackie, 'Henry VIII and Scotland', *TRHS*, 4th ser. XXIX (1947), 93–114.
[2] *Ibid.* pp. 103–9.
[3] The roots of the claim by Henry VIII had a basis in the Saxon kingdom of Alfred the Great. The matter was first effectively maintained by Henry II in 1174, however, when he captured William the Lion of Scotland.

whatever his own natural inclination might be. That was the meaning of Sadler's work from 1537–40, as England renewed Henry VIII's policy of gently wooing Scotland. Sadler's failure to shake Beaton's position in James V's favour was thus a doubly bitter defeat for Henry VIII, the result of a policy contrary to his own more martial tastes and, more important even than that, it had merely continued the process by which Anglo-Habsburg relations were strained.[1]

War loomed large in English thinking in 1540. Causes for war, real and imagined, were, of course, never lacking between ancient enemies. In 1541, when the temporary reconciliation of Valois and Hapsburg underlined the futility of Cromwell's policy, Henry VIII actually humbled himself to the point of travelling to York, in order to meet with James V. Unfortunately for the peace, so rapidly failing of its own accord, James failed to appear, apparently yielding to clerical councillors who suggested it would be easier for a Scot to enter than to leave England.[2] Henry was not a man to be trifled with. Proud, anxious, in failing health, but always quick to hear tunes of glory, the deeply angered king brooded over the injury to English pride. More important, however, than any wound to Henry's vanity, was James's total rejection of Sadler's scheme for reform at a time when the Protestant cause seemed to be making real headway in the lands north of the Tweed.[3]

Less dramatic, but more deeply ingrained, factors militated against the dying peace. Border unrest was again endemic and contributed to the tension. Beyond the normal friction all along the frontier was a special list of grievances. Chief among them was the flight of Dr Robert Hilliard, Bishop Tunstal's secretary and agent, a staunch Catholic who had refused the oath of supremacy and had then fled into Scotland, carrying with him a considerable knowledge of the disposition of English affairs in the northern counties. Demands for his return had been ignored. James also harboured other English criminals, especially the political rebels who fled after the failure of the Pilgrimage of Grace.[4] Scottish reluctance to extradite such men contravened the laws

[1] See ch. 5.
[2] John Knox, *The History of the Reformation in Scotland, 1494–1558*, ed. David Laing (Edinburgh: Woodrow Society, 1846), I, 76.
[3] See below for factors influencing English thought on this matter.
[4] Sturge, *Tunstal*, pp. 233–4.

regulating the Marches, by which all parties agreed to surrender such refugees to the justice of their native land.[1] Uncertainty about geography, especially that of the 'debatable lands', increased the chance for misadventure at a time when the men of both nations needed little provocation to go out and destroy each other.[2] Differences in the fertility of the frontier soil, nearly always in Scotland's favour, encouraged marauders alleging the doubtfulness of the boundaries. While the English borderer was proud of his wild and rugged hills, he could only rarely resist the gentler and more productive lure of the Scottish lowlands.[3] Finally, at the end of this catalogue of incentives to war, we ought to note the sheer exuberant love of combat that flavoured political life in that tough frontier country. Sir John Dudley, a great soldier himself, noted that Scots and Englishmen co-operated only long enough to stage collusive raids on one another in which no real harm was done, prompted by their fear of union, which would forever end their legacy of riot and war, a preference amounting almost to a sporting institution.[4]

Even admitting these factors, war and its consequences might have been avoided, if European diplomacy had moved in quieter channels in the 1540s. Events since 1537 had required Henry VIII to win Charles V's friendship anew. As Anglo-French enmity waxed as a consequence of the Franco-Scottish marriage, it became doubtful that Henry would continue to rule England without an ally to contain the French on the continent. England had to fall back again on Wolsey's pro-imperial policy of the days before Pavia, not out of natural aptitude or preference for such an alliance, but because it was the only reasonable thing to do. Ironically, the policy which had ruined Wolsey and over which Cromwell had also stumbled was to be taken up by Sadler and Wriothesley.[5]

The necessity to cultivate Charles V brought to light a stark contra-

---

[1] William Nicholson, *Leges marchiarum* (London, 1705), pp. 80–93. Extradition was to follow within ten days of the request. For the law of the Borders in the sixteenth century see D. L. W. Tough, *The Last Years of a Frontier* (Oxford: Clarendon Press, 1928).

[2] The best contemporary sketch of the frontier and its demarcation was that made by Sir Robert Bowes in his 'Book of the State of the Frontiers and the Marches', printed by John Hodgson, *History of Northumberland*, 3 vols. in 8 parts (Newcastle-on-Tyne: Thomas and James Pigg, 1825–58), part 3, II, 19–41.

[3] See William Camden, *Brittanica* (London, 1695), p. 847.

[4] *HP*, I, 261, Dudley to Henry VIII, 19 Dec. 1542.

[5] Sturge, *Tunstal*, p. 231.

diction in English objectives of such magnitude as to be ignored only at great risks. England was committed to reforms in ecclesiastical matters which were unacceptable to the emperor and only slightly less offensive to some English councillors. At the same time, Scotland was ruled by a king and cardinal thoroughly hostile to church reform in the English mode.[1] True, the Scots had a good number of Lutherans and Calvinists in their midst, including some of the nobility.[2] It was also true that a number of trimmers and ransomed captives were in English pay.[3] What mattered most, however, was that religious conversation of an evangelical sort closed the ears of those who counted most. This confusion of ends and means led England to accept a policy that mixed threats and blustering with a brand of sweet cajolery, thereby giving the Scots confidence in their view of the situation: England was tied to contradictory goals and therefore would never be able to go to war. How could England hope to pursue reform and also win Charles and James?

That was the situation in which Henry VIII characteristically reacted to the abortive York Conference. Increasingly violent speeches against the Scottish king were united to the efforts of a team of royal antiquarians whose only mission was to supply Henry with new proofs of his most extreme suzerainty claims. The result was his manifesto of 1542, in which he made the most aggravating claim of all: that he was ruler of Scotland in his own person.[4] At the same time, Sir William Paget sent news out of France which indicated that the French accepted the inevitability of an English war.[5] Since English efforts to achieve *rapport* with Charles V were slow in developing, the terrible prospect of a two-front war faced Henry VIII.

---

[1] Robert S. Rait, 'The Scottish Parliament Before the Union of the Crowns', *EHR*, xv (1900), 209–37 and 417–44.

[2] Gordon Donaldson, *The Scottish Reformation* (Cambridge University Press, 1960), pp. 1–30.

[3] BM Arundel MSS. 97, fo. 58a, a list of pensions, among them one for Angus at £300. Angus and his family were long absent from Scotland as a result of a series of bloody disputes dating back to the Hamilton–Douglas Edinburgh street brawl of 1520 famous under the rubric 'Cleanse the Causeway'. Their actual exile stemmed from the events of the regency struggle in 1528. In 1538 several of the Angus relatives remaining behind in Scotland were executed. Hence the Douglas family was a natural point of attraction for pro-English Scots. See Hume Brown, 'The Scottish Nobility and their Part in the National History', *ScHR*, III (1906), 166–7.

[4] Thomas Berthelet, the royal printer, published the claims as *A Sentence Conteyning the Just Causes...Wherein alsoo Appeareth the Trew and Ryght Tytle that the Kinges Most Roiall Maisetie hath to Soveraynte of Scotlande* (London, 1542).

[5] Lord Herbert, *The Life and Reign of King Henry VIII*, p. 549.

The English Wooing of Scotland in 1543

The last turn of the screw came on 17 August 1542. Sir George Bowes attacked a party of Scots near Halydon Rigg on that day, breaking the formal peace which had endured since 1513.[1] The war thus begun was a peculiarly sporadic one, even when one considers the intermittent character of early modern warfare in general. Throughout the late summer and the early fall of the year, actions of no great consequence were gladly waged on both sides of the border. Then, in November, James summoned the chivalry of Scotland to do battle with Thomas Howard, that duke of Norfolk who as a tough, young earl had commanded the forces at Flodden Field. The whip with which England had scourged Scotland thirty years before had not lost its sting. On 24 November 1542 the Scots were routed at Solway Moss. Almost at the same time, James V fell ill under conditions that were to be fatal.[2]

An event at Edinburgh mitigated partially the bitterness of those Scottish reverses, for Mary of Lorraine gave birth to the long-awaited heir to the king of Scots.[3] A new life for an old, surely, but hardly a fair exchange, since the child was a girl, a fact which could not fail to dampen the joy stemming from the insurance thus given to the succession. To the English, always suspicious of things Scottish, the birth of Mary, queen of Scots, seemed to be marvellous. Birth and death so coincided as to give substance to a remark uttered long afterward by Toby Matthew, the grasping Elizabethan bishop of Durham, to Burghley: 'There [Scotland] is a court and a kingdom as full of welters and uncertainties as the moon of changes...'[4]

The die cast at Solway and that thrown at Edinburgh might well have caused Englishmen to puzzle the results. The ancients had believed that strife was the father of all things. Might not that wisdom be applied in the present case? War and the pangs of birth, coupled with James V's mortal sickness had presented England with a reprieve. Scottish events joined the renewal of hostilities between France and the Empire in such a way as to grant England a breathing space and something more.

---

[1] Mackie, *TRHS*, 4th ser. XXIX, 112.

[2] Knox, *History of the Reformation in Scotland*, I, 77–89.

[3] Confusion about the health of the child is well demonstrated in *HP*, I, 254, 262, 337 and 339. Sir George Douglas supplied Viscount Lisle with correct information on 17 Dec., five days after Mary's birth and two days after James V's death (*HP*, I, 260).

[4] *CSPD addenda*, p. 345, 15 Jan. 1593. I wish to thank Dr Richard C. Barnett of Wake Forest College for this reference.

England had a marriageable prince of Wales. Scotland now had an infant queen who also happened to be Henry VIII's grand-niece. England also had a host of prisoners taken at Solway, many of them of great noble families, and all of them *en route* to London at the express command of the English king and council. The Scots had been obliged to give hostages to fortune, not the least of whom was their king, whose death had turned the clock back to 1286, the last occasion on which an English prince had been offered to a Scottish queen in such circumstances. All at once, England's hand had been fortified, and where death had frustrated England's plans in 1286 perhaps Edward would live to marry Mary.[1]

The onrushing war seemed, by a twist of fate, to have given Henry VIII all the aces in the game. For two months after Solway Moss he quietly observed the other players, measuring the strength of their position against his own, before deciding that diplomacy and deceit were more to his advantage than the continuation of that strange winter war on the borders. To accomplish his aims, Sir Ralph Sadler, the principal secretary of state and Scottish expert on the council, prepared to leave for Edinburgh. The council, meanwhile, tried to arrange things in a way that suited England's new-found power.

First of all, the council turned to the Scottish captives. After a number of long hearings in the Star Chamber, with Audley presiding, Henry VIII solicited from the leading nobles and knights captured at Solway Moss written promises to support English manoeuvres in Scotland. Angus and his brother Sir George Douglas, although they were not prisoners and in fact were English pensioners for a number of years, voluntarily entered into similar agreements of a fundamentally treasonous nature. All pledged to forward the Reformation and to work for an Anglo-Scottish alliance based on a marriage treaty uniting Edward and Mary. Implicit in the agreements was an undertaking not to stick at violent means in the efforts to overturn Beaton and the Guise faction. Once the noblemen had made their pledges and had in writing bound themselves to be 'assured' lords and supporters of the English plans, they were paroled to English keepers, after signing further indentures to the effect that they were to surrender themselves if they failed to live up to their

---

[1] In 1286 Edward I, the 'hammer of the Scots', tried to marry his son to the Scottish heiress, but the 'Maid of Norway' died before the contract could be drafted.

bargain. Sadler was granted the custody of Lord Monkeith, while other councillors received the 'honour' of other Scotsmen.[1]

Apart from the somewhat melodramatic air of the entire affair, in which men were bound to commit treason 'on their honour', further aspects of the matter of the 'assured' Scots merit our consideration. The two Douglases were about to return to Scotland for the first time since their exile at Methuen's hands. What is more to the point, they were the acknowledged leaders of those who swore to be good Englishmen.[2] Whether or not English councillors could really trust their 'Englishmen' was a capital question, but, if they could, then England would have at long last performed the miracle Sadler despaired of in 1540: they would have invented leaders for a Scottish Reformation!

While these matters were being regulated in London, two important bits of news reached the council. Sir John Dudley sent word that Beaton had already moved to fill the power vacuum created by James V's impending death. It was only natural that Beaton had carried great weight in the early moves to establish an interim council of regency.[3] His looking to France for aid was just as much a matter of course.[4] At the same time the first confirmed reports of the birth of Mary, queen of Scots, and tales of her robust health reached the court.[5] This last was accompanied by the less agreeable news in which it appeared that Beaton and James Hamilton, the earl of Arran, were conspiring to control the regency.[6]

Although the English were quite ignorant of the detailed course of events in Scotland, having only reports and rumours to go on, they nonetheless moved quickly to capitalise on the initiative so suddenly thrust upon them. Henry VIII's claims to Scotland were again announced;[7] at the same time a bullying reply was sent to the official word of the death of King James.[8] The English told the Scots that Solway Moss resulted from Scottish breaches of the peace.[9] Apparently, the

[1] Holinshed, *Chronicle*, III, 830; see also *SP*, v, 232–3.
[2] The full list is supplied in *HP*, I, 252.
[3] *HP*, I, 254, Lisle *et al.* to Henry VIII, 12 Dec. 1542.
[4] *Ibid.* p. 260, enclosure I, Sir George Douglas to Lisle, 17 Dec. 1542.
[5] *Ibid.* p. 254, enclosure I, Lisle to Henry VIII, 12 Dec. 1542.
[6] *Ibid.* p. 267, same to the same, 30 Dec. 1542.
[7] Wriothesley, *Chronicle*, I, 140, for the prisoners' oaths. See *SR*, III, 938, 34–5 Henry VIII *c.* 27 for the statute referring to James V as a usurper.
[8] *HP*, I, 264, 21 Dec. 1542.
[9] *Ibid.* p. 266, 29 Dec. 1542.

English council had taken the king's lead and had decided to be very aggressive, perhaps in the hope that such conduct would frighten the Scots into a marriage pact. For on the heels of the stern admonitions and some exceedingly bellicose threats, Scotland was assured that England desired nothing more than a peace based on a *parentado*, the English adding that many Scottish noblemen were already minded to support the hoped-for treaty.[1]

On 3 January 1543 Arran, who had been named governor of Scotland, was designated director of the regency.[2] Hence, he received the inquiries and also the diplomatic hint that Beaton ought to be banished from the council of regency.[3] Dudley, Viscount Lisle, who was Henry VIII's emissary at this stage of the negotiations, knew first hand that his king considered Arran's appointment to be in derogation of Henry's suzerain rights, rights which the English king meant to protect.[4] Behind the royal resentment lay a correct deduction about Scottish politics: if Arran remained as governor, it would be impossible, or nearly so, to get control of the young queen, to capture Beaton and the major Scottish forts and castles, all of which was a part of Henry's duplicit scheme for Scotland.[5] Henry was one of those rare individuals gifted with powers of polyphonic mendacity when faced with a difficult situation and he intended to use his gift.

Given the duplicity of his scheme for ruling Scotland, timing was the key to success for Henry VIII. Arran was a weak man and a trimmer who would not stand up to anybody as formidable as Beaton. In fact, the English were of the opinion that Beaton had in reality manipulated the forces that brought Arran to the governorship,[6] and this assumption was the basis for the plan put into effect in 1543. Instructions were issued to Sir Richard Southwell to the effect that Arran's attitude was crucial: the governor was to be told his co-operation was expected.[7] Whether or not even Arran could be deceived in the prevailing circumstances is

---

[1] *HP*, I, p. 269, 4 Jan. 1543.

[2] For the machinations surrounding the Arran nomination and appointments see Andrew Lang, 'The Cardinal and the King's Will', *ScHR*, III (1906), 410–22.

[3] *HP*, I, 275–6, 8 and 9 Jan. 1543.   [4] *Ibid.* p. 275, 8 Jan. 1543.

[5] *Ibid.* p. 276, 9 Jan. 1543.

[6] See Lang, *ScHR*, III, *passim*, as well as *SSP*, I, 138; *HMC Eleventh Report*, IV, 219–20; R. K. Hannay, 'The Earl of Arran and Queen Mary', *ScHR*, XVIII (1921), 258–76; *idem*, 'On the Church Lands at the Reformation', *ScHR*, XVI (1918), 52–72.

[7] *HP*, I, 276 (pp. 367–76), undated instructions issued for Sir Richard Southwell, supplementing earlier instructions.

now a moot point, but he must have heard the rumours in which his expendability was the major item of conversation.[1] Furthermore, the governor was faced with the paroled prisoners, men who were sworn to undercut him when it suited England's interests.[2] Englishmen, who marvelled when the Scots were at peace among themselves, and the 'assured' Scots, wore malevolence with an open face.[3] Thus, when Arran wrote to the council in London, requesting a truce, since peace was the *sine qua non* of reform, the time was ripe to dispatch the parolees.[4]

English observation of the changes effected by the return of the Douglases and their co-conspirators encouraged the hopes of success. Lisle reported that Angus and Sir George Douglas were restored to the council in Edinburgh immediately after arriving in Scotland.[5] It was his opinion that Beaton could be arrested almost at will, although when Arran actually moved to do just that Lisle suspected the governor's motives.[6]

This raised the problem of the adequacy of the intelligence being sent to the English council. Lisle was a soldier, and a very good one at that, but he confessed that he was insufficiently informed about the Scottish council and personalities at court to be of much use in evaluating the reports filtering down to him on the borders. True, the difficulty of interpreting events would have been there for any observer. Sir George Douglas fed English optimism, but he was decidedly ambivalent in his dealings with Lisle and the Scots. His influence over his brother Angus was complete; he was on good terms with Arran; he had Beaton's confidence, while all the time alleging his fidelity to England. It became clear in England that his conduct was the vital element in Henry VIII's success, in so far as the Scottish lords were concerned. But understanding Douglas seemed to be a full time job, necessitating the sending of a representative from London sufficiently skilled in things Scottish to solve the ambiguities inherent in Douglas's conduct. Douglas himself said the same thing in a letter to Charles Brandon, the duke of Suffolk,

[1] *Ibid.* pp. 371–3.
[2] *Ibid.* p. 374.
[3] *HMC Salisbury MSS.* IV, 345, Roger Manners to Sir Robert Cecil, 2 Aug. 1593.
[4] *HP*, I, 281.
[5] *Ibid.* p. 286, Lisle to Henry VIII, 21 Jan. 1543.
[6] *Ibid.* p. 289, same to the same, 28 Jan. 1543.

allegedly on Arran's behalf, when he noted that the paroled lords needed an expert diplomatic consultant, since the Scots themselves were 'hardly fit ambassadors' in the business at hand.[1] Finally, it seemed that Arran wanted a resident English ambassador for other reasons. Understanding the position of the former Scottish captives, the governor meant to deal with an open foe, in place of so many secret ones, in the matter of the truce and treaty. He justly told the English that the intolerable posture of distrust had to be eliminated, if anything useful was to happen along the lines desired by Henry VIII.[2]

The English advisers could hardly miss the implications of those remarks. Southwell, Lisle and Suffolk were not adequate to the delicate business of making peace, nor could they always interpret the situation with clarity and insight. Since events were moving very rapidly in the wake of the return of the Douglas brothers, it was imperative that somebody be sent to Edinburgh, fully equipped to conclude the peace, to understand the factions ruling in Scotland and to forward the underground movement designed to set Beaton by the heels. Sadler was the obvious choice for the mission.

A few days after Arran's letter to Suffolk made known the governor's views, Sir Ralph Sadler rode northward in the company of Sir Francis Bryan. At Newcastle they talked with Suffolk, Tunstal and Parr, the leaders of the council there. What they learned was alarming. Apparently the duke of Guise had pledged his willingness to intervene in Scotland in order to protect his kinswomen.[3] Furthermore, the Scottish people deeply resented Beaton's arrest; not a priest would bury, baptise or proclaim the bans.[4] It was said that any indiscreet action by the English party among the Scots would doom Sadler's mission before it was started. Sadler gravely sent this news on to the council, admonishing them *quieta non movere*!

The immediate consequence of Sadler's first statement in reaction to the situation in Scotland was striking. Henry, deciding that turn-about was fair play, asked that a Scottish plenipotentiary be sent to London.[5] That constituted a *de facto* recognition of Scottish sovereignty, in the

[1] For Suffolk's activities see Sadler's accounts in PRO, E 101/674/2 and E 351/211.
[2] *HP*, I, 290, Arran to Suffolk, 30 Jan. 1543.
[3] *SP*, v, 244–7, Suffolk *et al.* to the council, 26 Jan. 1543.
[4] Lang, *ScHR*, III, 419, and also *SP*, v, 249.
[5] *SP*, v, 247, Henry VIII to Suffolk *et al.*, 30 Jan. 1543.

language of modern analysis, and the move had practical consequences, whatever the state of diplomatic theory might then have been. Arran's prestige at home was greatly enhanced, an outcome not at all in line with English policy. This fact was emphasised by the governor's significant action in calling a parliament for 12 March, to meet either in Perth or Edinburgh. Although some Englishmen thought that the governor would use the meeting to strike at Beaton with an old English device, a parliamentary condemnation, Lisle was wary, and rightfully so, since Douglas immediately alleged that the forthcoming parliament made it impossible for the assured lords to deliver Beaton as they had sworn to do. The fact that Beaton's arrest had taken place at Dalkeith, a Douglas stronghold, had already aroused many Scots against England's agents. The abuse of parliament would make the position of the parolees impossible.[1] Douglas counselled patience.

Patience was, however, not Henry VIII's long suit. Pushed by Sadler for an immediate grant of truce, Henry, who considered that he had the high cards in the game, felt annoyed.[2] Despite Sadler's warning that Arran might revolt to the other party, if alarmed, the English king let it be known that he intended strong action if he did not get what he wanted.[3] Perhaps that was partly Sadler's fault, since the Newcastle dispatches had built Henry's confidence by telling of the strong support for the marriage among the Scots.[4] Sadler had even boasted that the earl of Murray and other Catholic leaders wished both the marriage and the concomitant peace. That the Catholic earls supported the governor ought to have aroused the suspicion of Sadler, since Arran spoke of his own enthusiasm for the doctrine of Christ as found in the English church. To a certain extent it had in fact done just that, as we have seen above. But, all things considered, Sadler's belief that it was possible to reconcile all factions about the proposed marriage and against the cardinal fed the strange mixture of petulance and confidence that characterised Henry VIII's disposition in 1543.[5] A truly diplomatic nature would have exhibited greater scepticism, when faced with that particular *embarras des riches*. Sadler and his friends, however, harmonised

---

[1] *Ibid.* p. 250, Lisle to Suffolk, 2 Feb. 1543.
[2] *Ibid.* p. 256, Suffolk *et al.* to the council, 7 Feb. 1543.
[3] *HP*, I, 296–7, Suffolk and Sadler to the Privy Council, 11 and 12 Feb. 1543.
[4] *Ibid.* p. 298, Suffolk to the Privy Council, 13 Feb. 1543.
[5] *Ibid.* pp. 299, 301, 303, 305 and 316.

the discordant notes.[1] Why even the arch-conservatives Bothwell and Buccleuch would dance to the English tune![2]

The English councillors reacted accordingly. Tunstal, convinced that all was well, took time off from his temporal cares in the north, where he played an important but obscure role,[3] and journeyed to Morpeth, where he had promised to deliver some Lenten sermons.[4] Henry, for his part, hurried forward the arrangement of a truce and the marriage that would follow.

In Scotland, however, events belied English expectations. The deep rifts which existed among the Scottish noblemen had been closed overnight. The sympathies of known conservatives, Murray, Huntley and Argyle, were quite different from those of the governor, whose principal support came from Glencairn, Cassells and the Stuarts.[5] At the same time, the Douglases had ample reason to dislike the governor and the seven bishops, for the role they had played in driving them out of Scotland in the first place.[6] The same was true for followers of Lennox. Finally, the Guise family was hardly likely to follow Arran's lead, since they had refused to endorse the regency arrangements at all and were ultimately to replace Hamilton with one of their own number in that position.[7]

Of course it cannot be denied that such a situation might provide a basis of optimism on the grounds of *divide et impera*. A multi-factional split within the regency council could conceivably play into English hands, since the assured lords in theory would function as a unit.[8] Unfortunately, Sadler soon disabused the English of any complacency on those grounds. He informed Henry VIII that the great Catholic leaders had laid aside their intention to boycott any parliament convened

[1] *HP*, I, p. 305, Sadler to the Privy Council, 19 Feb. 1543.

[2] *Ibid*. p. 320, Suffolk to the Privy Council, 1 March 1543.

[3] Lapsley, *AHR*, v, 440 ff.

[4] *SP*, v, 260, Suffolk to the Privy Council, 3 March 1543.

[5] Brown, *ScHR*, III, 167.

[6] James Fraser, *Chronicles of the Frasers: The Wardlaw Manuscript*, ed. William Mackay (Edinburgh: Constable, 1905), p. 133, for a contemporary view of the Douglas position.

[7] For a contemporary view of the responsibility of the Guise for the instability of the regency during the 1540s see John Manningham, *Diary of John Manningham*, ed. John Bruce (Westminster: Camden Society, 1868), pp. 118–26, where some excerpts from a poem in the *speculum principis* tradition entitled 'The Tragicall Historie of Mary Quene of Scottes...' are published.

[8] For the composition of the Council of Regency see Joseph Stevenson, *Selections from the Unpublished Manuscripts in the College of Arms and the British Museum Illustrating the Reign of Mary Queen of Scots* (Glasgow: Maitland Club, 1837), p. 2.

by Arran, for reasons of their own, not yet known to Sadler. They had agreed to come in peace to Edinburgh, in a grand display of Scottish unity. The bishops and clergy had also agreed to come.[1] A 'rump' parliament composed of reformers and assured lords was therefore circumvented, with the full body, traditionally the battle ground of factions in cases of minority governments, apparently ready to unite in the avowed purpose of resisting English attempts to subvert the kingdom.[2] What Sadler found in Edinburgh was neither simple unity nor simple disunity. What exactly the disposition of factions would eventually be was unknown to him; but he did perceive that the parliament would not bend to English wills.

The spectre of a united Scottish representative assembly filled the English council with anxiety, and they determined to send Sadler on to Edinburgh without further delay on the borders. In that way, they hoped that he would directly influence the parliament. In a letter dictating their thoughts to him, the council and the king noted the nature of

the long tract of tyme, whyche hath unfrutefully passed sithin the decease of the late kinge, and how slenderlie we be advertysed and answered from all parties in Scottlande, we have hens found it necessarie by som gud meanes to deciphre what ys intendyd towardes us, and thothre thynges promysed by the erle of Angwishe and suche othres as were latly here. And forsamuche as you, Syr Ralph Sadleyr, have nowe hitherto bene sundrie tymes in Scottlande, by reason whereof you have there and of thaire maners there gud acquayntance, and also that you be privy not onlie to the thynges which were promysed here, but also to all the proceedynges and advertysements sithens that tyme, we thynke no man shal soo wel sarve us in thys purpos as you.[3]

Formal instructions were to follow.

Luckily, a draft of these papers is preserved with the Hamilton Papers now in the British Museum, although no trace of them survives in Sadler's own state papers.[4]

Although it is a rather academic point as to whether Sadler was truly an ambassador by virtue of his commission, he did enjoy wide discretionary powers in a highly complex situation.[5] Once again, his tasks

[1] *HP*, I, 325, 8 March 1543.   [2] See Rait, *EHR*, xv, *passim*.
[3] *SP*, v, 261, 13 March 1543.   [4] *HP*, I, 330, 13 March 1543.
[5] 'Quicunque ab alio missus', said Behrens, was the usual definition of an ambassador in our period: B. Behrens, 'Treatises on the Ambassador written in the Fifteenth and Early Sixteenth Century', *EHR*, LI (1936), 616–27, for the entire subject of the style and powers of ambassadors.

were graded in line with a series of goals set for English policy in Scotland. One of his tasks was to persuade the governor that only a minister plenipotentiary could perform the required duties in London. Another was the expenditure of secret funds for the purpose of hiring additional Scottish agents for intelligence purposes. He was also to urge that Sir Robert Erskine, the secretary of state to Hamilton, be replaced by James Drummond, since the former was a well-known conservative ill-disposed to the Reformation. More important than any of these tasks, Sadler was to sound out the Douglases on the complicated business of the structure and mobility of Scottish factions. In the hope of clarifying the possibilities of a marriage alliance, Sir Ralph was also to speak with Mary of Guise. Finally, and most vital of all, he was to counsel Arran, the Catholics, the other Guise supporters and the Protestants to remember with whom they dealt, emphasising that Henry VIII was a great and proud king who was rapidly running out of patience.[1] While it is only hinted at in the draft instructions, there can be no doubt that Sadler's ultimate goal was to pave the way for a transformation of the regency arrangements, perhaps with the intention of securing the rule of one of the paroled lords or the Douglas family.

In principle the English plan was sound, but the timing proved to be poor. When Sadler arrived at Alnwick, he learned that the parliament had already met and adjourned.[2] The Scots had stayed at Edinburgh just long enough to upset the carefully laid plans of the English council and king. They had ratified Arran's appointment, petitioned for Beaton's freedom and drawn up instructions for their ambassadors to Henry VIII.[3] Sadler at once realised it would be a 'busie peice of business' to get those decisions revoked. He therefore recommended that he be allowed to press the rest of the points in his commission, while leaving the government of Scotland alone, reasoning that Arran was a weak man but not a fool. If, as Sadler believed to be the case, any English move to revoke his powers might 'well alter the airate erle' to the other side, then Henry VIII ought to keep a policy of watchful waiting as far as the regency question was concerned. Lord Lisle concurred in Sadler's advice.[4]

[1] *HP*, I, 330 and enclosures.
[2] *SP*, V, 262, Angus to Lisle, 16 March 1543; *HP*, I, 332, Lisle to Suffolk, 16 March 1543.
[3] Their instructions are printed in *SSP*, I, 59–63.
[4] *HP*, I, 333, Lisle and Sadler to Henry VIII, 17 March 1543.

Sir Ralph's position was sound and statesmanlike. Henry, however, reacted in that mercurial fashion for which he was rightly famous. Even while the Privy Council wrote signifying the king's agreement with Sadler's thoughts, they wrote independently to Lord Parr authorising the use of English troops to aid the English pensioners in Edinburgh.[1] Sadler, according to the new royal letters, was to have the right to decide when force was justified as the situation developed.[2] By the time the new instructions were sent out, however, Sadler was already on his way to Edinburgh to implement his own advice to the council.[3]

These problems well illustrate the difficulty faced by Sadler in his embassy, the chief of which was the unreliability of the king's moods. In attempting to form a judgement of his success as a diplomat, it will be well to recall that before he arrived on the scene the initiative had passed to Arran and the Scottish factions. Furthermore, as Suffolk noted in a rather prophetic statement, that Scottish parliament which so upset the king had had a startling beginning and an abrupt end, sure portents that the whole affair of the regency crisis and the marriage would not be easily managed.[4]

Suffolk's impressions were confirmed by Sadler's first talks with the governor, Mary of Lorraine, Douglas and others of the regency council. After a very pleasant reception given in his honour by Arran at Holyrood, Sadler retired to his quarters.[5] Sir George Douglas came to him at once, anxiously advising against any actions that might precipitate discontent, in the course of the discussion heatedly denying that he had entered into any such agreements as those sworn to by the paroled earls. He emphasised that he never promised to deliver strongholds or to capture the infant queen of Scots, arguing that such questions were academic, even if promises had been made, since circumstances simply did not allow such things to come to pass. For the time being, Arran held the upper hand. Douglas told Sadler that Glencairn and Cassels, as well as the other 'Englishmen', also thought immediate action impossible. These views were echoed by Mary of Lorraine herself, who told

[1] *Ibid.* p. 336, 20 March 1543.
[2] *SP*, v, 267, Henry VIII to Parr, 17 March 1543.
[3] *HP*, I, 334, Lisle to Suffolk, 17 March 1543.
[4] *SP*, v, 269, Suffolk to the council, 17 March 1543.
[5] *HP*, I, 337, Sadler to Henry VIII, 20 March 1543.

Sadler that events in Scotland were driven by an impetus of their own and were not to be controlled from London.[1]

The views expressed by Douglas and the Guise queen-mother necessitate that we pay close attention to Sadler's own pessimism as expressed in his first letters to England from Edinburgh. The first thing noted by Sadler was the way in which the old factional lines had been blurred by the threat of English domination after Solway Moss. It was clear that Arran had been able to prevail on the clergy to unite with the nobility, although it was likely that the idea was Sir George Douglas's, a man distrusted by Lisle at a time when Sadler still found him to be reliable.[2] Sadler found that the leading earls, Glencairn, Maxwell, Cassels and their friends were still faithful to their undertakings, but urged that Bothwell and his group no longer be numbered among the English adherents.

The first consequence of the realignment was that Arran prospered. Of course his waxing power was inimical to English interests, necessitating that all further plans be made about the centre of the governor's new role. The previous designs to overturn Arran with the aid of pensioners and other agents were worth less than the vellum on which they were written. In the matter of the peace and the marriage, Henry VIII now had to deal with fully accredited ambassadors from a stable government. Furthermore, the French let it be known that no *coup de main* would be tolerated. Hence, out of fear of a complete victory for Beaton in the event of a move against Arran, Sadler thought it best to work with the governor, while playing on the mutual antagonisms of the Scots, without resorting to force. That strategy would also increase the utility of the assured lords, since they might well practice subversion in peaceful surroundings but not in conditions of open war. A hard bargain determined by mutual self-interest was within the compass of the Scottish parolees; but open treason was another thing, even to the treacherous race of Scots, Sadler carefully and correctly noted.

The upshot of all of this was simple: the English had to trust the bonded lords and the Douglases, although the latter had already given some indications of unreliability. No action could be encompassed that

---

[1] *HP*, I, p. 338, Sadler to Henry VIII, 23 March 1543.
[2] *Ibid.* p. 339, Lisle to Henry VIII, 24 March 1543.

might embarrass the leaders of the factions siphoning information to England. At the same time, Sadler was not completely pessimistic. He urged Henry VIII to have confidence in the treaty and the possibility of the hoped-for marriage. It was Sadler's view that all the desired goals could be had as consequences of the marriage of Edward and Mary. Hence his quietist policy was the opposite of surrender; it was in fact a Trojan horse tactic. Sadler tried to convince the king that Scots and Trojans were equally slow learners. If only the marriage could be brought off, no matter with how much biting of the lips, all would follow. Arran would be Henry VIII's puppet. Beaton, who occupied no place in the English plans, could be eliminated by some means, perhaps murder, the course actually advised by Sadler and finally implemented. That would be God's holy work, Sir Ralph believed.[1]

Sadler found Beaton's position even more difficult to understand than that of either Arran or Douglas. Conflicting tales about the cardinal were current in Edinburgh, most of them *ex parte* testimony of one kind or another. Mary of Lorraine claimed that she and the cardinal were the true supporters of an English marriage, since that would spell the defeat of the governor's grasping ambition. Arran, she said, wanted the infant queen as the wife of his own son, and she implied that Arran would never allow the delivery of the child into English keeping. For her own part, she feared the Protestants so much that she came to see that safety lay only in the protection of the English king:

For it is seldome seen that the heir of the realme sholde be in the handes of hym that claimeth the succession of the same, as the Governour is now established...the second person of thys realme. And if her daughter faileth, looketh to be the kinge of the same.[2]

Mary had put her finger unerringly on the crux of the matter. Sadler's mission finally amounted to this: he had to decide who really wished the marriage to take place? Only by finding the answer to that question could he successfully analyse the power struggle waged by Arran, Beaton, Douglas, Angus, Lennox and others. The marriage was the central article of any treaty. The friends of the marriage had to be the basis of English hopes.

As the sequel will show, it was precisely that which Sadler failed to accomplish. While his concept of policy was undoubtedly correct,

[1] *SSP*, I, 77.   [2] *Ibid.* p. 87.

while his king's blustering was disastrous for the success of his mission, it is an inescapable fact that Sadler never mastered the realities of Scottish factional politics, a truth best demonstrated by pursuing the dilemma of the marriage in the wake of the parliament held at Edinburgh. In trying to form some just estimate of Sadler's skill as a diplomat and his value to his fellow councillors and his king, we can do no better than follow him to the day of the marriage treaty, ostensibly the crowning achievement of his career.

Sadler's initial confusion is clearly related by Lord Parr, his good friend and close associate in border affairs, in a letter of 27 March:

Mi lorde. Aftur mi righte hartie commendacyons. Your lordshypp shall understond that I have travelled here, as much as mi powre wytt wooll sarve me, to deciphre thinclynacyons and intent of thiese men here towardes the kinges maiestie. But the matyers are so perplexed that I know not what to judge of them. In myn opynyon they had lever suffre extremyte thanne cum to thobediance of Inglond. They wooll have thaire realme free, and lyve wythin themselves aftir theire owne lawes and customs. And undoubtedlie the kyrkman labour by all the menes they can, to empeche the unitie of thiese twoo realmes, uppon what groundes you can coniecture. I thinke assuredlie all of the spirituallitie and the whole temporallitie of thys realme do deseyr the marriage, and to ioyne with us in perfait amyte. In whiche case I thynke they wooll utterlie abandon Fraunce, and in tyme they wooll fall to the obediance and devocyon of the kinges maiestie, whereuppon the erle of Anguisshe and his brothre, with thothre lordes...do make a perfitt foundacyon. For mi parte, I cannot judge the sequela, but shal wisshe to God that all thynges may succeede...[1]

Matters were further complicated by every new bit of news. Douglas told Sadler that Mary of Lorraine was not to be trusted and that she was always maligning the cardinal. In his view, it was Mary who really wanted to keep the infant out of English hands. Sadler did not know what to make of Douglas's words, since the Frenchwoman had spoken well of Beaton.[2] Time to work out the puzzle was not afforded Sadler, however, since rumours that the cardinal intended to throw off his captivity reached Sadler. Indeed, it was reported that the cardinal was about to be moved to St Andrews, one of his own strongholds, from Dalkeith, a Douglas castle. If that happened, Sir Ralph vowed, he

[1] *SP*, v, 271, 27 March 1543.
[2] *SSP*, I, 88, 90–1, Sadler to Henry VIII, 27 March 1543.

would never again trust either Angus or Douglas.[1] Then, before Sadler had even the slightest chance to check those rumours, Arran confessed that a match between his own son and the infant queen had been proposed, while vigorously denying that the initiative came from his own family. The governor claimed that the queen-mother had made the first suggestion. Furthermore, Arran declared, Beaton was in French pay.[2] The governor's story completed the circle of mutually contradictory charges and counter-charges. All sides were stigmatised as against the marriage. At the same time, depending on the source of information, all were trying to arrange either a Tudor or a Hamilton marriage for Mary, queen of Scots.

It was up to Sadler to unravel the tangled threads. His touchstone for doing so was his own Protestantism. He fell back on Arran, who seemed to him to be a sincere Protestant, the only one among the many principal figures involved. Early in the negotiations for the marriage, Sadler had formulated his central axiom upon which his diplomacy was based. The governor was lacking neither in good intentions nor in faith. He lacked great strength of character and supporters in sufficient number.[3] English hopes had to turn upon Arran and also upon the Douglases, despite the many obvious signs of their double-dealing. The policy of gradualism which he espoused was in reality that of Sir George Douglas and the governor. In the flush of his own enthusiasm for reform, Sadler made the error of mistrusting all Catholics on principle, while looking favourably on all who claimed to have true religion at heart.[4] In that way, Henry VIII's ambassador became the prisoner of an ideological preference in an age of rival ideologies, with the inevitable consequence: the reality of powerful clan feuds and selfish political rivalries, so much in evidence in Scottish politics, never were accorded their due weight by Sadler.

While his ambassador was trying to formulate a policy, seeing the matter more clearly from a distance, Henry neared the end of his rope. The king realised the difficulty of Sadler's task, but he pushed relentlessly for action and a quick conclusion of the business, instructing Sadler to inform the Scots that fair words were not holy water. The

---

[1] *Ibid.* I, p. 89; *HP*, I, 340, Privy Council to Sadler, 25 March 1543 and 339, Lisle to Henry VIII, 24 March 1543.
[2] *SSP*, I, 93.   [3] *Ibid.* p. 94.
[4] *Ibid.* pp. 90–9, Sadler to Henry VIII, 27 March 1543.

assured lords had lagged in their correspondence with the king; they had made no move against the cardinal; they had allowed Arran's rule to be proclaimed by the parliament. Angus and the others were to act at once or forfeit the place of trust and confidence reserved for them in Henry VIII's heart. The king advised a simple end to the problem: the young queen should be seized and given to the English. The French were to be abandoned at once![1]

What Henry never seemed to grasp, however, was that Scottish affairs moved of their own accord, as Mary of Lorraine had shrewdly remarked. His fulminations did not alter the fact that Beaton was allowed to go from Dalkeith to St Andrews. Nor did they alter the wisdom of Douglas's view that the cardinal's liberty ultimately was the governor's fault and that of the earl of Huntley and that England had better 'kepe in with Fraunce' as a result.[2] Sadler, at a loss to understand the accomplishment of what he had believed to be a mere rumour, decided to dine with Arran in order to arrive at the truth.

The dinner with the governor was held on April Fools' Day, appropriately enough, and served only to add to the confusion. Arran swore oaths to the effect that Douglas had lied, that the removal of the cardinal was not a veiled way of setting Beaton at liberty. Making no headway in that matter, and distressed to find Douglas and Arran at each others' throats, since he hoped to see them working together for England's aims, Sadler moved to the Guise–Arran marriage plot. In that matter Arran was more guarded in his replies, shifting the ground whenever he could, but admitting that he had aspired that high, only to abandon his own advancement when he had found out that Henry VIII wished to have the young queen as a daughter-in-law. On the pure note of the governor's unselfish devotion to England and Scotland, the conference came to a close. Sadler had heard what he wanted to hear.[3]

The round of informative but confusing dinners continued. On 2 April Sadler dined with Mary of Lorraine again. She quickly branded Arran a liar. Sadler could see merit in both her story and the governor's and did not know which to credit. Yet both could clearly not be true,

[1] *HP*, I, 343, Henry VIII to Sadler, 30 March 1543.
[2] *SSP*, I, 104–8, Sadler to Privy Council, 31 March 1543.
[3] *HP*, I, 345, same to the same 1 Apr. 1543.

since they were mutually contradictory in the details of who first proposed a Guise–Hamilton marriage.[1] Once again, Sadler chose to side with the governor, on the grounds that Arran was eager for the gospel, while the queen-mother was a papist. The ambiguities of Arran's position were chalked up to his weakness and not to any duplicity.[2] Thus April brought no clarification of the main problem. Getting possession of the infant queen meant mastering Arran. That in turn required that Beaton, whose great will to triumph and character cannot be doubted, be kept in custody, things beyond Sadler's power to effect.[3]

In retrospect, April was the decisive month for the history of Anglo-Scottish relations for many years to come. During that month Beaton regained control over the diplomatic situation. At the same time, Sadler lost his office of principal secretary of state. Although there can be no certainty that a connection existed between the two developments, it is true that the first green shoots of spring came just at the moment when the fight for the marriage was really lost, although the treaty was pushed to a conclusion in an elaborate charade staged for England's benefit. To what extent Sadler's demotion on grounds of administrative necessity hindered his diplomacy must remain uncertain. But we may be allowed to think that more than mere coincidence was involved.

The paradox of the lost marriage needs careful examination, if it is ever to be properly understood. In order to persuade Arran of the wisdom of collaboration, Henry VIII dangled before the governor's eyes the prospect of marrying his son to Mary while Arran's son took Elizabeth Tudor as a bride. The offer was made by Sadler in unconditional terms, although of course it was understood that the Anglo-Scottish match had to be sealed before England insured the

---

[1] *Ibid.* p. 346, same to the same, 2 Apr. 1543.

[2] Sadler's ardour for the Reformation exceeded that of his sovereign. While Sadler reported that he could set great cartloads of Bibles and New Testaments to work for the English cause more effectively than soldiers among the Scots, Henry VIII outlawed Tyndale's translation at home. Scotland's own council surpassed Henry in this matter also on 3 March 1543, when it voted to allow the lieges to possess the scriptures in either Scots or English (*APS*, II, 414–15); see also *HP*, I, 348.

[3] For Knox's account of Beaton see *The History of the Reformation in Scotland*, I, 84–150. R. S. Rait, in his introductory essay to Annie I. Cameron, *The Scottish Correspondence of Mary of Lorraine, 1543–1560* (Edinburgh: Constable, 1927), pictured Beaton convincingly as a great Scottish patriot seeking to protect the Scots against the old English enmity.

future of the house of Hamilton.[1] Sadler was instructed by the king to treat Arran with a mixture of flattery and scorn, alternating threats and cajolery to carry the governor into the English fold. Sir Ralph's reaction was immediate: any threat of force against Arran would end any chance of success in the main business, since the 'hoole realme of Scotland wyl stonde faste with Arran, and dye rathre all yn a daye, than they woulde be thrall and subiecte to Englande'. The landing of a party of French soldiers under Lennox on the west coast near Dumbarton had given new courage to the independent Scots, offering proof that the French meant to be a true ally in all weather. Sadler's advice was once again of a cautionary sort.[2]

But Henry was no more prepared to give up the game than he was to stand still in the face of new threats from across the Channel. He warned Sadler that Lennox[3] might combine with Beaton in an attempt to remove the queen from Linlithgow to Sterling, far away from English influence.[4] Angus was also alerted to watch Lennox's movements closely, while at the same time the council wondered about the likelihood that Lennox could be bribed by an offer of marriage between Lady Margaret Douglas and the earl.[5] Sadler found the new situation baffling and destructive of his own schemes.[6] Angus had failed to act on Sir Ralph's suggestion that Beaton be moved to the Douglas castle of Tantallon, near the frontier and English support.[7] In the light of Lennox's appearance with French soldiers, it hardly appeared likely that Angus would even attempt such a manoeuvre in the future.

Thus informed, the Privy Council in London wrote urgently, asking that Sadler leave no stone unturned in his efforts to force Arran to move the queen from Stirling,[8] where Mary of Lorraine knew some measure of independence.[9] The council correctly surmised that Lennox's safe

---

[1] *HP*, I, 348, Henry VIII to Sadler, 4 Apr. 1543.

[2] *Ibid.* p. 350, Sadler to Henry VIII, 6 Apr. 1543.

[3] See the *DNB* for Matthew Stuart, fourth earl of Lennox, naturalised as a Frenchman in 1537. He returned to lead the Guise forces, only to rediscover his ancient hostility to the Hamilton family, especially the governor.

[4] *HP*, I, 352, Privy Council to Sadler, 13 Apr. 1543.

[5] *Ibid.* p. 355, Privy Council to Angus, 17 Apr. 1543.

[6] *Ibid.* p. 356, Sadler to Henry VIII, 18 Apr. 1543.

[7] *Ibid.* p. 350, for the description of that Douglas castle lying just beyond North Berwick.

[8] *Ibid.* p. 353, Privy Council to Sadler, 13 Apr. 1543.

[9] The dowager preferred Stirling to Linlithgow, perhaps for sentimental as well as strategic reasons; it was part of her dowry. See her letter to Suffolk in *The Scottish Correspondence*, no. 1, as well as nos. 5–6, Huntley to dowager, 25 March 1543.

return to Scotland was a stumbling block making Sadler's task still more difficult.[1] The ambassador was totally at a loss for a course of action in those circumstances. Cassells and Glencairn warned him to eschew any direct move against the queen, since that would set the governor's teeth on edge, making him impossible to deal with effectively.[2] It still remained Sadler's decision, however, that would immediately affect the course of events, no matter what advice came from London or the Scots. He decided to gamble, perhaps sensing that such a course of action would win the king's own support. On 19 April he told Arran that in his opinion the queen ought to be moved. The governor retorted that she was as safe in one place as she was likely to be in any other. Both Linlithgow and Stirling were approved residences, as a result of the parliamentary decisions taken in March.[3] But Arran did agree to follow any reasonable plan of action in regard to the queen's safety. Sadler went to bed at 2 a.m. that night with the feeling that he had gambled and won.[4]

When he awoke the next morning, all appeared lost. The governor had out-schemed Sadler and on the 20th disavowed the agreements of the previous night. What Sadler discovered stirred his worst fears. On the same night during which he had apparently won over Arran to the English point of view, the abbot of Paisley, the governor's natural brother, had arrived at Holyrood.[5] He immediately assumed the functions of chief adviser to his kinsman.[6] The abbot was, of course, a loyal churchman, a friend of Beaton's policy, sworn to push the English out of Scotland.[7]

Two days later the first tangible results of the palace revolution were known to all. Arran dismissed as court preachers the strongly Protestant nominees of Glencairn. Sadler took the move as the first sign that Arran was about to join Beaton.[8] Such was the view from Edinburgh,

[1] *Ibid.* nos. 10–15.   [2] *HP*, I, 356.
[3] *SP*, v, 271–80, 14 Apr. 1543.
[4] *SSP*, I, 142–52, Sadler to Henry VIII, 19 Apr. 1543.
[5] For the career of John Hamilton, abbot of Paisley, upon whom the English wasted so much money and hospitality, see Hannay, *ScHR*, XVIII, *passim*. Ironically it was upon Sir Ralph's own recommendation that Paisley received an English safe-conduct (see *HP*, I, 346).
[6] *HP*, I, 360–1.
[7] R. K. Hannay, Jane Harvey and Marguerite Woods, 'Some Papal Bulls among the Hamilton Papers', *ScHR*, XXII (1924), 25–42, for proof of the assertion that Paisley was guilty of simony in his translation to St Andrews in preference to Beaton's own nephew as a condition of amity between Beaton and Arran.
[8] *HP*, I, 362.

although the full details of Arran's bargain, including a simoniacal transaction made with Beaton by Paisley in which the governor's son gained a church pension of £1000 p.a. for life, contingent on his entry into holy orders, were then unknown.[1]

Sadly, Sadler admitted that the bishop of Rome had outfoxed the English. Faced with the developments of 22 April, Sadler advised Henry VIII that the position of the assured lords was now untenable and that he had to allow them to look to their own safety. He also told the king that he himself was in danger, advising that the Scottish agents in London be detained as an earnest of his own safety as well as the well-being of the paroled earls and lords.[2]

The events of the 22nd were significant in that they fully underlined the international scope and importance of Sadler's mission. Rome was bent on beating the English at all costs. At the same time, a new alliance, involving France, Scotland and Denmark, was being formed by Paul III, word of which Sadler sent to Henry VIII.[3] The English terms of peace, which included the *parentado* as the sole necessity, had touched off the powder keg of counter-reform diplomacy. Europe would explode, if need be, on behalf of the queen of Scots.[4]

Henry therefore resorted at last to tactics of a milder sort. On 25 April the details of the new approach to Arran were sent to Sadler. The governor was to be shown that the Scottish nobility considered him to be a bastard,[5] a fact the cardinal would publish when it suited his convenience.[6] Sadler was to let Arran know, as a friendly gesture, that the Scottish clergy seemed likely to follow the cardinal's lead and destroy the house of Hamilton. After all, in their eyes, Arran was a heretic.[7] 'Or', said Sadler, 'can you thinke that you shal contynue as governour whan thadverse partie that wolde have made themselves by a forged wyll regentes withoute you…shal have authoritie?'[8] Realising that these new tactics could have the reverse of the effect intended, which was to frighten Arran into a decidedly pro-English stand, Henry also

[1] Hannay *et al*. *ScHR*, XXII, 39.   [2] *SSP*, I, 158–60, 22 Apr. 1543.

[3] *HP*, I, 357, 18 Apr. 1543.

[4] *Ibid*. p. 362, 364 and 367 for the details of the Catholic reaction.

[5] *SSP*, I, 157, Henry VIII to Sadler, 20 Apr. 1543.

[6] *HP*, I, 364, Henry VIII to Sadler, 25 Apr. 1543.

[7] Knox, *The History of the Reformation in Scotland*, I, 84.

[8] *HP*, I, 364 and also the comments in George Buchanan, *Rerum scoticarum historia* (Edinburgh, 1582), XV, i.

empowered Sadler to distribute bribes among the Scots and to inquire among the pensioners as to when and where an army could most conveniently enter Scotland, omitting Douglas, who was under suspicion for his past double-dealing.

The conference with Arran did not go well. Neither did the talks with the pensioners have a hopeful outcome. The governor was not so easily alarmed; the lords could not be won to immediate military action, although they renewed their promises and took the proffered gold. The main bright spot was the realisation that Arran and Lennox hated one another and made war on the other's dependents whenever the chance arose. Sadler believed this to be a result of the cardinal's friendship with Lennox, which the governor resented intensely. Despite this one encouraging fact, the main conclusion seemed inescapable. The likelihood of the queen passing into English hands was remote. Durable though the nobility might be, and however much Lennox and Arran might oppose one another, Beaton seemed equal to all of them and he intended to prevent the realisation of any plan that would see the young queen in English hands.[1]

The coincidence of the cardinal's release and Sadler's demotion late in April was ominous.[2] In the sixteenth century impetus was sustained in diplomatic work by the knowledge all had of the high standing of the ambassador.[3] At a crucial time in the intrigues in Scotland, Sadler's labours were hampered by his dismissal, although the reasons given for his loss were certainly adequate.[4] The fact of the cardinal's being at liberty, Henry VIII's renewed threats of invasion, and Sadler's personal eclipse combined to doom the mission of 1543.

The end of the real business upon which he had first gone to Edinburgh can be read in the correspondence of May and June. The chief item of business was the extension of the truce until 15 July, a thing required for the atmosphere in which the details of the treaty were being worked out between Sadler and the Scots.[5] In so far as the treaty was concerned, whatever the reality of politics might be, Sadler could do no

---

[1] *HP*, I, 365, Sadler to Suffolk, 28 Apr. 1543.

[2] *SSP*, I, 168, 26 Apr. 1543.

[3] Behrens, *EHR*, LI, 620.

[4] Henry could ill afford an absentee secretary, it was claimed. This was at best a half-truth, since sixteenth-century secretaries were often abroad for long periods of time by virtue of their position as cardinal agents in royal control of diplomacy.

[5] PRO, SP 1/178, fo. 115, Sadler to Parr, 29 May 1543.

better than to advise Henry to accept the terms Douglas carried to London, since it was unlikely that any immediate delivery of the queen could be obtained.[1] In effect, Sadler advised his king to play an elaborate game, while the real issues were already beyond his control.

Arran and the council had sent Douglas on his way to London with stipulations that were in themselves a systematic refutation of the *raison d'être* of Sadler's mission.[2]

Whatever encouragement might be derived from the estrangement of Beaton and Lennox, the latest development in the welter of Scottish party strife, Arran still bent like a willow in the wind and was on the verge of openly casting his lot with Beaton.[3] The assured lords seemed to realise that the cause for which they had been sent home was beyond recovery. Their pessimism was hardly allayed by the rumours of Henry VIII's alliance with the emperor and the stilling of Protestant preaching at home. While Henry VIII's zeal for the Reformation waned, they could hardly be expected to risk their positions and perhaps even their lives for the English marriage.

The sense of hopelessness which pervaded Scottish thinking was amply reflected in Sadler's letters. Although Henry still pushed the marriage treaty, and this was dominant in Sadler's letters, which were a perfect looking-glass of English indecision in matters of high policy, other matters occupied Sir Ralph's time.[4] Minor border problems and the internal aspects of Scottish politics vied equally for the first place, a condition unthinkable while there was still some real hope of gaining possession of Mary, queen of Scots.[5] A long note on the details of the insipid war between Lennox and Angus illustrated the fact that the original mission was relegated to the background of chatty intelligence briefs, reports which would be of great value only in the event of re-newed warfare between England and Scotland, hardly what Sadler was sent to accomplish.[6] While his own view of the situation had become more realistic, in so far as the factionalism of the Scots was concerned,

---

[1] *HP*, I, 371, Sadler to Privy Council, 6 May 1543.

[2] *Ibid.* p. 376, Sadler to Henry VIII, 7 June 1543. By the terms agreed upon, Mary was to return to Scotland if her husband died before an heir was born. The text of the Scottish proposals is printed in *APS*, II, 425–6.

[3] PRO, SP 1/178, fo. 170, Sadler to Parr, 7 June 1543.

[4] *SP*, v, 302–4.

[5] *Ibid.* pp. 158, 170 and 189; see also *HP*, I, 384–5.

[6] *SSP*, I, 199–209.

that new insight had come too late, a fact amply demonstrated in a letter to Suffolk:

Neverthelesse, the state of this realme is so perplexed, that it is hard to judge what will follow; for all this while the feares of our warres hath made them sit still and agree togethir. But whan the pece shalbe concludid, it is not unlike that the warre whiche nowe goes on will begin here among themselfes in earnest, the realm being divided as it is into sundrie partes. There is one partie whiche be called hereticks, and the English lordes, which is the Governor and his partie. Anthre partie there is, that whiche be called Scribes and Pharisees, which is the clergie and their partakers. And then there is the thirde partie, whiche seemeth to be neuter, and be alwaies readie to take the better and the stronger partie, if there wil come anie business betwene them.[1]

The events in Scotland had not waited on Sadler's growing insight into the situation there. It had taken him the entire spring season to realise that the Scots had played on English willingness to believe in the possibility of *rapport* without ever giving up their own factional and national interests, which dictated unity in regard to the English intruders, even to the point of co-operating in deceiving the English ambassador. The degree to which this was true was once again shown by two letters, one from late June and another from early July. These relate the futile efforts of Sadler to gain an interview with Arran, for the purpose of pressing the arrest of Lennox, Argyle and Beaton. The best that Sadler had been able to do was an interview with David Panter, the governor's secretary.[2] Alleging that Arran was ill and bedridden at Hamilton House, Panter made certain slips that led Sadler to the conclusion that Arran was totally committed to Beaton.[3] The second bit of news was even more terrible. Sadler had learned of a French fleet cruising in the Channel. He told the council with Henry VIII of his own warning to Arran, that a naval venture in Scotland would spell doom for the governor and the plans to move the queen to Linlithgow. The only reply was that the queen could not be moved at that time; she was teething![4]

It was against that background, then, that Henry VIII played out the

[1] *Ibid.* p. 216, Sadler and Douglas to Suffolk, 9 June 1543.
[2] David Panter, the abbot of Ross, was a cohort of Beaton and deeply involved in the simoniacal translations of 1543.
[3] *HP*, I, 386, Sadler to the Privy Council, 21 June 1543, also *SSP*, I, 221-4.
[4] *Ibid.* p. 392, same to the same, 2 July 1543.

farce of signing the treaty at Greenwich, binding England and Scotland together in perpetual amity by bonds of marriage to be had between the infant queen of Scots and Prince Edward.[1] Expressing the hope that speedy ratification in Scotland would follow, the English king congratulated Sadler upon the occasion of the Greenwich signing.[2]

The royal correspondence with Sadler must be compared with a letter written by Lord Parr, who was busily summing up his own impressions of the situation in Scotland, if an adequate appreciation is to be had of the degree to which Sadler allowed false hopes to enter his thinking. Parr cut through the fog of godly oaths, stating that Arran was all promises, but in essence could be counted on only for falsehood and fraud. He told Suffolk, his correspondent, another man of action not accustomed to the refinements of diplomacy, that Scotland was motivated solely by national sentiments which were contrary to England's goals. The Scots would never allow their queen to marry out of the country, no matter what treaties were signed in London and Edinburgh. It was a matter of public knowledge that Angus and his friends were English pensioners and therefore suspect among their countrymen. Who in his right mind would count on them for much? Furthermore, change of front, clearly discernible in April, was itself based on recognition of Henry VIII's deceitful practices with regard to the whole Hamilton clan. In short, the Scots had out-manoeuvred Henry and Sadler at their own game. They had skilfully bought time while the French party waxed and the campaigning season of 1543 passed by without a renewal of the hostilities which had almost ended Scottish independence. Thus, the consolidation of the victory won at Solway Moss had eluded the English.[3]

One can scan Parr's letter and write it off as the expression of military frustration when faced with the complexities and realities of diplomatic life. Yet Parr was right in every particular. Whatever the reasons for the diplomatic failure, Parr realised that Sadler's new instructions, by virtue of which Sir Ralph was now to press for the ratification of the treaty, and by which Sadler and his wife were to have the tutelage of the queen, were based on a total misreading of the true situation.[4] Sadler's own complaints about his new commission showed this to be the case,

[1] *HP*, I, p. 395, Henry VIII to Arran, 3 July 1543.   [2] *Ibid.* p. 399, 3 July 1543.
[3] *Ibid.* p. 397, Parr to Suffolk, 6 July 1543.   [4] *Ibid.* p. 399.

especially when he told the council in London that Scotland was a realm out of order and ready to 'grow *de malo in peius*'.[1] Nevertheless, he had to go through with the job of winning the consent of each Scottish councillor to the draft treaty, dealing with each in turn, never telling two men the same story, and deceiving all about the thoughts of Henry VIII.[2]

Even in July Sadler seems to have believed that the form of the draft treaty represented some substance of victory. He entered a traverse of Parr's exacting analysis, declining to admit that Beaton's league against the governor was intended to scuttle the treaty. Nor would he admit that the Guise faction had fooled him and his king any more than he would admit that Arran was a trimmer.[3]

Sadler was wrong on all counts, an assertion for which proof is now available. As Parr had rightly stated, Mary of Lorraine had conspired with Beaton from the beginning.[4] There is also proof that Arran negotiated with Paul III as early as 14 May, eagerly promising to aid the papacy, at the right price and at the right time.[5] Sadler was also mistaken about the character of the internecine strife in Scotland, which led him to false optimism about the success of the English cause.[6] Not even an attempt on his life by irate English-haters had jarred him sufficiently to make him recognise that national feeling in Scotland was more important than love for church reform and the gospel.[7] His own ardour for Protestantism had undercut his diplomatic talents in every way possible.

On the surface of things, the Scottish hostility had dissolved when the trumpets heralded the peace along the High Street in Edinburgh.[8] Amidst so much rejoicing, who could cavil over the queen's removal to Stirling, so much closer to the centre of Beaton's power?[9] Linlithgow had been too small to quarter the retinue of the royal child, and Sadler,

---

[1] *Ibid.* p. 401, 8 July 1543.   [2] *SSP*, I, 246–57.

[3] *HP*, I, 405, Sadler to Suffolk, 13 July 1543.

[4] See *The Scottish Correspondence*, nos. 10–15, and *The Warrenden Papers*, ed. Annie I. Cameron, 2 vols. (Edinburgh: Constable, 1931–2), no. 10, dowager to Charles V, 5 June 1543.

[5] *The Warrenden Papers*, I, no. 7, Arran to Paul III, 14 May 1543, where Arran placed Scotland under papal protection. In return he wanted church patronage taken out of Beaton's grasp. See also no. 8, Arran to Christian III of Denmark, 5 July 1543, a plea for Danish aid.

[6] *HP*, I, 415, 418 and 425.

[7] *Ibid.* pp. 408–9, Sadler to Henry VIII, 16 and 17 June 1543.

[8] *Ibid.* p. 426, same to the same, 26 July 1543.

[9] *Ibid.* p. 419, same to the same, 22 July 1543.

whatever he felt about the incident, was too happy to notice closely that the harvest season and the removal coincided. Defeats seemed to dissolve in the general optimism of the treaty's signing, since the peace, which Sir Ralph had always thought would entail all the other English objectives, was a reality. Unable to see behind the masks worn by the nobility of Scotland, Sadler misread the significance of the waning summer of 1543. To the Scots, the peace signified the end of foreign intervention in their affairs, leaving Scot free to fight Scot in diehard combat, while Sadler spent his energy preparing for the ceremonies of ratification.[1]

Parr was not so easily deceived.[2] At the very moment in which Henry VIII and his emissary had their vision clouded with the ceremonial aspects of their 'triumph', the soldier shrewdly analysed the true situation. In his view, it was possible to believe that Beaton lied to Arran about his desire for peace and that the governor lied to Sadler on that subject, each for his own good reasons. If that was the case, then the possession of the queen gave the Guise supporters the upper hand, whatever the public by-play might seem to say.[3] Since Sadler had always assumed that *at least one* of the parties genuinely wanted the peace, he had been in no position to realise that the 'revolt' to Beaton was perhaps being staged for English eyes, as Parr put it.[4] By the end of June the cardinal's forces were said to number 30,000, while Arran and the English supporters, assuming they were true allies, commanded only 10,000 men.[5] On the very eve of the signing in London the rebellion against the English policy 'so craftelie wroughte by the cardinall' was on the verge of success.[6]

That is not to say that Henry VIII was left totally without resources. That king had always acted on the ancient maxim: *si vis pacem bellum pare*! In case the cardinal's party felt itself strong enough to resist the treaty, Sadler was authorised to deal with Arran in the matter of in-

[1] *HP*, I, p. 425, same to the same, 26 July 1543.
[2] *Ibid.* p. 427, Parr to Suffolk, 26 July 1543.
[3] *Idem.*
[4] *HP*, I, 414, Parr to Suffolk, 18 July 1543. The details of the increasing disenchantment with Arran appear in the same volume, nos. 435–8; see also PRO, SP 1/181, fos. 1–5 a. That the governor lied is proved by the *Balcarres Papers*, especially entries dated 12 and 17 July and 11 Aug. 1543, the former being a letter from Antoinette, duchesse de Guise to the dowager, while the other two were from the dowager to David Panter.
[5] *HP*, I, 418, Parr to Suffolk, 22 July 1543.
[6] *Ibid.* p. 419, Sadler to Henry VIII, 22 July 1543.

vading Scotland. Nothing better illustrates how completely both the king and his envoy were deceived about the roles played by the governor and his supporters. Treason, of course, had been one of the alternatives all along, but on 4 August Sadler put the proposition in naked form:

That in case the numbre nowe to be sent shall not soo misdoubt the cardynall, as he and hys accomplyces shalbe glad to yeld to the ratyficatyons of the treatyes the...kinges maiestie wooll prepare a greter furnyture for that purpos; not doubtyng but the Governour wooll in case of that necessyte delyver unto his maiestie the holdes[1] which he hath promised...Assuryng the said Governour that performyng the same...hys highnes wooll not fayle to ayde and assist hym both by see and lande, to make hym kinge of the rest beionde the Frith.[2]

The season for launching a campaign was not yet passed when Arran received the new demands. He therefore decided to play the game a little longer. The governor arranged a new conference of all parties, with the result that all pledged to work for the peace with renewed vigour. Sadler believed that they swore truly.[3] Beaton, who had once been offered an English bishopric in exchange for Roman beret, on the condition that he came over to the English side, solemnly vowed that he was no enemy to the peace.[4] That Sadler 'misdoubted of', although he urged Henry VIII to retreat from the former position in the technical details of ratification. Where once it had been urged that only Arran's seal was required, in his capacity as governor, now Sadler counselled his king to let the Scots have their ceremonies in full parliament, since they put great stock in glorious occasions. England's would be the more substantial victory.[5]

Meanwhile, the governor refused to be moved to overt treason by either threats or bribes. He was not interested in Scotland beyond the Firth of Forth, whether as king or as governor. Parliamentary action on the marriage was the only way; failing that, there would be no marriage. Masks had been dropped in favour of a hard line, for at the same time

---

[1] Castles and various fortified positions are indicated.
[2] *HP*, I, 439, 3 Aug. 1543, a draft in Wriothesley's hand, much corrected, but finally marked 'stet' in the margin. The original is in BM Add. MSS. 32651, fo. 185*b*, from which the quote is taken.
[3] *HP*, I, 443, Sadler to Henry VIII, 5 Aug. 1543.
[4] *Ibid.* p. 653; see also PRO, SP 1/181, fo. 12*a*, 6 Aug. 1543, Sadler to Wriothesley.
[5] *HP*, I, 445, Privy Council to Sadler, 9 Aug. 1543.

news reached Sadler that Beaton was encouraging French intervention. Furthermore, the neutrals had given their word to the cardinal that they would resist any move not sanctioned by the parliament.[1] Then, before Sadler had assimilated that intelligence, the first news of a Beaton-Douglas accord came to him.[2] That was swiftly followed by Huntley's declaration that he would rather fight and die than come to heel before Henry VIII.[3]

As if on cue, the Scottish burgers joined the nobility in the new attitude of overt hostility to Henry VIII. The king's policy of confiscating certain Scottish ships bearing French wines and other goods to and from Scotland had alienated the eastern portmen, previously so avid for reform. They were restive under the restraints imposed upon their trade by a foreigner who treated them as the victims of perpetual subordination to London in matters of trade.[4]

Realizing how much hostility to England was on the rise, Sadler advised Henry VIII to speed the ratification under whatever conditions could be managed. It was under such circumstances that Sadler exchanged great seals with Master James Fowles, the chief registrar of the great seal of Scotland, at Holyrood House on 25 August 1543. To make certain that nothing was lacking in the fine ceremony designed by Arran, 'Christes bodie sacrat (as Papistes call yt) was braken betwix the saide Governour and Maister Sadler, Ambassadour, and recaibed of thaim both as a signe and tokin of thaire mindes...'[5] Underlining the actual power structure that prevailed, Catholic forms were used in ceremonies enjoyed by the cardinal and his followers, who must have known that Marcus Grimanius, a papal legate, was then on his way to Scotland in the company of de la Brossé, a French ambassador, and other agents of the Valois and Guise party.[6] Sadler took Roman communion as a gesture fitted to the occasion on which Henry VIII won his treaty.[7] The symbolism was more profound than he suspected.

---

[1] *Ibid.* p. 446, Sadler to Henry VIII, 9 Aug. 1543.

[2] *Ibid.* p. 452, same to the same, 17 Aug. 1543. See also *The Scottish Correspondence*, nos. 17–18. Argyle came in on 17 August, according to a note in the *HMC Argyle MSS.* pp. 484–5, nos. 215–16.

[3] *The Scottish Correspondence*, nos. 16–17.

[4] *HP*, I, 451, Sadler to Henry VIII, 16 Aug. 1543.

[5] Knox, *The History of the Reformation in Scotland*, I, 103–4. See also *APS*, II, 425 and Sadler's account in *HP*, I, 460, Sadler to Henry VIII, 25 Aug. 1543.

[6] *HP*, I, 461, Sadler to the Privy Council, 25 Aug. 1543; for La Brossé, see II, 102, n. 61.

[7] *Foedera*, XV, 5.

The sequel unfolded swiftly. War between England and France had already broken out by the time of the ratification.[1] Scottish ships bound for France were seized by English captains, while Henry VIII reasserted his suzerainty in Scotland.[2] The power of the Guise family was openly committed on behalf of Beaton, who overnight had picked up the high cards in the game.[3] After months of oscillation for English consumption, Arran hopped nimbly into the Catholic camp.[4] On 4 September the governor fled to Beaton at Callendar House, out of range of English reprisals. The day of deception had finally passed.[5]

Sadler's position rapidly degenerated from that of ambassador to that of a hunted enemy agent. Townsmen in Edinburgh repeatedly threatened his safety, focusing their pent up resentments on the English representative and the most conspicuous sign of the scourge of Scottish shipping.[6] Sadler complained that the Scots were unreasonable people, living a life of such 'bestlie libertie, that they nevar regarde God nor Governour, ne yet justice, or anie goode policie doothe take place among them'.[7] In order to safeguard his ambassador, Henry VIII urged Angus to use force to extricate Sir Ralph from any difficult situation, while at the same time threatening to destroy Edinburgh, if Sadler was harmed.[8] As a result of those imperious statements, Sir George Douglas managed to arrange Sadler's flight from Edinburgh to Tantallon, the famous Douglas castle,[9] from whence he was rescued in a daring amphibious operation[10] that later provided Sir Walter Scott's hero in *Marmion* with a great adventure.[11]

Beaton, in the meantime, had consolidated his victory. Mary was

[1] *L & P*, xviii, ii, 30.

[2] *Ibid*. p. 46.

[3] *SSP*, iii, 137.

[4] Knox, *The History of the Reformation in Scotland*, i, 116 and 173.

[5] *HP*, ii, 11, Sadler to Suffolk *et al.*, 4 Sept. 1543. For the details of Lennox's position and its effect on Arran's revolt, seen from the Scottish side, see *The Scottish Correspondence*, nos. 24–49.

[6] *HP*, ii, 10, Sadler to Suffolk, 4 Sept. 1543. For the real danger in which Sadler found himself a letter from Sir Andrew Otterbourne to the dowager proves illuminating: *The Scottish Correspondence*, no. 28, 13 Oct. 1543, where it is related that Sadler was blamed for instigating the sack of the friars which took place in Edinburgh on 3 Sept. 1543.

[7] *HP*, ii, 2, Sadler to Henry VIII, 1 Sept. 1543.

[8] *Ibid*. p. 19, Suffolk to the Privy Council, 8 Sept. 1543.

[9] *Ibid*. p. 73, Sadler to the Privy Council, 25 Oct. 1543, Sir Ralph did not arrive at Tantallon until 10 Nov. 1543 (*ibid*. p. 92, Sadler to Suffolk).

[10] *Ibid*. pp. 203–18.

[11] Sir Walter Scott, *Poetical Works*, ed. James Black (Edinburgh: Constable, 1852), p. 85, n. 1 to canto v.

crowned queen of Scots at Stirling,[1] despite Henry VIII's fulminations.[2] Immediately before the coronation, Arran recanted his heresies and was given absolution by Beaton and the bishops of Scotland.[3] In a rather futile gesture, the English council wrote Douglas and his friends, accusing them of rank duplicity and blaming him for the ruin of their vision of a united kingdom. Their exact words are worth noting: 'As yet his maiestie was sure nother of marriage, amite, peax, nor hostages for the performaunce of the same, nor no castles nor holdes delivered to his maiesties handes, nor yet non of thothre promises observed amonge you...'[4] The council's indictment of the governor was a confession of the total failure of English diplomacy in Scotland, a recognition sealed on 3 December, when the Scottish parliament denounced the treaties of Greenwich, giving as the ground of their action that Henry VIII's capture of Scottish merchantmen violated the accords.[5] Even if just, the reason given was ludicrous. It was not because a few loaves of bread and some casks of wine were kept from Scottish ports that the treaties were a dead letter. While they alleged such things in an outburst of rather plebeian national enthusiasm, the Scottish nobility and the burgesses knew that cardinals and queens had had more to do with the affair than had sea captains.

Certainly the historian recognises that there were more complex reasons for the *débâcle* of English policy than those alleged on 3 December. While there can be no doubt that Henry's actions against Scottish shipping had played into Beaton's hands and delivered to him the support of the commercial classes which he might not otherwise have obtained, thus providing him with a united national opposition to England, there can be even less doubt about other facets of the situation. Scots had managed to subordinate religious feeling and motives of self-interest long enough to resist Henry in the wake of the military disaster of 1542. Henry's entire scheme demanded a revolution in popular religious and political views sufficient to make England and Protestantism preferable to France and the old faith. At best, the English plan could have succeeded only with the help of an extraordinary conjunc-

---

[1] *HP*, II, 30, Parr to Suffolk, 13 Sept. 1543.

[2] *Ibid.* p. 34, Suffolk to Henry VIII, 16 Sept. 1543.

[3] According to the eye-witness report of Sandy Pringle, one of the Douglas agents (*HP*, II, 30)

[4] *Ibid.* p. 127, Privy Council to Sir G. Douglas, 1 Dec. 1543.

[5] *APS*, II, 431.

tion of signs. Instead, the actions of the English king himself seemed bent on destroying the favourable aspects of the situation. When, in the early part of 1543, it looked as if the marriage had real potential, Henry was not satisfied with the prospect of ruling Scotland through his son. With the substance of union a real possibility and perhaps within his reach, the king lunged at the ancient shadow of suzerainty and absolute rule in his own name, an action that implicitly supports Dr Elton's view of the Henrician revolution and the coming of sovereignty as Cromwell's work. Henry VIII, so far from having a modern conception of monarchy, made claims more extensive than those of Edward I in his own behalf: James V and his father and his father's father had all been evil usurpers, and Mary of Lorraine's daughter could be neither more nor less.

The inconsistency of English policy and the temper of the king was a heavy burden for any diplomat. The Scots were not fools. The king's bad faith and his outrageous suborning of the nobility weakened Sadler's posture. The offer of a kingdom to Arran, with treason as the sole condition of the gift, was a blunder calculated to hammer out of discordant elements a national opposition fundamentally opposed both to a puppet régime and direct English rule.

Then, there was the inadequacy of Sadler's own account of Beaton, a churchman clever enough for the English and his own nobility too. He matured his plans to accord with the climate and geography of Scotland, keeping the queen in the western regions, where the French had easy access to the chief strongholds. The governor's conversion was announced only after the end of the campaigning season. While Scottish farmers took in their grain in peace, Beaton gathered the fruits of his political labours. He had concealed from his enemies with great cunning the important changes in Scottish politics brought about by the death of James V. The old assumptions made by Sadler, that one could still divide the Scots along the old clan and religious lines, were no longer valid in that simple form. Paradoxically, Beaton's greatness as a leader lay in the fact that he was both the man least and most motivated by religious considerations, with the possible exception of that *politique*, Sir George Douglas, for whom self-interest amounted to the highest principle.

None of this is said to escape the obligation of facing up to Sir Ralph

Sadler's share in the failure of his mission. Although we think that the lion's share must go to the lion, Henry VIII, Sadler thought to much in religious terms. His criterion of truthfulness was too often the intensity of the gospel light. His narrow views kept him from effectively exploiting the real rifts in the Scottish factions, especially those between Arran and Lennox, Angus and Lennox and the numerous highland–lowland groups of the same religious persuasion but different clan loyalties and territorial pretensions. Last, but certainly not least, Sadler failed to exploit the genuine tensions between the townsmen and the pastoral folk in each party.

On the level of high politics, Sadler failed to give due weight to the ambition and skill of Mary of Lorraine. If the cardinal's murder in 1546 was the result of Sadler machinations, that does little credit to either him or his diplomacy. The French dowager and her daughter were not so easily dealt with. Marry in England they might not, but they would marry in France, due in no small part to the lack of perception in crucial matters showed by Sadler in 1543, a lack that robbed the re-forming party among the Scots of a *modus operandi*. I refer here to the way in which Sadler fed Henry VIII's optimism at the earliest stages of the affair, with the result that the king was determined to pursue a very bold policy in a blustering way. Instead of seeing the deep divisions in Scottish politics as potential to be developed, Sadler treated them as bits of reality that might be manipulated by a religious touchstone, hoping to forward English diplomacy by delivering whole cartloads of *New Testaments* to his English friends in Edinburgh. Meanwhile, the cardinal and Mary of Lorraine busily mended their fences.

This reading of Sadler's mission makes it out to be doubly doomed: first of all, it was in a very real sense a fool's errand, as Parr so ably pointed out; secondly, the means to the end were wrongly chosen. Sadler himself came to share that view, expressing himself bitterly on the issue in 1563, before an Elizabethan Commons hotly debating the queen's marriage policy and the Scottish succession problem. It was Mary, queen of Scots, whose claims were being discussed, and in 1563 Sir Ralph Sadler, then nearly sixty years old, had some right to speak on the subject. Turning to the House in his role as a Scottish expert, Sadler reminded his listeners that he had once been sent to Scotland in pursuit of an illusion:

I pray you geve me leve to aske you a question, in the wordes I wyll rehearse unto you. If, said he, Maister Otterbourne,[1] with whom I spake in Scotland in '1543, your lad was a lass, and our lass was a lad, wolde you then...be so ernest in thys matyer? And colde you be congenial that our lad sholde marrie your lass and so be kinge of Englonde? Wee coulde be well contente with it, if wee had the lad and you the lass. But I cannot beleve that your nacyon colde agree to have a Scotte to be a kynge of Englonde. And though the hoole nobilitie of the realm woulde consent to yt, yet our comen pepul, and thr stones in the stretes, wolde ryse and rebel agenst yt...Whereby you may betar understande the affectyon and disposityon of the Scottes in that case. And even as he said, it followed; for by and by, aftur the treatye was ratyfied, the Governour and the nobilitye revolted from it...Nowe if thys proud beggarlie Scottes did so much disdayn to yelde to the superioritie of Eng- londe...whie sholde we, for anie respecte, yelde to their Scottish superioritie. Surely, for mi parte, I cannot consent to it...ye and the stones in the strete wolde rebel agenst it.[2]

Only time, and the accession of James VI and I, would show Sadler to be a poor prophet in both his generation and the next too!

[1] A Scottish diplomat and secretary of state. Otterburn was pro-Douglas in the late 1530s and early 1540s and was under suspicion as being 'over good an Englishe man' (*HP*, II, 106). By 1543, however, he opposed the Douglas-oriented paroled lords and the conclusion of the marriage treaty, since he had come to believe, correctly, that Henry VIII intended to absorb Scotland by that means. A reliable account of his views is that by John A. Inglis, *Sir Adam Otterburn* (Glasgow: Jackson, Wylie and Co., 1935).

[2] London, Inner Temple Library, Petyt MSS. 535/4, fos. 287a–b. A view of Sadler's mission similar to mine but more flattering to Henry VIII is expressed by Gladys Dickinson, in her preface to *Two Missions of Jacques de la Brosse* (Edinburgh: for the Scottish Historical Society, 3rd ser. XXXVI, 1942), pp. 6–9, esp. p. 7, where she wrote: 'intrigue was wrapped within intrigue until the English ambassador was wholly unable to disentangle the skein'.

7

THE POLITICS OF SURVIVAL

I have done your errand to Master Sadler whoe I perseyve remaynith in this and in all thinges ours aftur the olde manar...

SIR EDWARD SEYMOUR to Sir William Paget

It is obvious that Sir Ralph Sadler's continued prominence in Henrician politics was in no way due to diplomatic triumphs. His very strong hold on a variety of offices, including his place on the Privy Council, a body just achieving its full importance in the Tudor system of governance, can in fact best be analysed within the framework of his Cromwellian heritage. Embarking on his labours, both administrative and diplomatic, under Cromwell's *aegis*, Sadler survived the demise of his powerful patron for reasons inextricably linked to the very nature of the Cromwellian system. It is therefore necessary to consider the immediate impact of that organisation of power practised by Thomas Cromwell, even if only briefly, if we are to comprehend Sadler's survival in 1540 and the role he played between Cromwell's death and the death of Henry VIII in 1547.

Cromwell's revolution in government included an extension and improvement of certain features of the technique utilised by Wolsey. The cardinal had used his own dependents in government work in a somewhat different way than that employed by earlier manipulators of quasi-bureaucratic affinities. Where the medieval nobleman of political influence had maintained a vast clientage, the basis of his power remained territorial. Within that limitation, which was also the strength of his position, the lord's clients envisioned careers in their master's retinues in terms of domestic and official service. As the connection with the old territorial base became more tenuous during an age of shifting patterns of adjustment to new conditions which undermined feudal relations, official patronage tended to become the pabulum of life. For that very reason, the fall of a great figure like Essex, a transition figure incompetent to maintain his position once cut off from office, threatened all his followers with immediate ruin. The downing of their master isolated the clients in the sustained struggle for place and profit, a struggle intensified by the exigencies of dramatic and uncomprehended inflation. Wolsey and Cromwell, neither of whom had inherited a great territorial basis for their power, saw the danger of their situation and were thereby forced to make of the client-patron relationship something new, flexible and capable of adaptation to changing circumstances. Thus the iron immutability of earlier affinities gave way to a relationship in which the master's ruin did not necessarily mean the end of the world for his followers.[1]

Factions and affinities formed about the great Henrician ministers, to be sure, but they consisted for the most part of men whose final loyalty was not related to the territorially based armed bands of the great patron. While the clients in Wolsey or Cromwell's service might divide along social, religious or regional lines at any single moment, they were basically tied to the monarchy by the character to their twofold service. The *sine qua non* for Cromwell's men, as for the cardinal's agents in the previous decade, was *place*. They were rewarded by their master with a *niche* in the service of a rapidly expanding government. Mere personal loyalties still counted for a great deal, but office alone conferred on the clients stability. Whether or not one was employed high on the ladder, as was the case with Sadler in 1540, or lower down the rungs, as John Hales found himself situated in the late 1530s, the common tie extended beyond the immediate patron, in this case Thomas Cromwell. Both Sadler and Hales were also the king's men in a way that was not true of Henry Sadler a generation before. Sir Ralph's father was simply Belknap's steward who happened to do some official work in a strictly unofficial capacity. That dual loyalty was precisely the thing that had eluded Essex's followers, who were cut off from office by Burghley's son Robert Cecil. Hence, when the Cromwellians were suspect, they were not generally found wanting in loyalty to the king, while Essex's men followed their master to ruin in an abortive revolution. It might even be argued that the difference between Cromwell and Essex as aspirants for power is more readily perceived in their followers' fate than in their own, since they both made work for the executioner.

[1] David Mathew, *The Social Structure in Caroline England* (Oxford: The Clarendon Press, 1948), pp. 2–5, for the germ of the analysis here made. Mathew saw the mid-sixteenth century as a critical time in the changing client-patron relationships.

This means that Sadler's survival in 1540 depended in the final analysis on the fact of the place secured for him by Cromwell several years before the crisis ever developed. Since the 1520s Sadler was known at court. From the early 1530s on, without interruption, Ralph had been an official servant of the Crown and the monarch. He had thus had ample opportunities to demonstrate his efficiency and loyalty to the dynasty, thereby escaping the stigma that might be attached to the purely personal retainers of a man suspected of high treason. In this regard it is worth noting that it was Sadler who sat beside Henry VIII opening the letters of John Wallop, the English resident ambassador at Paris, in which Francis I congratulated Henry on the occasion of Cromwell's imprisonment. Whatever his inward feelings might have been, Sadler discreetly masked them as he copied out Wallop's gleeful letter for the council's benefit,[1] shortly before he made still another copy for the eyes of the duke of Norfolk, one of Cromwell's bitterest critics.[2] No doubt he laboured under the dual burden of anguish and suspicion. But he laboured, and that was the important thing.

Norfolk, who was no tender-minded respecter of the delicacy of Ralph's situation, perhaps clucked in approval when reading the neat translation from the French original made by Cromwell's personal choice for the secretaryship. He might even have understood the copy, which was not made at the order of the king or council, as a gesture of propitiation on Sadler's part, since there could be no doubt that the shifting factional alignments had played a key role in bringing Cromwell to the Tower. What was beyond supposition was that the conservatives now commanded the council in which lesser men had no choice but to follow where Brandon, Gardiner, Norfolk and the turncoat Wriothesley led.[3] Behind the first rank stood some important members of the episcopal bench, especially Stokesley and Bonner.[4] There was also Tunstal. But he was more a figurehead than anything else. Although at one time he had been reckoned a wise head in council, of late the man once reputed the best civilian lawyer in Europe had developed a dream-like habit of mind.[5] Whether senility or recognition

[1] BM Harleian MSS. 288, fo. 47.
[2] BM Cotton MSS. Caligula E IV, fo. 42.
[3] Hughes, *History of the Reformation in England*, II, 69.
[4] Sturge, *Cuthbert Tunstal*, p. 188.
[5] For Tunstal's decline in power see Brewer, *The Reign of Henry VIII*, II, 113.

of his old maxim that 'the first place under the king is a slippery one' provoked his trances, Tunstal avoided full participation.[1] Roland Lee, the former Cromwellian who had gone over at the first anxious moments, was more vital in the new order than was the bishop of Durham.[2] Most of the other highly placed clergymen were almost without exception conservatives, or Henricians, to distinguish them from the reactionary band of true papists.[3] Many of the leading laymen also chose that posture, whatever their genuine inclination might have been. Sir Anthony Browne was almost too conservative for his own fellow councillors,[4] and the diplomatic brothers Wooton were tied to Gardiner by old bonds.[5]

That galaxy of stars of the first and second order was beyond comparison as a force illuminating the condition of politics in the wake of Cromwell's arrest and execution. A small number of important men truly uncommitted to any party geed and hawed with the bishops, led by able *politiques* like St John, the financial expert who was to achieve lasting fame as Elizabeth's expert on exchequer matters.[6] Then there was the enigmatic Paget, Sadler's close friend, a Cromwellian by training who had been made secretary to Anne of Cleves, but who had also kept open his connection of longstanding with Gardiner.[7] Sir Edward North,[8] Sir Edward Montague[9] and John Bromeley[10] rounded out the uncommitted group who played along with the dominant party. The last two were judges, a fact which might well explain their indecisive conservatism.

Obviously, there were not many men of the first rank or the second left with which to form the nucleus of a reform party. But there was Cranmer to lead them and he had the king's confidence. Unfortunately,

---

[1] *L & P*, xiv, ii, 750: One of Tunstal's men quoted the motto: 'Lubricus est primus locus apud reges.'

[2] Hughes, *History of the Reformation in England*, I, 266.

[3] Smith, *Tudor Prelates and Politics*, pp. 305–8.

[4] Gladish, *Tudor Privy Council*, p. 23.

[5] Pollard, *England under Protector Somerset*, p. 21.

[6] Sir William Paulet; there is no study of this important man.

[7] See Gammon's 'The Master of Practises' for all matters of Paget's career. Suffice it to say here that he was a London man of low birth. Catching Gardiner's eye was the beginning of a career that involved civil law studies in France followed by a number of administrative positions related to the secretariat.

[8] The treasurer of the court of Augmentations from 1541–6.

[9] Chief justice of the court of Common Pleas.

[10] Chief justice of the court of King's Bench.

in matters of state he was no match for Gardiner. Despite his strong hold on the affections of Henry VIII, Cranmer was as truly a cipher in politics as was Gardiner the chief integer.[1] The archbishop was seconded by Audley, the decidedly Protestant chancellor of England.[2] He was, however, no counter-weight to Norfolk. A few more names that might be added to the list were nothing more than a slender hope for the advancement of either religion or the Cromwellian polity. In 1540 Sir John Dudley and Sir Edward Seymour were men of great promise, stars clearly on the rise, and the same was also true of Sir John Russell, Sir Edward Herbert and Sir Anthony Denny, all able courtiers and good administrators.[3] Apart from the chancellor and the archbishop, Sadler's reform-minded colleagues were not the equals of the men who led the Henrician faction.

To make matters worse, the currents of diplomacy moving toward England with the Channel tide bore little of comfort to the reform party. The international situation favoured the conservatives after the Cleves *débâcle*. A malign fate constrained Henry VIII once again to favour the pro-imperial policy which had ruined Wolsey. In order to ward off the spectre of a war on two fronts, a possibility already treated in some detail in the preceding chapters, the English needed Charles V. Thus religious reform had to be discounted and a softer line pursued in matters touching the Church. This played into the hands of Gardiner and Norfolk, who were able to control the council and the administrative machinery, while at the same time dominating the episcopal bench. Clearly, any basic alteration in the pattern of politics would have to wait on the passing of the war scare, until 1546, at which time the Scots were beaten and the French, for reasons of their own, sued for peace. In the meantime, Sadler and the others of a like mind had to preserve their consciences while conforming their actions to the necessity at hand.

That was not an easy thing for a man of strong religious convictions, and Sadler was such a man. As nearly as we can tell from the surviving materials, Sir Ralph was a convinced believer in the reformed religion for all of his mature life. Although he preserved a good number of close

[1] Hughes, *History of the Reformation in England*, II, 69.
[2] Gladish, *Tudor Privy Council*, p. 23.
[3] Russell (later the earl of Bedford), Dudley (later the duke of Northumberland) and Seymour (later the Protector Somerset) were all clearly stamped as men of measured merit by 1540.

friendships with more conservative men, Wriothesley and Lee, for example, his closest companions were Protestants like Hales and Stephan Vaughan among laymen and Hugh Latimer and Holgate among the bishops. His personal agents, John Somers, Thomas Avery and Gregory Raylton, a fair sampling of the lot, were men far to the left of the Henrician settlement. Raylton, his 'inwarde manne' in high politics and diplomacy, was a very stern and forbidding Calvinist.[1] No wonder the leaders of the Catholic League in Scotland in the 1570s listed Sadler with the 'precisians' responsible for the misgovernment of England.[2]

Still other evidence supports the view that Sadler was sympathetic with the advanced reformers. His own position was most carefully stated in a letter to Leicester in 1568, when he remarked that the fate of true religion in England would be at the mercy of the continental powers in league with the papacy, if ever the European leaders of re-form were destroyed: 'The Reformacyon of relygyon in Englonde is the next marke they have to shoote at...', Sadler wrote, full of gloom and foreboding.[3] During the height of the Puritan classical movement, Sadler was of comfort to its leaders who knew him as a friend at the council board, where it was noted by archbishop Parker that he himself was 'outweighed and defaced' by Sir Ralph's protection of 'precisians'.[4] A little closer to home, apparently Sadler selected his sons-in-law with an eye toward their correctness in religion.[5] Thus it was no small matter for such a strong Protestant and a 'favourer' of religion, as an Elizabethan bishop of London labelled Sadler, to survive the full tide of the Henrician reaction of the 1540s.[6] All that we hear of Sadler in matters of conscience, whether the reports stem from Elizabeth's reign, from his Scottish diplomacy or from the record of his activities in the

[1] John Strype, *The Life and Acts of Mathew Parker*, 3 vols. (Oxford: The Clarendon Press, 1821), II, 191; for Sadler's household, see ch. VIII below for Hales, Raylton and Somers.

[2] Strype, *Annals*, I, ii, 363: Cecil, Mildmay and Bacon were also blamed.

[3] *HMC Report on the Pepys Manuscripts in Magdalene College*, pp. 151–2, Sadler to Earl of Leicester, 21 March 1568.

[4] Patrick Collinson, 'The Puritan Classical Movement in the Reign of Queen Elizabeth' (London University: unpublished Ph.D. thesis, 1957), p. 121, n. 3, where Collinson shows Archbishop Parker complaining to Cecil that he was 'outweighed and defaced' by Sadler's protection of 'precisians'.

[5] PCC Register 11 Baker for Edward Elrington's will; for Sir Edward Baeshe see *Collections of Original Letters from the Bishops to the Privy Council.* Edited by Mary Bateson (London: Camden Society, 1893), p. 60.

[6] Bateson, *Collections of Original Letters*, p. 61.

radical days of Protector Somerset, indicates that Sir Ralph was under severe strain in the 1540s.[1]

One piece of evidence gleaned from his personal correspondence best illustrates the hopes of Sadler, better even than the letters from Scotland in which he argued the primacy of scripture in the manner of a true 'gospul Christian'.[2] When the marriage between Catherine Parr and Henry VIII was celebrated, Sir Ralph heralded the event in joyous tones. Writing to the new queen's brother, his old friend Lord William Parr,[3] Sadler pondered the implications of the known Protestant views of queen Catherine:

Thys revyved my troubled sprytes and tuned all my cares to reioysyng. And my lord I doo not onlie reioyse for your lordshyppes sake...but also for the real and inestimable benefitte and cumforte whiche thereby shal ensue to the hoole realme, which nowe with the grace of God shalbe stored with many precious juelles.[4]

Sadler expressed his belief that the new queen would favour reform. That in itself would dispel the woe which arose from the fettering of the word of God, which had been all but banished from England. The mouths of the 'precious juelles', Latimer and his fellow reformers, would be once more opened; they would no doubt be restored to court again. However circumspect Sadler had been in public between 1540 and 1543, in private he made it abundantly clear that the conservative reaction was perverse and ultimately wrong.

The necessity for circumspection had been forcefully impressed upon Sadler in the dark days following Cromwell's fall. He had been caught up in the anti-Cromwellian purges and agitations instigated by Gardiner and his supporters on the council. At first the bishop struck at Sadler in an indirect way, through the family of Heron of Hackney which was dependent on Sir Ralph. Giles Heron, the head of the family, was an old man who had served Sadler in some household capacity for a space of time on more than one occasion. He and his sons were imprisoned and examined by the council.[5] The gist of the charges was sought by

---

[1] See the *DNB* article on Sadler.　　[2] *SSP*, I, 323 and 50–343 *passim*.
[3] Parr was created baron before he became Henry's brother-in-law.
[4] *SSP*, I, 323, 20 July 1543.
[5] Joan Heron Newman, earlier Giles Heron's wife, a Hackney resident, was also closely questioned. For the details see BM Royal MSS. 7 C XVI, fos. 152–3. Giles and John Heron were the sons of Sir John Heron, the early Henrician chamber treasurer; furthermore, Giles was the

Sadler, who was informed by the council that the Herons had practised conjurations against the king.[1] The situation was complicated when John Heron, a brother of Giles, was hauled before the council and charged with having practised 'astronomie and necromancie sithens the perturbacyon of the late erle of Essex'.[2] That charge cleared the air, since it made manifest the fact that Cromwell was the real object of the inquiry, at least in the persons of his *relicta*. By opening charges relating to the dark and occult arts touching his servants, the council might well be led to a direct attack on the principal secretary himself.

Sadler was not dismayed by the investigations. He maintained the suits of his servants before the council, securing the release of the Herons. The king himself wrote to Sir Ralph, declaring that he might keep his servants at work, since the trial was one of 'thair trewth and a purgacyon of theim from all suspycon rather than anie ignoynie or shame' in them.[3] John Heron, for whom Sadler also intervened, was also released after giving testimony that was vague, confused and entirely inconclusive.[4] But he was arrested again in late September, only to be cleared on that occasion also, upon the condition that he was not to use 'or exercise anie maner of necromancie, astronyme, calculacyon or other experymentes'.[5]

While the move against the Herons came to nothing, they were small and inconsequential men. Sadler, on the other hand, had a position at the heart of government and he owed it to the fallen Cromwell. In those circumstances the nervous investigations conducted throughout the summer of 1540 and on into the autumn of the year, inquiries which were designed to check on everybody whose path had crossed Cromwell's, had to be anxiously watched by Sir Ralph Sadler. Even Wriothesley was charged with slander against the king, although the charge was adjudged maliciously made. Before the slanderer of Wriothesley was arrested, however, the secretary was questioned on a number of rather

son-in-law of Sir Thomas More, having been More's ward before marrying Cecily More (cf. *L & P*, III, 2,900). Giles Heron was later executed.

[1] BM Arundel MSS. 97, fos. 145*a*–146*b*; also *Proceedings and Ordinances*, VII, 11, 24–5.
[2] *Ibid.* p. 30.
[3] *Ibid.* p. 25.
[4] PRO, SP 1/163, fo. 169*b*, Lord Maltrevers to Henry VIII, writing to tell the king that he had refused to honour Sadler's request for a position in the garrison on Heron's behalf. He went on to state that he would never give employment to any man who 'hath bene anie cause of suspycon', even though the principal secretary of state made the request.
[5] *Proceedings and Ordinances*, VII, 30.

ticklish points.[1] Further evidence of the near hysterical temper of the time was provided when Lord Leonard Grey, an old friend of Cromwell from the days of the Dorset connection, went to the block for treason.[2] Even better evidence of nerves rubbed raw came to light during the interrogation of William Gray, a former dependent of Cromwell. His crime, treason: the evidence, he had scrawled Melanchthon's name in the margin of one of his books.[3] It all seemed likely to add up to a purge on a grand scale. The remaining Cromwellians, high and low alike, were being carefully sifted.

Sadler conducted himself with caution through the months immediately following Cromwell's death. Yet it seems likely that his maintenance of the Herons increased the distrust already felt toward him on the part of the leading conservatives. Early in 1541 the full sessions of the council were dominated by Gardiner and his supporters; their main care was to mask their real intentions from their prospective victims. For that reason they appeared to shrug off the disturbances in Lincolnshire caused by Sir John Neville. Other signs of unrest provoked no overtly stringent repressive measures. As Pollard so incisively remarked, 'their practice was to veil their *practice*'.[4] In that way they might hope to catch the big fish while the minnows swam quietly on their way.

The full force of the purge was unleashed on 16 January 1541, with all of the celerity that characterises the mature plot. Sadler was arrested. An eye-witness to the seizure of the principal secretary told Chapuys that a gentleman of the chamber who had recently been in Scotland on an embassy and who was also one of the men to whom Cromwell gave the secretaryship had been sent to the Tower in company with the poet and courtier Sir Thomas Wyatt. Messengers had also been sent to secure the servants of those taken.[5]

---

[1] *Proceedings and Ordinances*, VII, pp. 100–2.   [2] *Ibid.* p. 90

[3] *Ibid.* pp. 93–107. The case was certainly a bizarre one, even amidst the others involving men proscribed for reading Protestant books.

[4] Pollard, *Henry VIII*, 402.

[5] *CSPSp*, VI, 1 and 150, Chapuys to Mary of Hungary, 17 Jan. 1541. The text of the original is supplied from a transcript of Les archives Imperiales de Vienne, Tome 232, fo. 74, in PRO, PRO 31/18/3, a sheaf of pages not numbered but arranged chronologically.

'Madame. En linstant mesures du patrement de ce courier ay estre adverty par personne qui a este te moiny en laffaire, qui uni de deux, a qui Crumwell peu avant sa ruyne resigna lestatt de premier secretaire, a estre constitue prisonnier en la tour, et que puis uny heure M. Huet a estre apprehendere en sa maison et aussi mis en la dict tour. De Londres le XVIIᵉ de Januir XVᶜ XLI.' *L & P*, XVI, 461, note, correctly identified Sadler as one of the victims.

Although not mentioned by name in the report, it seems beyond doubt that Sadler was the victim of the plot. He had attended the council daily until 15 January, along with Wriothesley. But from the 16th to the 20th his name fails to appear among those at the council board; Sir Thomas Wriothesley was the sole secretary in attendance.[1] That circumstance, joined to the rather full report made by Chapuys, is also given additional weight by the evidence of Marillac, the French resident in London. Marillac was usually a step or two behind Chapuys in the game of gathering news to send to Francis I, but on this occasion he sent an accurate report of the 'unexpected and important new event'.[2] He related how two highly regarded courtiers and officials had been taken prisoner at Hampton Court on the evening of the 16th. On the following morning, he reported, they were taken to the Tower, with their hands tightly bound, under heavy guard by twenty-four armed men. Marillac[3] rightly asserted that both men were persecuted because they were Cromwell's relics. He noted that even so great a man as Wriothesley had not escaped questioning. The Cromwellians seemed bound to descend more quickly than they had climbed the ladder of fortune. In still another letter, although he did not name Sadler, he expressed his belief that the Cromwellians were at an end. Almost all of the conservatives who had formed the league against Cromwell were united in the purge of the surviving dependents of that minister. No war, Marillac noted in genuine horror, could be more terrifying than the one then being carried on by Englishmen against one another. The

---

[1] *Proceedings and Ordinances*, VII, 116–120.

[2] Paris, Archives des affaires étrangères, Tome IIme, fos. 5–7, M. de Marillac to Francis I, 18 Jan. 1541, a précis of which was deposited in the PRO (PRO 31/11/3) by Armand Baschet.
'Cest en substance Sire que ceste nuite passee par londre de ce roy deux gentilhommes de sa cour fort estimmez et nommez par deca ont este menez de Hampton cour, prisonniers en ceste ville, et lesa lon veu ce matin estre conduirez les poinys lies par 24 archers, jusques a la grosse tour de londres, ou ils sont detenues. Dont luv est M. Hoevt et lautre prisonnier Sire, est uny gentil-homme de pays du nord, peu cogneu a moi car il este bien peu souvent a la court. Totesfois, il a bien haut charge aultrefois lambassadeur devers le roy discosse. La cause pourquoy les personnages dessus surnommez ont este prins, Sire, ne se peult encores entendres: et asee grande difficultes en seura lon la verite, daultant que par un loy failte au dernier parlement on condempne iey les gens sans les oys; avec ce que, depuis quony homme est prisonnier en ce pays, en le dict grosse tour, il ne ya personnage vivant qui ose sentremettre crime que celluy qui est arrestre. Tant y a, Sir, que le lestime que ce soit les reliques de Crumwell, veu mesnement que le prive secretaire de ce roy Nommez M. Voyezley estant parvenu en lieu on il est par le moyen du dict Crumwell est en grande bransle de descendre plus vistement quil neste monte, car il a desja estre interroge et examine surplusieurres articles asses chitouilleaux et se dict communement quily en a beaucoup daultres qui ne sont point hors de dangereures.'

[3] For Marillac's limitations as an ambassador see Mattingly, *Renaissance Diplomacy*, p. 244.

deep hatred which was Cromwell's legacy would allow nobody any rest until all of his remaining followers, including Sadler, were brought down. God alone knew the end of such events.[1]

The verdict of Chapuys and Marillac was echoed by John Wallop, the ambassador to Charles V. He wrote from Spain to inform Henry VIII of Charles V's views on English politics. As Wallop reported the conversation, the emperor flitted about before getting down to what was really on his mind. Then, he spoke candidly; Charles began to show that he knew the direction of political events in England. According to Wallop the emperor

receyved newes how that Wyat was taken and sent to the Towre, aftur suche sort as befor thys tyme he had nevar harde of any, hys handes beyng manacled togither, askyng me what I thoughte the same to be for and whether he was of the Lutherian secte or not, havyng sayd that at hys beyng in Spayne[2] he was muche troubled for such lyke thynges... Then aftre he beganne to enter agayn the matyer of the purpos of the late privie seale[3] an hys muche naughtines pretendyd intencyons in tyme to cum aswel concernyng your hyghnes as my lady Marye[4] and how muche ye were beholden unto God that those thynges came unto your knowlidge, meanyng by a favor, as I colde perceave, that Wyat and thothre sholde be of that affynyte, saynge that he was very gladde when he furste harde saye that your hynes dyd reforme the Lutherian secte...[5]

These reports reinforce one another on the vital points. It is clear that the Gardiner-led conservatives wished to fix in the king's mind the association between Lutheran ideas and Cromwell's servants and government officials patronised by Cromwell. By doing so they hoped to play on the king's known dislike for the continental brand of reform, which had about it a populist element that alarmed kings and aristocrats alike. Hopefully, this alarm would trigger the destruction of the politicians of a Cromwellian persuasion.

Here the plotters failed. On 25 January Marillac wrote to Francis I, informing him that the purge had fallen short of its mark, that Wyatt and Sadler had been tried and acquitted.[6] Although Sadler's name is not to be found in the list of those questioned and freed,[7] he was once

---

[1] PRO, PRO 31/3/11, fos. 293–5, undated.
[2] Wyatt had served in Spain from 1537–9.
[3] Cromwell is obviously meant here. [4] Princess Mary Tudor.
[5] *SP*, VIII, 517, 26 Jan. 1541. [6] *L & P*, XVI, 482.
[7] *Ibid.* pp. 449, 461, 466, 469, 470, 474, 482, 488, 506, 523, 534, 611 and 641.

again at the council board after his brief and inexplicable absence, inexplicable, that is, on any other hypothesis.[1] The irony of the situation
was underlined by Sadler's opening of the Wallop letters in which the
discomfort of the 'sectarians' was recited. Sir Ralph had survived still
another crisis.[2]

Why the purge failed remains a mystery. There is not a shred of
evidence to support Pollard's thesis, which was that Sadler regained his
place by abjuring his former opinions on religious and political questions.[3] I have been unable to find any material showing that Sir Ralph
ever joined the faction opposed to Cranmer's opinions. Although it is
tempting to see in Sadler's support for the imperial alliance some
evidence of a change of heart, we must remember that Sadler was an
Englishman well aware of the nature and degree of the French threat
which seemed a good deal closer than did the dangers of weakening the
zeal for reform by virtue of a pro-Spanish policy. Sadler had spent
many years trying to dissolve the 'auld alliance' without success; that in
itself is sufficient to explain his diplomatic preferences after 1541. In much
the same way the Castilian subjects of Charles V were more alarmed by
Turkish piracy in the western waters of the Mediterranean than they
were by Lutheran depredations in Saxony. The perception of immediate danger was a powerful determinant of actions that will not
yield to a simple religious touchstone.

A far more likely explanation of the failure of the purge in so far as it
concerned Sadler hinges on the king's recognition that Sir Ralph was a
man who had given long and faithful service to the Crown and,
furthermore, that he was a politician without power. While he was a
man of proven ability in a variety of capacities by 1541, Sadler never
achieved the substance of power as secretary of state. Unlike Cromwell
at home or Cobos in Spain, Sadler had never become anything more
than a good bureaucrat in the wake of his appointment to the secretaryship. Another facet of this explanation lies in the very condition of
Henrician politics after Cromwell's fall. The king was at times indolent,
but he was never a fool. He must have realised that Gardiner's succeeding in the purge would have created a disequilibrium by virtue of
which the king would be the biggest victim. Having just shed one

[1] *Proceedings and Ordinances*, VII, 120.
[2] *L & P*, XVI, 174 and 594–5, for Sadler's knowledge of the plans for trapping Wallop.
[3] *Henry VIII*, p. 403.

overly powerful minister Henry, like his daughter Elizabeth, did not intend so soon to create another all-powerful faction able to oblige the king in matters of state. By balancing the distribution of power and rewards the king could count on hearing two or more sides of every suit or matter of policy. He would also have alternative agents of government at hand should the present advisers of greatest influence cease to perform up to expectations. That, plus the way in which Cromwell had developed the clientage system in a way advantageous to the state, are enough to explain the survival of Sir Ralph Sadler and a dozen men like him. In the absence of political parties and with no standing military force, the balancing of faction was a necessary and simple rule of the practice of the arts of obedience and coercion. Men like Sadler were exactly what was needed; men skilled and loyal and also without the substance of power.[1]

Whatever the ultimate reasons were, Sadler's restoration to favour was swift but not complete. Although he was given the very delicate task of examining Cromwell's correspondence and making a calendar of it along with Tunstal, a task that must be viewed as a vote of confidence, he clearly lost influence at court.[2] In 1541 the privy council apparently was divided into two groups due to the king's increasing absences from court locations in and about London. Part of the council peregrinated with Henry VIII, while the other part remained in London at all times. The council with the king had the king's ear and was thereby in a favoured position. To nobody's surprise, Wriothesley and the leading conservatives dominated that segment of the original council. The council remnant in London, on the other hand, was responsible for the execution of the formal orders it received from the men in contact with the monarch. It consisted almost entirely of Protestants, among them Cranmer, Audley, Baker, Seymour and Sadler.[3] Wriothesley was thus in an advantageous position on two counts and steadily moved ahead of his co-secretary in influence and power. Sadler's absence from court was a serious limit set to his career by the circumstances of politics, since only a truly great blunder seemed

---

[1] Walter C. Richardson, *History of the Court of Augmentations*, p. 67, describes Sadler as one of the Cromwellians 'whose varied contributions to a great gain in national administration' has not been adequately assessed by historians, calling for a biography (n. 20).

[2] *Proceedings and Ordinances*, VII, 121, for the commission, and *L & P*, xx, i, 506, Sadler to the Privy Council, 11 Dec. 1545, for a retrospective account of the work done in 1541.

[3] Pollard, *EHR*, xxxvII, 50–1.

likely to loosen the hold on power enjoyed by the men grouped around Gardiner and Norfolk.

In the autumn of 1541 there happened just such a mischance. While Gardiner was abroad on an embassy, Cranmer and his supporters busily gathered evidence relating to the apparent misconduct of Catherine Howard, Norfolk's niece and Henry's fifth queen, a girl placed in the king's path by Gardiner and Norfolk in the wake of the Cleves fiasco.[1] Realising that the king was more sensitive in marital than in most other matters as a result of his long run of bad luck, Gardiner had hoped to cap the fortunes of his faction with a love match between the ageing monarch and the comely and playful Catherine. That was the error in judgement which came to haunt the great bishop, as the malign fate which pursued Henry's marriages once more revealed itself.

During the summer of the year of his fifth marriage, the king made his usual northern progress. From July until October the court ambled about the green and golden countryside, often visiting places familiar to the young queen as childhood haunts. Perhaps the heady air got the best of Catherine or perhaps she was simply a vicious and jaded girl. Be that as it may, and there is no suggestion that such a choice exhausts the possibilities, at Lincoln and at Pontefract castle she met secretly with Thomas Culpepper, a cousin to whom she had once been engaged. She was aided in those ill-considered trysts by yet another cousin, the weak-minded Jane Rocheford. Then, to compound felony with felony, in August she conspired to know Francis Dereham, a handsome retainer of the dowager duchess of Norfolk and the queen's private secretary. It is not a matter of record how long these affairs lasted. But on 2 November 1541 a maid-servant of the queen deposed to Cranmer that Catherine had carnally known Culpepper, Dereham and a youth named Manock before her marriage to Henry VIII.[2]

That testimony was the handle on the whip which the Protestants needed to scourge the Gardiner faction. The bishop's party went reeling in disfavour at the first disclosures. On 11 November Sadler was installed as the secretary attendant on the king. On that same day he

---

[1] She was the daughter of Lord Edward Howard, a younger son of the second duke of Norfolk, Henry VIII's lord admiral. She was a dependent of Agnes, the dowager duchess, her grandmother, at Horsham House in Norfolk. Henry married her secretly in 1540.

[2] For the basic facts see the recent book by Lacey Baldwin Smith, *A Tudor Tragedy: The Life and Times of Catherine Howard* (London: Jonathan Cape, 1961).

wrote to Cranmer on behalf of the council with the king, informing his friend that Catherine had confessed her premarital sins and had been removed to Sion House. Some members of the full council were deputed to investigate the problem fully, although it was made clear at the outset that Henry wished to spare the girl's life, humiliated and grief-stricken though he was.[1] Sadler also wrote privately to the archbishop in greater detail, emphasising that the king was minded to question the queen in detail about Culpepper and the other men, 'if her wittes are suche that she could stand the strain'. Furthermore, he revealed that Audley had spoken out against the queen in Star Chamber, declaring that there 'was an appearance of grete abominacyon in her'.[2]

The elaborate investigation that ensued was mirrored in the letters written between Sadler and the council. Sadler's correspondence showed the full extent of the disaster which visited the Conservative faction by virtue of queen Catherine's misconduct. It revealed that Cranmer had the chief role in the inquiry, since marital affairs were traditionally church causes. Audley, naturally enough, served as the archbishop's chief agent. Seymour had charge of the queen's personal effects, while Sir Ralph handled the details involved in the co-ordination of the various processes. That all of the men named were members of the faction opposed to the Gardiner–Norfolk axis was no mere accident. It was in fact a warning to the Conservatives that the king could and would intrust his affairs to their enemies when it suited his purposes. The punctuation to that message came in the form of a commission to try Culpepper for high treason. Several of the most eminent Conservatives had no place on the commission.[3]

Southampton and Wriothesley were selected out of the so-called Henrician group and thus participated in the sifting of evidence that threatened to ruin Norfolk and Winchester. Under an order signed by Sadler, those two men visited the dowager duchess of Norfolk and persuaded her to surrender to Audley's questioning.[4] While she visited the chancellor's quarters they searched her home at Lambeth, and their colleague Sir William Petre searched at Horsham for incriminating

---

[1] *L & P*, XVI, 1,331, 11 Nov. 1541.

[2] PRO, SP 1/167, fos. 145–6, 12 Nov. 1541. Other details are related in *L & P*, XVI, 1,332–4.

[3] PRO, KB 8/12/1, the indictment and other records on the Crown side of the case.

[4] *L & P*, XVI, 1,409, a series of questions put to the dowager and others naming the men inculpated.

evidence. Wriothesley notified Sadler that the queen's servants could be made to tell what Sadler and his companions wanted to know and that a transcription of testimony already taken would be handed over to the commissioners. Armed with such material, 'they could picke owte what served for thair busines' and in so doing satisfy the king.[1] Meanwhile, Sadler urged Southampton and Sir Anthony Browne to press the ladies of the court for information, in that way collecting data damaging to the duchess. As Browne confessed to Sadler, the old duchess 'hath so entangled herselfe I thinke she will be harde to winde herselfe owte again'.[2]

Sadler did not confine his activities to the direction of other inquiries. He questioned one Elizabeth Welkes himself, wheedling testimony out of her that delighted him for its 'good mattre'. Then, on 6 December, Sadler learned of the most damaging piece of evidence yet uncovered. One of the retainers of the duchess deposed that the old mistress of the Howard faction had broken into the trunks of Dereham and made off with a bundle of letters. At the same time Sadler gained information of Lord William Howard's complaints to the effect that his cousin was being made to suffer for youthful indiscretions committed before her marriage under strange circumstances.[3] That information, obtained under extreme pressure, and in consideration of Lord Williams place as an important commander at Calais, contributed to the already dark picture of the Howards bent on frustrating the inquiry.

Salder's conduct from start to finish was ruthless and efficient. The formal denial of a charge meant little or nothing to him. When he realised that much of the data gathered was merely circumstantial he solicited the opinion of the law officers of the Crown. They informed him that on the basis of what was in hand charges of treason could be supported only with serious difficulty. They were willing to go before Star Chamber in so far as the case related to Dereham and Culpepper. But they were as reluctant as many of the councillors themselves to widen the net in a political purge.[4] It was at that point that something of Sadler's mind in the case appeared most clearly. He wrote to the council in a rather haughty tone, informing them that the king *wished*

[1] PRO, SP 1/168, fos. 58–9, a letter to Sadler, 4 Dec. 1541.
[2] *Ibid.* fos. 85–6, 5 Dec. 1541.
[3] *SP*, I, 696, council to Sadler, 6 Dec. 1541.
[4] PRO, SP 1/168 fos. 102–3, council to Sadler, 7 Dec. 1541.

the judges to believe the charges against the old duchess, especially that of concealing evidence touching Dereham. It was enough that the record showed the Howards knew of the queen's 'naughtie lyfe', whether or not the purloined letters could be produced. The king's will as expounded by Sir Ralph did not stick at matters of procedure. It was the duty of the council, Sadler wrote, 'to picke owte from the testimonie geven' the facts necessary for the condemnation of the Howards and their dependents.[1]

Sadler pictured himself as the instrument of the king's will; that was no doubt the case. But the plain fact is that he relished the view which urged the councillors to set aside legal haggling, when it suited the king's purposes to do so.[2] Marillac confirmed this picture in relating that Henry had called for a sword with which to slay Catherine, so great was his rage against her sins.[3] Sadler, realising this to be the case, showed once more that he was Cromwell's heir. Not for nothing had he played a part in the examination of Fisher and More in 1535.

The advantage gained by Sadler's side was pressed home. On 8 December Sadler wrote to the council again in the king's name, informing them that the Howards were to be placed in confinement, Dereham and Culpepper were to be executed and the retainers of the Howards who had traded their Norfolk livery for immunity as witnesses for the Crown were to be released.[4] The time of rejoicing was at hand for Sadler and his companions. Power was once more in their grasp; the ruin of the Howards seemed imminent. The future looked wondrously bright and attractive.[5]

The hoped-for triumph never came. The Gardiner–Norfolk faction's hold on power was dealt a severe blow, but it proved to be only a temporary one. The queen and Lady Rocheford were executed in February, 1542. Other members of the Howard family lost their property and their freedom. Norfolk's prestige as the premier peer was shaken as was Gardiner's power on the council. Surely the balance of

---

[1] *SP*, I, 699–701, Sadler to council, 7 Dec. 1541.

[2] The report that Anne of Cleves had given birth to a son, while his own adulterous queen proved barren, spurred the rage of the king at a time when no stimulant was necessary.

[3] *Correspondence politique de MM. de Castillon et de Marillac, Ambassadeurs de France en Angleterre, 1537–1542,* ed. Jean Kaulek (Paris: Germer Bailiere, 1885), p. 370.

[4] *L & P,* XVI, 1,430. Mary Lasselles and other servants gave 'gude testimonie' for the Crown.

[5] *Ibid.* pp. 1,431, 1,437–8, 1,444, 1,467 and 1,472.

power had shifted. But the hoped-for purge never materialised in the political arena.

Henry VIII was never a fool. Early in 1542 his attention was diverted from private woes to public dangers in the form of European menaces to English peace. Foreign affairs once more came to the aid of the Henricians. War seemed inevitable in 1542. As we have already observed, the peace with Scotland hung by a slender thread. In the light of that recognition, Seymour and Dudley were charged with preparing a war plan against the Scots.[1] Henry regretted that he did not have two other war-makers of equal skill to launch against France, since the renewal of hostilities with England's perpetual enemy seemed likely in the event of a war with Scotland.

On two counts these facts favoured Gardiner. He was the chief exponent of an Imperial alliance.[2] Then, the very necessity of girding for war in the wake of the promotion of the Protestant faction had a paradoxical effect. Financial necessities removed Sadler from the political arena for a while, as he was commissioned to help extract the 'love money' or forced loans of 1542 by privy seal letters in the council's name.[3] War preparation also robbed the Cranmer faction of the services of its two most promising men, since Dudley and Seymour were shortly to leave court for the campaign against James V. Thus Cranmer, who was neither an able diplomat nor a military expert, was left alone on the council attending the king and he lacked the skill to combat Gardiner in politics.

Henry VIII therefore had no choice but to turn to men experienced in the business at that time most demanding attention. Gardiner came to the fore as naturally as a cork comes to the surface of water. Whatever his demerits, the bishop of Winchester was a brilliant diplomat and a skilled administrator with a long apprenticeship under Wolsey behind him. He was immediately given charge of the imperial negotiations, while the soldiers and financial experts passed from the scene.[4] Although it is true that Gardiner personally could exercise no political influence while he was away on the imperial embassy, when he returned

[1] *HP*, I, 243, Hertford to Wriothesley, 29 Nov. 1542.
[2] Hughes, *History of the Reformation in England*, II, 4; Muller, *Stephen Gardiner and the Tudor Reaction*, pp. 102–3.
[3] PRO, SP 1/170, fo. 122, Robert Dacres to Denny, 13 May 1542.
[4] See ch. 6 for the details of Anglo-Scottish problems in the 1540s.

early in 1543 his influence was higher than ever before.¹ Furthermore, shortly after Sadler's completion of the work in connection with the forced loans, Sir Ralph received orders to depart for Edinburgh. That further depleted and demoralised the faction sympathetic to reform in religion and the continuance of Cromwell's policy in administration and politics.²

An observer at court in the early months of 1543 would have been a little baffled by the oscillations in English politics. With Sadler, Dudley and Seymour absent, and with Audley in failing health, Gardiner's group moved against the reform already avowed and partly achieved. *The King's Book* of 1543 overturned the earlier doctrinal reforms and was the chief sign of the second wave of reaction. Another, and perhaps a more potent omen, was the trouble brewed against Cranmer himself at Gardiner's urging. The archbishop was formally charged with promoting heresy in the still mysterious affair known as the prebendaries' plot, from the fact that the Canterbury prebends attacked their bishop.³ Although their case was not sustained, chiefly due to the strong role played by the king himself, who ordered that Cranmer be allowed to supervise the hearing of the charges and the sifting of the evidence in his own case, the plot alarmed the Protestants.⁴

Gardiner clearly intended to use his regained power to 'shoote at some of the hede deer'. He missed Cranmer. But one of his shafts lighted on Sir Ralph Sadler. On 24 April he was deprived of the office of principal secretary of state on the plausible grounds of his prolonged absence in Scotland. To compensate him for the loss, the office of master of the great wardrobe was put in his hands.⁵ He was retained on the council, but it was a blow to his friends to lose their share of the king's ear in the person of a secretary who was also an advanced reformer.

Sadler's removal from office was symbolic of the movement of affairs in 1543–4. Design and circumstance once more combined to place the reigns of government in the hands of the same men who were nearly ruined in 1541. The leading Protestants were absent on royal business, pressing home the war effort against the Scots and the French,

¹ See Gairdner's signed article in the *DNB*.
² Hughes, *History of the Reformation in England*, II, 16.
³ *L & P*, XVIII, 546 (pp. 291–387).
⁴ Muller, *Stephen Gardiner and the Tudor Reaction*, pp. 107–12, for that rather lurid development.
⁵ See below for the exact circumstances.

thus leaving a clear field at home for the Henrician conservatives. Audley died and he was succeeded by the ambivalent Wriothesley, a move that added materially to the gloom which surrounded Sadler's friends. That is not to imply that Wriothesley and Sadler were not on good terms, for they remained good companions from the earliest days of their common service to Wolsey and Cromwell. But the imperial ambassador expressed the plain truth when he remarked that the party in power during the war years was sympathetic with the Empire and the slowing of religious innovation, and they ruled all.[1]

Less than a year later that same observer had cause to make a new evaluation of the situation. The final stage of the revolution in power which went on throughout the last seven years of the king's life puzzled Van der Delft, Charles V's agent in London. It has often confused later political observers as well, since the solid phalanx of the conservatives which appeared unbeatable in 1544 was broken once and for all in 1545. Van der Delft had to admit that 'Seymour and Dudley are the only nobles of a firm age and ability for the task of managing affairs' once the wars came to an end. Almost overnight it seemed to Van der Delft that the world had been made over. The conquerors returned from the field to find themselves giants in politics, a thing not puzzling in itself, but strange in the circumstances of English politics in the 1540s. For a change in leadership implied a swing back in the direction of Cranmer's reforming ideas and those of the new lords of the council. To the Catholic ambassador the change signalled that England was once more awash in a sea uncharted and inhospitable to the merry old England eulogised by Brandon and Norfolk.[2]

The final political convulsion of Henry VIII's rule benefited a small group of men of reforming temperament. Chief among them were Cranmer's old allies, especially Seymour, Dudley, Paget, Rich, Lee and Sadler, as well as a number of lesser lights in the administration who were shortly to shine more brilliantly. The nagging question that emerges from the brute facts of their prosperity is that of deciphering how they came to be a tightly knit faction capable of grasping power on the eve of the king's death. Or, put in another way: what was the antecedent connection between Sadler, Paget, Dudley and Seymour?

[1] Hughes, *History of the Reformation in England*, II, 70.
[2] *CSPSp*, VIII, 150, 152 and 320.

How did they come to depend on Paget for political leadership from 1543-6?

There is only the slenderest evidence to show that Sadler was a special friend of either Seymour or Paget before 1543. Dudley and Sadler had become good friends as early as 1540.[1] They had congenial minds, especially in matters relating to the Scots.[2] The only scrap of evidence relating Sir Ralph to Seymour before 1543, however, seems to indicate that they were not completely happy with one another.[3] So far as other men enter the picture, Sadler's close adherence to Cranmer in the adultery crisis of 1541 has already been exposed. Lord Parr, the king's brother-in-law, was a rather intimate friend of Sadler; they exchanged some very revealing letters about political matters[4] and they shared a distrust of Tunstal and Suffolk.[5] Their religious ideas were clearly of a sympathetic nature.[6] For others among the newly constructed party Sadler cannot be shown to have had special feelings of friendship.

The Sadler–Seymour relationship, which began so dimly as far as the surviving evidence goes, warmed into a comfortable relationship as a result of their common service in the North. Seymour came to repose a special faith in Sadler's handling of routine business and in his advice on military matters. A good case of the latter can be examined in the Scottish campaign of 1544. Seymour begged Henry VIII to let Sadler accompany the invading army even though the council had informed him that the king was against the idea from the start, since he wished to have Sadler on the Borders in order to care for business behind the lines. Seymour kept at his master and got him to change his mind, a thing not easily done with Henry VIII.[7]

The growing bond of sympathy and common endeavour between Seymour and Sadler was paralleled by a budding friendship between Seymour and Paget. Paget seconded the Seymour agents at court and

[1] PRO, SP 1/155, fo. 67b, Dudley to Sadler, 13 Apr. 1540.

[2] Dudley's ideas on that and other subjects are obscure. The best work is Charles Struge, 'John Dudley: Duke of Northumberland' (London University: unpublished Ph.D. thesis, 1927). For the Scottish problem see *HP*, I, 261, 265 and 299.

[3] *HP*, I, 243, Seymour to Wriothesley, 25 Nov. 1542.

[4] *SP* and *HP*, as well as *SSP*, are rich in materials concerning the service of both men on the borders.

[5] PRO, SP 1/181, fo. 93b, Tunstal to Parr, 3 Sept. 1543, and fo. 12, Sadler to Parr, 6 Aug. 1543.

[6] PRO, SP 1/179, fo. 158, Sadler to Parr, 5 June 1543.

[7] Hatfield House, Salisbury MSS. 231, no. 57, Council to Seymour and others, 21 March 1544.

looked after the earl's domestic interests in a variety of ways. He was the intermediary on Seymour's behalf in a number of property disputes in which the king was a party.[1] He also came forward on Seymour's side as a special agent, especially in matters related to Seymour's land dealings with the officials of the court of Augmentations.[2] Paget steadily coached his fiercely ambitious friend in the ways by which influence could be gained at court. They grew to be so much at ease with one another as to make jests of the most delicate sort about marital matters, with the usually sombre earl taking the initiative. The whole smacks of something more than mere political friendship, although the origins may have to be found in mere convenience.[3]

Paget was in fact the middle man in the forging of a new alignment during the 1540s. Although he has been classed in the past with Gardiner's followers, it was Paget's support that facilitated Sadler's revival at court and the rapid rise of the future Protector. In 1544 it was already the case that both men placed their complete trust in the powerful but patient secretary of state.[4] All three laboured in good time to convince the king that Gardiner was personally responsible for the inefficiency and downright dishonesty of the war effort in the North. In this they had the support of Holgate, the new archbishop of York, a man who owed his election in no small measure to the support of Sadler and Seymour.[5] Again, the same triumvirate conspired to outwit the king and in so doing to fleece Tunstal of some £1,500 in lands, with the gain to go to Seymour.[6] In other cases of a less suspect nature they constantly demonstrated their growing loyalty to one another and their sense of common purpose. Mutual solicitousness was their rule of conduct.[7]

---

[1] PRO, SP 1/203, fo. 98.

[2] Longleat, Bath MSS., General Correspondence of the Seymour family IV, fos. 92–9. I owe thanks to Dr Marjorie Blatchford Bindoff, currently editing these papers for the HMC, for permission to use her transcripts on deposit at Quality Court.

[3] PRO, SP 1/202, fo. 52, Seymour to Paget, 9 July 1545: 'I perseyve ye find faute with me for that I have wreggtin ij tymes and send nevar a letar to mi wyfe, as thow ye wold be notid a gud husband and that no sich faute colde be found in onie othre. I wolde advyse you leve of sich quarels or ells I wille tell mi ladie sich talles of ye as ye shal repent the begynnyng. To home I prai ye I may be commendid wyth all mi harte.' Michael Bush, of Manchester University, is now at work on a life of Somerset to replace Pollard's. He has advised me that his view of the Paget–Seymour relationship is very much the same as mine.

[4] Hatfield House, Salisbury MSS. 231, nos. 71–4, 21 and 22 March 1544.

[5] *Ibid.* no. 80. See also *HP*, II, 220, and *L & P*, XIX, i, 336 and 411.

[6] Richardson, *History of the Court of Augmentations*, p. 265. See also PRO, SP 1/197, fos. 228–9, Paget to Sadler, 2 Feb. 1545.

[7] PRO, SP 1/200, fo. 129, 1 Mary 1545, and fo. 225, 3 Oct. 1545.

The most decisive document for an understanding of their common effort is a letter written by Seymour to Paget in 1545. During the better part of that year the secretary and Sadler were preoccupied with the disordered state of the royal finances and the effort to pay for the war against France and Scotland. As Professor Richardson has amply demonstrated, every sort of expedient was tried with little long-range success.[1] Paget wished to overcome the difficulties inherent in the multiplicity of temporising measures and to that end devised a scheme which he sent to Sadler and Seymour for comment. Although the text of Paget's note has not survived its tenor can be reconstructed from that of Seymour's reply. Seymour reminded Paget of the need to 'kepe secretlie' the correspondence in question, perhaps fearing that Paget's preoccupation with many other 'melancholie matiers' might breed carelessness. Passing from admonitions to the substance of Paget's design, which was to 'borrowe some of the plate in all the churches', Seymour noted that the idea was uncomfortably like that held by the fallen Cromwell. In his own cramped and awkward hand, not trusting the matter to a secretary, the earl spelled out his reaction to the plan at some length:

I thynke it is the most redie and present relyffe than canne nowe be had for the Kinges Maiestie and not onlie lest chargybull to hys highnys subiectes but all so in mi opinyon a thynge whyche all menne wouldbe or att lest oughte to be best contentyd with. For Goddes servis whyche consisteth not in juelles plat or ornamentes of gould and silvar verily can not be tarnyshed nor be anie thynge diminisshed therbi and those thynges betar imployed for the wele and defens of the Reaulme, whyche beyng wel perswadid to the pepull shal satisfi them. The worst that I can see in yt is that a bruit may arise thereof that the Kinges Maiestie is dryven to shifte for monie whyche nevartheless I thynke it is as muche suspectyd of and is spoken of in all partes. But I refer mine owne opinyon to you and othres who can see moe deeplie and weighe thynges. I have done your errand to Master Sadler whoe I perseyve remaynith in this and in all thinges ours aftur the olde manar...[2]

At the time of the writing of that letter, which has something about it of a conspiratorial air, secrecy and alert caution were required, since the day of open and victorious partisanship had not yet arrived.

[1] Richardson, 'Some Tudor Financial Expedients of Henry VIII', *EcHR*, 2nd ser. VII (1954), 33–48.
[2] PRO, SP 49/8, fos. 45–6, 9 July 1545.

24 October 1545 brought Sadler and Seymour back to the council board, however, after an absence of better than two years, and that tipped the balance toward Paget and his companions. The first sign of the shift in the political scale came in the form of Paget's openly revealed preference for the Protestant councillors so recently returned to the council. The timid but astute courtiers of inferior rank read the portents, swore great oaths, but dutifully fell into line.[1] Then Wriothesley left the camp of the Conservatives, just as he had defected from Cromwell on earlier occasions of alarm. That convinced even the most sceptical that Gardiner's innings was about over.[2]

Meanwhile, signs of the impending change in the power structure continued to accumulate. Seymour, Dudley, Cranmer and Sadler figured very prominently in the reception held for the French peace commissioners, while Norfolk put in one of his increasingly rare appearances at court.[3] Van der Delft began to report that the Protestants were beginning to dominate the council sessions.[4] Paget forced Gardiner to halt the persecution of sectarians of an anti-sacramental character in Essex a few scant months after it was begun.[5] The last doubts were cast aside when Dudley slapped the face of Gardiner before the entire council and was mildly punished with a short-term banishment from court.[6] The gains were rapidly being consolidated as 1546 wore on its way.

The Protestants capped their revolution in the old manner. Sadler, who had been at ease for the first time in years, resting in the grand new home he had built at Standon, came up to London early in December, 1546, for no reason in particular. The courts were not in session. Nor was parliament meeting. There was no special council business outstanding. The only sign of anything resembling political activity was a seemingly innocent letter to Paget, inquiring whether or not anything worth knowing was about to happen.[7] The answer must have been affirmative, although it has not survived. Sadler cut short his vacation

---

[1] Pollard, *Henry VIII*, p. 416. Between July 1543 and May 1545 council minutes are lacking, a critical loss for political history.

[2] Hughes, *History of the Reformation in England*, II, 10.

[3] BM Cotton MSS. Vespasian C xiv, fo. 67 and Cotton MSS. Appendix xxviii, fo. 101, undated protocol memoranda.

[4] *CSPSp*, viii, 150 and 320.   [5] Pollard, *Henry VIII*, p. 415.

[6] Hughes, *History of the Reformation in England*, II, 71.

[7] PRO, SP 1/225, fo. 229, Sadler to Paget, 3 Dec. 1546.

and rode into London. On the 12th of the month, after a long meeting of a group of councillors at Seymour's house, an order went out for the arrest of Norfolk and his sonneteering son, the talented earl of Surrey.[1] Great Norfolk, the special bane of all of the old Cromwellians, was down at last![2] The new *clique* had decided to strike at the head of the opposition, and it was rumoured that they were set to move against Gardiner himself.[3] That rumour became reality on the 26th December, when the king struck the bishop's name from the list of men selected to execute the will of the dying ruler.[4] The Henricians were cast out of power on the very eve of the new régime, a fact of the gravest significance for the future of the kingdom and Prince Edward Tudor as well.

Henry VIII died in January of the new year, clutching the hand of his Protestant archbishop, a sure sign of the new dispensation in politics. Seymour assumed the headship of the faction which, as Chapuys noted, was for all purposes the government of England.[5] The council of regency numbered twenty-nine men in all. Not one of them was a peer of a dozen years' standing.[6] The most powerful voices belonged to Seymour and Dudley, while Cranmer, Sadler and Paget, as well as a number of lesser men, formed the inner council of the new régime. Sir Ralph Sadler's place was especially secure. The old king had shown him the highest favour, singling him out for the large bequest of £200 and, more vital still, a place on the committee charged with the oversight of the instrument of succession.[7]

After many years of oscillating fortunes and great risks Sadler's patient work and cautious but tenacious political gamble had paid off. Efficiency, experience and fidelity to the twin ideals of reform in church and state won for him a new place in the new order. The men Father Hughes described as 'wicked from ambition, or from greed, or from cowardice, or wicked from the deliberate consent to evil in the

[1] Gladish, *Tudor Privy Council*, p. 24.

[2] BM Cotton MSS. Titus B 1, fo. 94, Norfolk to the council, undated.

[3] *CSPSp*, VIII, 371, Van der Delft to Mary of Hungary, 24 Dec. 1546.

[4] Such was the version given by Paget and recorded by Foxe, *Acts and Monuments*, VI, 163 ff. Foxe believed that Paget coaxed the king to omit Gardiner's name (*ibid.* v, 691).

[5] *L & P*, XXI, ii, 605 and 756, both dated 29 Jan. 1547, Chapuys to Charles V.

[6] Gladish, *Tudor Privy Council*, p. 24.

[7] *L & P*, XXI, ii, 634; Gardiner stated that Sadler's reward was slated at £100 before Paget 'corrected' the king's will. On that version, the evidence of the Paget-Sadler friendship is all the more important.

hope that good may come of it' triumphed in 1547.[1] Thus, if we believe the words of one of the victims, the earl of Surrey, the process was complete by which 'catchpoles' of Paget's breeding, or Sadler's, 'ousted the old aristocracy'.[2]

[1] Hughes, *History of the Reformation in England*, II, 75.

[2] At his trial, Surrey expressed his view of the matter very succinctly: 'Thou Catchpole,' he addressed Paget, 'thou hadst better hold thy tongue, for the kingdom had never been well since the king put mean creatures like thee in the government.' Quoted in Emmison, *Tudor Secretary*, p. 64.

8

PLACE AND PROFIT:
THE EXPLOITATION OF OFFICE

I wulde rathere geve you £40 than hym a pennie who nevar dyd me
anie gud.   ARTHUR PLANTAGENET, Lord Lisle to Sir Ralph Sadler

Political ambition certainly played a part in the making of Sadler's
fortunes, but it was the exploitation of office that highlighted Sir
Ralph's rise within Cromwell's affinity. So far we have dealt with
the details of successive phases of Sadler's rise to a prominent role in
Henrician public life. Now we must turn to those elements that perhaps
loomed largest in Sadler's mind: the enjoyment and advantage inherent in
the place patronage had secured for him or any other politician of the era.

Since Henry VIII lacked both a mature, well-ordered bureaucracy
and political parties, the stability which he desired in government
depended in the final analysis upon his ability to reward and advance
his agents. Place and profit thus helped secure for the monarchy the
support of the politically powerful classes. By the distribution of offices
and of the real wealth and prestige implicit in place, the king preserved
and extended a system of governance whose roots lay in the medieval
past. The undoubted end of the system was to win the confidence of a
rather small number of aristocrats and professional people, for without
their aid civil government was truly impossible. Hence, Tudor men
recognised that the scramble for the rewards of office was an honourable
part of public life, as Thomas Wyatt implied in urging the king 'to
butter the rook's nest' in order to mitigate the unrest resulting from the
monastic dissolution of 1536.[1] Such thoughts as those of Wyatt or his
contemporary Sir Richard Grenville, father to the great Elizabethan
sea-dog, who told Cromwell that his purchases of monastic lands were
designed to insure the opinions of his heirs in religious matters, are read
erroneously as councils of cynicism.[2] They simply expressed the Tudor

[1] Lloyd, *The Worthies and States-men of England*, 1, 89.
[2] Alfred Leslie Rowse, *Sir Richard Grenville*, p. 35, quoted in Christopher Hill, *Puritanism and Revolution* (London: Warburg and Secker, 1958), p. 45.

truth that a man was known by his friends and that friendship was measured in material terms as well as in the finer stuff of inner loyalties. That was the meaning of Sir William Cecil, when in Elizabeth's time he admonished his sovereign to gratify the nobility and the great magnates and other chief men: 'binde them fast to you...whereby you shall have all men of value in your realm to depend on yourself only'.[1] Cecil's advice passed for an axiom in Tudor political circles.

Wyatt, Grenville and Cecil all made reference to a special feature of the middle part of the Tudor régime. The years from about 1540 until 1560 witnessed an unprecedented expansion in the number and variety of rewards open to those loyal to the dynasty. In addition to the traditional medieval avenues of patronage Cromwell's revolution of the 1530s had placed at the disposal of the Crown vast amounts of land and other church possessions. The rising politician of the mid-sixteenth century found himself squarely in the path of a torrent of opportunity, a circumstance which points up the burden of this chapter, which is to discover how well Sadler moved with that current. To do so, we will examine certain problems attendant on office-holding. The chief focal point here will be the process whereby office was exploited for private profit, which is to say that we shall study the conversion of patronage into profit.

We must develop the inquiry within the framework of certain basic questions, or, rather, lines of investigation. Perplexity as to what Sadler did as an office-holder must be resolved first of all. His conditions of office, his routine labour and a number of totally commonplace details need some clarification if we are to understand the relationship between place and profit. All things hinge on profit and the profit-making potential of any position; therefore we also must obtain some indication of how a plurality of offices could be managed and exploited by a single official. Furthermore, the problem of sinecurism and deputation of duties is such a complex, as well as a necessary, line of inquiry if we are to understand Sadler's success, that we must pay special attention to the personalities involved in Sir Ralph's manipulations. The details of his career, then, might well throw some light on political-administrative techniques in general in the sixteenth century.

Once we have firmly in mind the details of Sadler's operation of the

[1] Quoted by MacCaffery in *Elizabethan Government and Society*, p. 98.

various offices entrusted to him we will be able to comprehend the basic issues of profit and power and their effect on Sir Ralph. From the latter viewpoint, Sadler's real problems began where the routine business ended. Although possession and efficient operation were pre-requisites of exploitation, which was all the more necessary in considera-tion of the inadequate or non-existent Crown fees and salaries, it was the technique of supplementing one's income that each incumbent sought to refine in a variety of ways. Beyond semi-official perquisites and allowances, either in cash or kind, there were possibilities that might well help build a modest fortune.[1]

These sources of profit were varied. The most important of them was that stemming from the sale of services to the public. The practice of Tudor administration condoned the exaction of sums beyond the fixed fees charged for the performance of even the most routine tasks. A shrewd enough or bold enough man could easily procure a tremen-dous addition to his ordinary income in this way. The flow of gratuities, favours and *douceurs*, in striking contrast to the 'rents' paid by the Crown in the way of a salary or annuity, were ample and extra-legal, although not illegal. Closely connected with this avenue of exploitation lay another; a host of satellites swarmed about the holder of high office, a mass of petty functionaries, clerks, ushers, messengers and others, as well as merchants eagerly seeking contracts and other benefits from office-holding friends—all anxious to tap the resources of the monarchy by courting the favour of the bureaucrat. Beyond the collection of fees, gratuities, *douceurs* for services and the sums realised by the peddling of influence, there was yet another potential source of great profit for the placeman: he might sell his office and thus make an extraordinary capital gain in an obscure but vital market which is as yet inadequately investigated.[2]

No mention has been made of the profits to be made by the official who participated in the supposedly booming land market of the mid-century, an obvious defect in any scheme that pretends to completeness in the matter of the profit-making potential of an official career and an important one, if we can judge importance from the amount of ink

---

[1] Quoted by MacCaffery in *Elizabethan Government and Society*, p. 104.

[2] There is nothing novel about this type of analysis. It represents the methods and problems suggested by numerous workers in the field of administrative and social history, among whom Pollard, Namier, Richardson, Elton, Aylmer and Neale stand out.

spilt in the 'storm over the gentry' in recent years. Here it can only be said that the problem of the relationship between office and landholding is reserved for a separate chapter for two reasons: Sadler's activities in the land market were important enough to deserve distinct treatment; that treatment requires a different set of questions from the one employed here. For those reasons, buttressed by the insight of Professor Trevor-Roper, who once remarked the rising gentry 'were almost without exception...office holders' in the first place,[1] we shall deal with first things first.

In the struggle for advancement the first goal was a patent of office setting forth the conditions and other particulars of the grant of place. A life grant was naturally the most treasured tenure, but most major offices were given *durante bene placito*. That was true of the secretaryship of state which Sadler enjoyed from 1540–3, a fact which explains the ease with which he was dismissed.[2] Since no patent was issued for the secretaryship during the sixteenth century, it was the least certain of Sadler's many appointments. As keeper of the hanaper in chancery Sadler had a life tenure in survivorship with Thomas Cromwell from 1535 to 1540.[3] Until well into Elizabeth's reign he held that office in co-tenancy with John Hales, his friend and agent co-opted after a period in which Sadler enjoyed the office alone as a consequence of Cromwell's death in 1540.[4] But in 1572 Hales died. Sadler then received a new co-keeper, his son Henry, with whom he held the place until his own death in 1587.[5] Thus this tenancy for life was in fact just that, since Sadler held the office from 1535 to 1587.[6] It is also worth noting that Henry Sadler not only inherited the position from his father but also held it until 1604, at which time he sold it for cash.[7]

---

[1] Hugh Trevor-Roper, *The Gentry 1540–1640* (Cambridge: For the Economic History Society Supplement no. 1, 1953), p. 10.

[2] *SP*, II, 623–4.

[3] PRO, C 66/700 pt. I, m. 29, 26 July 1540. As early as 24 Apr. 1535 Sadler and Cromwell were co-keepers, according to a copy of the grant enrolled in a precedent book in PRO, C 193/2, fos. 61a–64b. Accounts beginning in September 1535 also name both men: E 101/222/8 ff.

[4] See below for the particulars of the Hales-Sadler tenancy. The only official record of that co-keepership is the marginal gloss found in the patent rolls mentioned in n. 8 above; dated 24 Oct. 1545, the entry states that Sadler vacated the office and received it back in co-tenancy with Hales. Full particulars of the grant are supplied only by the entry in the hanaper accounts for 1547 (E 101/224/6/1).

[5] PRO, Index Volume 17411, fo. 36b.

[6] PCC Register 23 Spenser; PRO, C 142/215/259, Sadler's *inquisitio post mortem*.

[7] PRO, E 101, subsection 'Hanaper Accounts' and E 351, subsection 'Declared Accounts' each testify to Henry Sadler's long tenancy.

Life grants could, however, be terminated while the grantee was still alive. Although Sir Ralph had received a life grant of the mastership of the great wardrobe in 1543, he was forced to vacate the office upon the death of Edward VI.[1] He was similarly ejected from a number of other, less important offices under Mary Tudor, doubtless because his religious preferences proved unacceptable to his Catholic queen.[2] The other side of the coin of ejectment was reversionary rights: Sadler long held the reversion to a number of places in the central administration before he actually received the tenancy itself.[3] The accidents of politics and longevity thus affected his interest directly.

Once seised of any position, Sadler had to assume the full responsibility for getting the routine work done. Little is known about how this was handled in the case of minor offices, especially the positions in the land revenue system of the court of Augmentations. But for the central administration, with regard both to chancery and household places, the quantity and quality of the evidence is such that something can be said about Sadler's direction of the routine work.

From a variety of sources Sadler's working day can be reconstructed. Three of his posts were of a household nature; they were the secretaryship, the mastership of the great wardrobe and the position of gentleman of the king's chamber, the last a post of great dignity but little actual work. The incumbent of any of these offices normally lived within the verge of court and was obliged to take his meals with the household, breakfast being served at 10 a.m. and supper at 5 p.m.[4] According to Sadler's own testimony, he rarely slept past 4 a.m. while he resided at court.[5] In such circumstances, in order to fortify himself for the long day, he took a light repast upon arising and then the midmorning meal assumed gargantuan proportions, especially on the weekdays and Sundays devoted to council business.[6] Since we know

[1] Sadler's patent of appointment was not enrolled, but notice of the grant dated 24 Apr. 1543 is found in BM Stowe MSS. 571, fos. 6 and 17, as well as in PRO, E 351/3025–6. For local revenue positions and accounts see Hackney Public Library, London, Thyssen MSS. Y 235; BM Losely MSS. 838; PRO, E 101/426/14, 17 and Folger Shakespeare Library, Losely MSS. L.b. nos. 22, 82 478, 489, 492–4.

[2] PRO, E 403/2244–5; E 315/235, fos. 41*b*–43*a*; C 66/692 pt. 7, m. 20; BM Stowe MSS. 571, fo. 17 and various *VCH* indices.

[3] The offices were those of warden of St Buriana the Virgin, Cornwall, and the notaryship in chancery. For these places see PRO, C 66/668 pt. 1, m. 7 and C 66/664 pt. 1, m. 26. The reversion of the chancery office appears in *L & P*, VII, 601.

[4] BM Add. MSS. 45716, fos. 39*a* and 11*a*.   [5] BM Sloane MSS. 1523, fos. 29*a*–*b*.

[6] Gladish, *The Tudor Privy Council*, pp. 53–4.

that the council regularly met on Tuesday, Thursday and Saturday, sitting from 8 to 10 a.m. and also intermittently in the afternoons, we can assume that the regular business of offices such as the mastership had to be attended to on the other weekdays. Considering the press of his secretarial labours, we can easily understand Sir Ralph's complaint that he scarcely went to bed one day in seven before midnight, only to arise wearily with the light of candles in the pre-dawn hours.[1]

The rigour of the régime had its compensations. In return for long days spent in reading dispatches and writing accounts and memoranda, Sadler drew comfort from the fact that he was the king's man. His offices were spread throughout the city of London. Decked out in the green and white of the Tudor livery, or splendidly robed for some ceremonial occasion, he travelled his route from the chancery rooms in Holborn to those of the signet office in Whitehall, or even to the western reaches of the city, toward the wardrobe.[2] Since the pressure of work often did not allow for much commuting and time wasted in such bureaucratic progresses, Sadler fell back on the expedient of keeping living quarters at Hackney, Hampton Court, Westminster and Whitehall, each with a stable of good horses attached.[3] Costly though such practices were, they enabled him to save time, thereby increasing his capacity for work, which was his stock in trade.

This efficiency made profits possible and necessary as well. For the expenses incurred were vital to the mastery of the merely routine business, a truth the more easily comprehended by virtue of a close look at a group of offices mastered by Sadler in the early 1540s. The positions in question are the notaryship in chancery, the hanaper clerkship and the mastership of the great wardrobe. In order to recoup the outlay of money Sadler had to serve with maximum efficiency; to do that, he fell back on the practice of employing deputies in order to solve the problems occasioned by his pluralism.

The three positions had once all been great posts. In the 1540s they were important clerkships and nothing more, each with its routine concerned with the details of receiving and spending a part of the royal income. Each was a part of the administrative machinery of the Tudor

---

[1] We know this from Sadler's habit of dating his letters by the hour as well as the day.

[2] Aylmer, *The King's Servants*, pp. 150–3.

[3] BM Add. MSS. 45716, fos. 5*a* (court) and 28*a* (Hackney); see also *L & P*, xxi, ii, 528, Sadler to Mr Hanby (Westminster and Whitehall), 11 Dec. 1546.

monarchy which did not always make nice distinctions between fiscal, legal and other types of work. Although the notary in chancery was by origin primarily a legal position, by the sixteenth century its legal powers of a judicial sort had atrophied and matters of finance dominated the notary's schedule.[1] The hanaper had always been the treasury for the entire chancery.[2] The great wardrobe had been and still was a spending department of the household.[3] Together these offices demanded of their incumbent a certain skill in handling financial matters, happily for Sadler, just the sort of skill he had acquired during his long years of service to Cromwell.

A close look at the notaryship tells us little about the specific duties performed by Sadler, since surviving chancery records give little indication of Sadler's role in that office, beyond merely confirming his tenure.[4] We cannot say that the position was a sinecure, however, although Maxwell-Lyte was correct in his assertion that the notaryship had declined sharply from its past greatness, from a time when the notary was a judge in the chancellor's court.[5] We know also that Sadler was no trained lawyer, which raises the suspicion that his appointment in 1534 was part of the process by which administrative cares came to completely overshadow judicial concerns, since his predecessor, William Throgmorton, was a doctor of civil law.[6] But there was still routine administrative work to be done, especially the registration of writings addressed to the chancellor, work much like that done by the notaries of king's bench or common pleas, who registered writs, with this difference: chancery notaries held less remunerative posts than did their common law court counterparts.[7] All of this evidence points to one conclusion: considering Sadler's political status and his conditions of service to Henry VIII, his routine work at the chancery must have been attended to by a deputy.

[1] Henry Maxwell-Lyte, *Notes on the History and Use of the Great Seal* (London: HMSO, 1926), pp. 274–6.
[2] Richardson, *Tudor Chamber Administration*, pp. 36 and 108; see also Elton, *The Tudor Revolution in Government*, pp. 105–6.
[3] Aylmer, *The King's Servants*, pp. 26–30.
[4] PRO, E 101/222/10, m. 3r for Sadler's claim to office; PRO Index Volume 17411, fo. 81a, states that on 26 Dec. 1561 Raylton became co-keeper; *ibid.* fo. 82a notes Kempe succeeding him upon his (Raylton's) death on 7 Nov. 1572.
[5] Maxwell-Lyte, *Notes*, p. 275 (and n. 2).
[6] PRO, C 66/664 pt. 1, m. 26a; see also SP 1/83, fo. 209a.
[7] Aylmer, *The King's Servants*, pp. 117, 213–14.

Place and Profit: Exploitation of Office

The material relevant to the wardrobe and hanaper clerkships amply supports this surmise about Sadler's exercise of authority in clerkships of the middling rank. Administrative documents created in the course of daily work in each of those offices provide a view of that work totally uncoloured by political or other considerations in situations where profit-making was a distinct possibility.

The mastership of the wardrobe was originally a position of high trust. In the medieval period it had been a quasi-secretarial office within the household. By the 1540s, however, it had lost its great place in the governance of the kingdom and was merely a convenient office with which to endow a trusted councillor.[1] The duties were those common to any department handling large sums of money and substantial stores of materials. Keeping accounts and auditing those of subordinates; taking and checking inventories; drafting, revising and letting contracts; even the preparing of legal instruments, were all part of the charge of the master.[2] Nominally, he also supervised the work of the sixty or so craftsmen and women employed in making hangings and garments and other gorgeous effects for the palace and the royal retinue. In addition, the master was also the paymaster for the royal stables![3]

Surviving accounts and other documents indicate that Sadler was a careful custodian of his trust. Specimens of account books[4] and inventories in his own hand exist,[5] as well as a large number of warrants made by Sadler or his agents.[6] His records of monies assigned by tallies were always precise and neatly drawn.[7] He also kept careful notes on all wardrobe properties in London and the rents accruing from them.[8] He had a sharp eye for the ordinary details of the craft aspect of the wardrobe, or else he was simply practising some petty patronage, for he employed men and women known to him in their capacity as his tenants on wardrobe business.[9]

[1] Tout, *Chapters*, I, 21.
[2] Aylmer, *The King's Servants*, p. 155.
[3] *Ibid.* p. 30, for the household below stairs.
[4] PRO, E 101/423/9–11; E 101/426/14; E 351/3025–6.
[5] BM Harleian MSS. 1419, pts. A and B.
[6] See the citations in n. 4 above as well as: BM Harleian MSS. 304, fo. 139 and 6074, fo. 40*b*; Add. MSS. 11320, fo. 89*b*.
[7] PRO, E 101/423/10, fos. 9*a*–10*b*; E 101/426/14, fo. 79*b*.
[8] PRO, E 101/423/10, fo. 2*a*; E 101/426/14, fo. 3*a*.
[9] The fact that these men were Sadler's tenants is an inference from two lists, the first a wardrobe list (PRO, E 101/423/10, fo. 78*b*) and the second a Sadler rental (BM Add. MSS. 35824).

Certain extraordinary functions were attended to by the master himself. During the French war in 1544 Sadler accounted for monies and supplies earmarked for the war effort in the great wardrobe.[1] He also handled there some naval expenditures.[2] It is likely that these accounts are vestiges of the days when the wardrobe was a central armoury. But it may simply be the case that Sadler's work as treasurer for the Scottish war of the same period brought about blurring of normal administrative lines. Whatever the case, Sir Ralph was meticulous in his accounting in such matters.

In order to accomplish all of the work of the mastership, Sadler relied on a small coterie of officers with long years of experience at the wardrobe. The chief clerk, under-clerks, the auditor, chief cutter, porter and collector were men left over from the régime of Andrew, Lord Windsor,[3] a clear implication being that there was a limit on Sadler's ability to use such an office for patronage purposes. Such men were the professional core of the wardrobe, while the dozens of craftsmen might come and go and were of no importance in the administration of the office.[4] The fact that Sadler carried over Windsor's men is of interest in regard to the reputation for inefficiency and wastefulness, corrupt procurement and fraud, sinecurism and other practices of a suspicious kind enjoyed by the household spending departments of the sixteenth and seventeenth centuries.[5] It is difficult to say whether Sadler's use of these men contributed to the petty evils and larger malpractices; it is even more difficult to interpret the fact that Sadler introduced into wardrobe affairs men from his own rent rolls, to say nothing of the fact that he frequently made contracts with clothiers in partnership with his brother John Sadler. The available evidence is inconclusive on the issue of how Sadler's handling of wardrobe patronage affected the office's efficiency and honesty. His use of men known to him may well have been intended to correct long-standing abuses; it may also have contributed to poor administration.[6]

A similar question of reform and petty corruption enters at another level with regard to the wardrobe. Sadler insinuated some trusted agents of his own into the routine operation of the department. When he

---

[1] PRO, E 101/423/9.
[2] PRO, E 101/423/10, fo. 78a.
[3] PRO, E 351/3025, fos. 89a–b.
[4] *Ibid.*
[5] Aylmer, *The King's Servants*, pp. 31 and 42.
[6] PRO, E 101/423/10, an enrolled account of the items supplied by John Sadler and his partners.

could not serve in person, John Hales, Gregory Raylton and Thomas Cotton, his dependents and friends, served as his deputies.[1] Since the same names occur in other capacities, in connection with the hanaper, for example, the question of pluralism and patronage becomes more complex, especially with regard to the problem of the value of these men who stood outside the formal machinery of the offices in question.

The hanaper office was more important to Sadler than the mastership of wardrobe from some points of view, although considerably less lucrative. On the administrative side of chancery the keeper of the hanaper was next to the chancellor in dignity. He was directly involved in the sealing process and the delivery of instruments under the great seal, for as treasurer of chancery he collected the fees payable to the chancery staff for their exercise of the office of sealing and writing to the seal. The office at Westminster was an ancient one and had a well-established routine, in which the keeper had an important place. Although he was not an officer with much in the way of power in government or initiative, he held a place of trust and some influence on the whole matter of expediting grants and the patronage machinery.[2]

Just as was the case with the wardrobe, the hanaper brought with it a small staff of permanent officials a cut or two above the level of menials.[3] Furthermore, the keeper of necessity had close working relationships with the members of the larger secretariat composed of the privy seal and signet staffs. For that reason alone Sadler, while he was also secretary of state, was in an exceptionally good position to exploit the relationship of the various sealing departments. To do so he required efficient operation in all routine matters, a detail the more urgent when we consider his own frequent and prolonged trips abroad during the period of his active pluralism. Even while he was at work in England, his onerous council duties and his work on special commissions in financial matters, in which field he had special skill and was prominently employed during the anxious days of the French wars of the 1540s,[4] made it imperative to secure faithful deputies in his major clerkships.

[1] See below for the chancery and wardrobe activities.
[2] Elton, *The Tudor Revolution in Government*, pp. 99–100 and 105–6, as well as the references cited there.
[3] PRO, E 101/222–5, a group of related hanaper accounts.
[4] For evidence on Sadler's role in routine financial administration see *L & P*, XIX, i, 147(26), 267; XX, i, 125(9); XX, ii, 1,067, 1,068(28); XXI, i, 91, 211, 375, 471, 1,166, 1,383 and 1,537. See also Richardson, *The History of the Court of Augmentations*, pp. 112–13: in commenting on Sadler's

It is for this reason that we must once again turn to the matter of how the lay pluralist managed the details of administration while also attending to great matters of state, the Howard inquiries of 1541, for example, or the negotiations with the Habsburgs in 1542–3. Herein lay the importance of deputation in Tudor administration. Under-clerks were a quite normal part of the established machinery and were quite distinct from co-keepers although both categories of men were internally related to the office in question.[1] Again, neither the existence of the one category nor of the other is an evidence of sinecurism, since few posts were without functional responsibilities. The most that can be said is that the archaic character of some household institutions often made the routine work of such an office irrelevant to the business of daily administration in any immediately practical sense. Why, then, we may fairly ask, did Sadler employ his own dependents as deputies superimposed on the already cumbersome structure of proliferating household officers?

The answer to that question emerges readily enough from a consideration of the evidence found in wardrobe and hanaper records of the 1540s, especially the hanaper documents, which are notable in this respect.[2] About one-half of all surviving early modern hanaper accounts and subsidiary documents date from Sadler's hold on that office.[3] Yet from 1537 to 1587 there is no evidence to prove that Sir Ralph did the work of the keepership in person. As early as 1536 John Judde and Richard Snowe did the work.[4] In earlier accounts filed in Sadler's name the efficient agent was John Pexsall,[5] who was apparently a clerk of the Crown in chancery, close to the hanaper, but with no hanaper office whatsoever.[6] In a similar manner, Sadler was accountable for the accuracy of the particulars of all accounts in 1537,[7] but Judde, styled

---

vital role in late Henrician finance and efforts at retrenchment, Professor Richardson attributes Sadler's place in that endeavour to experience in war finance, an awareness of the problems inherent in the expansion of the revenue administration and a knowledge of the Cromwellian system, while condemning his lack of zeal for thorough-going overall reforms. Sadler was of course, as Richardson realised, necessarily cautious, given the conditions of politics in the 1540s.

[1] Aylmer, *The King's Servants*, p. 127. In the fifteenth century Sir John Fortescue commented on pluralism and performance by deputy. *The Governance of England*, pp. 150–3.

[2] *Elizabethan Government and Society*, p. 105.

[3] PRO, E 101/221–6, esp. 222/8 and 226/13.

[4] PRO, E 101/222/15, nos. 1–6.

[5] PRO, E 101/222/8, m. 25; Pexsall also drafted 222/211.

[6] PRO, E 403/2444, fo. 13a.

[7] PRO, E 101/222/10, m. 1a.

subclericus, actually filed and endorsed the books.[1] From 1537–41 Snowe, also called *subclericus*, received an official allowance towards robes used in the execution of his office.[2] But during all that time Sadler did not name a deputy despite the fact that his patent of office permitted him to use such a person.[3] It was in 1541 that he finally appointed Snowe to that position,[4] a post in which Snowe remained active until 1547, although he was eclipsed in office by John Hales of Coventry after 1543.

The importance of Hales at the hanaper after 1543 is a matter of some interest. His name first cropped up in 1540, when he endorsed some warrants in Sadler's name.[5] His appearance in the hanaper was no doubt due to his old friendship with Sadler, the two having met when both were dependents of Cromwell. As early as 1538 Hales relied on Sadler's influence to press a suit for some lands near Coventry.[6] In 1539 and again in 1540 Hales served Sadler as a general legal agent in certain business transactions involving lands in London.[7] High in Sir Ralph's favour and trust, Hales slowly began to take over the direction of hanaper routine. Between 1542 and 1545 he was styled 'clerke' or 'deputie', although in fact he was legally neither.[8] Then, on 24 October 1545, he was named co-tenant with Sadler, thus securing official recognition of the fact that he did the hanaper work.[9] Despite this change, some writers continued to refer to Hales as *subclericus* as late as November 1545, either because they lacked precise information or perhaps because the titles were popularly thought to be of equal dignity.[10] At any rate by 1547 Hales did all of the routine work of the keeper, and writers forced to correspond with the keeper noted him alone, dropping any mention of Sadler in their address.[11] In so far as the working of the office appeared to other men in government, Sadler had dropped from sight.[12]

---

[1] PRO, E 101/222/10, m. 4b.　　　　[2] PRO, E 101/222/15; 223/2, 5, 6 and 7.

[3] PRO, E 101/223/2, m. 2b.　　　　[4] PRO, E 101/223/8, m. 3b.

[5] PRO, E 101/223/3, a bundle of 91 parchment slips, chiefly copies of warrants, over a score of which are endorsed '*per me* Jo. Hales'.

[6] PRO, SP 7/1, fo. 40, Sadler to Wriothesley, undated; see also 1/138, fo. 73, Hales to Hanby, undated.

[7] PRO, E 303/17/376; E 326/B 5,608; E 318/967.

[8] Hales is first styled deputy in PRO, E 101/223/13, m. 2a, and clerk in 223/14, no. 1. Sadler referred to him as 'mi deputie' in E 101/224/5.

[9] PRO, C 66/700, pt. 8, m. 29a; E 101/224/5.　　　　[10] PRO, E 101/224/2.

[11] PRO, E 101/224/3, a file of over 500 subsidiary documents.

[12] PRO, E 405/115, m. 8b, a teller's receipt roll of 1547, recording a quittance issued to Hales 'clericus hanaperii'.

The interesting facts of Hales's rise are paralleled by those of his domination of the hanaper. Although he continued to use Snowe and other men whose careers in the office dated back to Cromwell's tenure, Hales slowly but steadily came to rely on Sadler's dependents to do routine work. On a number of occasions Gregory Raylton[1] and Thomas Cotton[2] appear as hanaper agents. The former was a long-time friend and servant of Sadler and was his 'inwarde man' during the trying days of Sadler's secretaryship and the Scottish mission of 1543–5.[3] Cotton was clearly also an old Sadler acquaintance, although his connection with Sadler is somewhat obscure.[4]

The significance of this development, however, is truly seen only in connection with the fact that the same group of men served Sadler in a similar way in other offices. Hales was especially ubiquitous as Sadler's general agent. While Sir Ralph was in the North as treasurer of the Scottish war in 1544 he deputed Hales to handle financial matters related to the war effort in London.[5] Furthermore, although Hales never enjoyed an official position in the wardrobe, accounts of that department reveal that he did much of the routine work there.[6] On nearly every page of the accounts and inventories covering the period 1543–7 we find the evidence of Hales acting for Sadler. He received money,[7] disbursed sums on contracts completed,[8] authorised payments on warrants dormant[9] and attested the accuracy of accounts related to monies assigned by tallies.[10] Hales did the work, although the official clerk-deputy was Richard Stoughton,[11] who had the aid of two under-clerks, of whom Thomas Cotton was one.[12] Hales's primacy was further

[1] PRO, E 101/223/15, nos. 7–21.   [2] PRO, E 101/224/6, m. 2a and 224/7, m. 1b.

[3] Raylton had a sound though unspectacular career. Under Sadler's patronage he rose to be household messenger (BM Add. MSS. 35824, fo. 37b), signet clerk (PRO, Index Volume 17411, fo. 10b and SP 1/200, fo. 129a), and, finally, clerk of the council (PRO, E 179/69/63, m. 1a).

[4] Cotton was apparently a member of Sadler's entourage after Cromwell's death (BM Add. MSS. 38136, fo. 66) and like Hales and Raylton steadily advanced in office. He became in succession Hales' deputy at the hanaper (*ibid.* fos. 26b–28b), clerk of Star Chamber (PRO, Index Volume 17411, fo. 10a), and a gentleman of the queen's household in 1563 (PRO, E 179/69/82, m. 9a).

[5] PRO, SP 1/187, fo. 23; 183, fos. 136, 195–6 and 204; E 351/211, fo. 13; and Hatfield House, Salisbury MSS. 231, no. 50, Privy Council to Hertford, 8 March 1544.

[6] All accounts give full lists of officers; Hales is never mentioned.

[7] PRO, E 101/423/10, fos. 82a–b.   [8] PRO, E 351/3025, fo. 2a.

[9] PRO, E 101/423/9, *passim*.   [10] PRO, E 101/423/10, fo. 1b.

[11] PRO, E 101/423/10, fo. 77a.

[12] PRO, E 351/3025, fos. 89b–90a; the other under-clerk was Andrew Walker.

attested by Cotton himself.[1] His testimony is buttressed by the fact that Hales was able to provide his brother Stephen with a clerk's position at the wardrobe shortly after his own first appearance there.[2] Despite this emphasis on Hales's power, a useful reminder of his dependence on Sadler was issued when Sir Ralph had his secretary John Somers supervise some wardrobe business.[3]

Hales was in reality simply the chief agent among a number of men to whom Sadler entrusted the routine work of his various offices. Since the persons involved were often the same, it is not at all surprising to find a certain overlap of documents from the several offices. Although the Crown often drew on the hanaper and wardrobe for funds in emergencies[4] and normally paid employees of the various offices out of cash on hand by virtue of warrants dormant, it was doubtlessly due to Sadler's pluralism that defalcations in wardrobe books occur for the salary of chancery officers.[5] The same can be said of the occurrence of hanaper writs and subsidiary documents in large numbers among wardrobe warrants for the 1540s.[6] What is more difficult to decide is whether the overlap confused or clarified the operation of the offices in question. Beyond a doubt, however, is the fact that the administration of two distinct departments, one still a household office and the other long since 'out of court', were interdependent due to Sadler's pluralism.

Another issue that suggests itself at this point is that of the overlap and its effect on the exploitation of the revenue potential of the offices in question. We know that the maximal exploitation of offices added handsomely to salaries, rents and other perquisites. But we have no hard data which enabled us to claim that Sadler intended to use the same agents in his various affairs in order to maximize administrative profits. What we do know is that such profits existed and that they were of several types. Annuities were of two basic kinds. There were *ad hoc*

[1] PRO, E 315/103, fo. 147b.

[2] PRO, E 101/423/11, fos. 27a and 73b.

[3] PRO, E 101/426/14, nos. 1–14, wardrobe warrants signed by Somers, who rose to be a signet clerk and a knight (E 179/69/93, fo. 3).

[4] PRO, E 101/222/11–15; 223/3, 13 and 14; 224/6, 7 and 12; 423/11 and BM Add. MSS. 5756, fos. 15, 60, 61–79, for warrants authorising payments made by Sadler to Brian Tuke, treasurer of the chamber, duplicates of which were made for Sadler's petitions of allowance upon defalcations.

[5] A warrant dormant was a standing authority to pay out recurring expenses. Payment was in theory made only upon the presentation of a petition supported by evidence of defalcation.

[6] PRO, E 101/426/14, no. 1.

rewards bearing that name, usually given for work well done. In the case of land revenue positions salaries were customarily paid in the form of small rents or annuities arising from the office in question. Thus salary, rent and annuity might all refer to the guaranteed yield of an office exclusive of the fruits of exploitation based on the fee system, the payment of gratuities or the yield of perquisites in kind. Before discussing any other forms of income, a survey of Sadler's profit from these sources so far mentioned is in order.

From a very early time in his career Sadler received extraordinary annuities for services rendered either to Cromwell or to the king. If we take 1540 as the peak year, the year in which Sadler held the maximum number of such grants, we find that they were worth £48. 13s. 4d. That sum was derived from the following sources: a £2 annuity given him in 1533 by the Crown;[1] a £6 rent given by the dean of Westminster in 1534;[2] a £20 reward for faithful service granted by Henry VIII in 1536;[3] and another £20 annuity from the Crown, given in 1540 but made retroactive to 1537.[4] This steady income of nearly £50 p.a. was supplemented by numerous grants of an occasional kind, the best example being the £200 bequest in the king's will in 1547.[5] Other examples are found in the remembrance books kept by Cromwell, which often carried notes to the effect that Sadler was 'to be held in the kinges most benigne remembraunce' on this or that occasion.[6]

For the same period of time the salaries or rents arising from a number of minor offices within the province of the court of Augmentations paid a substantial income, although the individual amounts were small. Despite the fact that no complete list of such offices held by Sadler exists, a compilation of income from minor positions in land administration shows that such posts were lucrative.[7] Over £40 p.a. came in

[1] The overlap in accounting is also explicable in the following manner: despite the reforms described by Richardson and Elton, the hanaper was still allowed to account either to the wardrobe or to the exchequer. In 1543 it is conceivable that pluralism increased corruption.

[2] *L & P*, VI, 1,624.

[3] Westminster Abbey Muniments Room, Deeds Register II, fo. 297, 15 May. Perhaps this should not be counted as income from office.

[4] BM Add. MSS. 38136, fos. 77a–78b, 9 Apr. 1536, 'in consideracione boni et veri et fideli servicii...'.

[5] PRO, E 315/235, fos. 43–4.

[6] *Foedera*, XV, 110, prints the will; *ad hoc* sums ranging from £5 to £40 are mentioned in *L & P*, XIV, ii, 782; VI, 1,508 and VIII, 653.

[7] BM Cotton MSS. Titus B1, fos. 470, 499 and 501.

from some dozen stewardships,[1] fourteen bailiwicks on royal manors,[2] four appointments as park keeper on royal estates,[3] revenue farmer of Shacklewood manor[4] and the constableship of Hertford castle, which carried the additional income owing the custodian of the manorial rolls there.[5] Of course there was profit to be had in all of these manorial offices from the processes of local administration and justice, as well as from the power and prestige of patronage in the localities. Unfortunately, little evidence of that kind has survived with reference to Sadler.

From this sprinkling of annuities and rents about £90 p.a. found its way to Sadler's pockets. But this figure underestimates the worth of these offices by virtue of the fact of our ignorance of other profit-making aspects of the positions in question. As the sequel will demonstrate, such income was of no little consequence when balanced against the money coming in from normal income in some quite major offices.

Of course official fees from major offices were important. Peck reported that the mastership of the wardrobe was worth £100 p.a. in salary and £15 in livery. He also valued the hanaper fees at £43. 13s. 4d., with an annuity of £40 beyond the 'rent' of that office.[6] He gave no specific time during which those figures pertained, but they are partially confirmed by material in Sadler's accounts. The wardrobe yielded £115 p.a.[7] At the hanaper the story was a little different. Officially,

[1] PRO, SP 1/103, fos. 234 and 270; C 66/692, pt. 2, m. 20a; E 315/235, fos. 41a–43b; 315/391, fo. 73a; BM Royal MSS. 7F XIV, fo. 79b.

[2] Beyond the notice of sources in the above note see also *VCH Staffordshire*, v, 26; *VCH Surrey*, III, 279, and BM Losely MSS. 838. The Folger Shakespeare Library, Losely MSS. L.b. 478 and 492–4 contain accounts showing the steward's income at several manors held by Sadler supporting this estimate.

[3] For the keeperships and parkerships see *VE*, III, 130; *L & P*, XIV, ii, 780 (42) and XVI, 1,500. See also PRO, E 315/235, fos. 41b–42a, where *per diem* expenses allowed for the posts as Nonesuch Manor are supplied. Folger Shakespeare Library, Losely MSS. 478, fo. 3, a schedule of fees for the seneschalships and parkers' offices at Nonesuch, Bansted, Walton and other Surrey manors, showing *per diem* allowances of 2d., as well as the total fees of £24. 6s. 8d. for all posts combined. This did not represent clear profit, since deputies charged with holding the courts, collecting the rents and caring for the properties were paid a total of better than £21, leaving only £2. 9s. 4d. clear (Losely MSS. 22). The only full schedule offered is in BM Royal MSS. 7F XIV, fo. 79b, for Hitchin Hundred and Ansty, Herts.

[4] Hackney Public Library, Thyssen MSS. Y 235, Sadler's accounts.

[5] PRO, DL 42/23/48, endorsed in a later hand '1547'. This duchy of Lancaster account is interesting in the light of the patronage opportunities reaped by Sadler many years afterwards, as chancellor of the duchy. An interesting example of such patronage with regard to lands administered by the duchy is that portrayed in Folger Shakespeare Library, Losely MSS. L.b. 512–15, Sadler to Sir William More, various dates.

[6] Francis Peck, *Desiderata Curiosa*, 2 vols. (London, 1732–5), I, ii, 12, and I, ii, 1.

[7] PRO, E 101/423/10, fo. 77b; E 351/3025, fos. 89a–89b.

Sadler had a salary or rent of £40, plus riding expenses of 18*d. per diem*, with a livery and 'the accustomed fees charged at the seal' as well.[1] Maxwell-Lyte thought that the riding money given for attending the ambulant chancellor of the early medieval period had by the sixteenth century become a stereotyped payment made for every day in the year.[2] Sadler's declared accounts show, however, that the number of days claimed averaged about 200.[3] Finally, Peck made no mention of the exact robes allowance of £2. 6*s.* 8*d.* p.a.[4] On the basis of the 200-day average claimed for riding money, plus the 6*d. per diem* awarded the keeper for purposes other than riding expenses,[5] the hanaper was worth about £65 p.a. to Sadler exclusive of fees taken for sealing documents,[6] which are discussed elsewhere.

The notaryship in chancery was not nearly so rewarding. The basic income from that post was a salary of £33. 6*s.* 8*d.*[7] There were no other regular fees of the kind paid the hanaper clerk. Nor, so far as I can tell, is there any evidence showing the nature of fees paid by clients for the handling of documents in chancery.

If we consider the two chancery offices together, the total salary level was roughly £100 p.a. Two indentures show that Sadler's half year's income from the combined offices from 30 September 1541 until 30 March 1542 was £47. 3*s.* 6*d.*[8] A year later the yield was £47. 6*s.* 2½*d.*[9] Five years earlier Sadler's annual petition for defalcations toward salary certified his income for the year at £98. 6*s.* 2*d.*[10] No further confirmation of the reliability of the £100 value seems necessary.

Two other salaries remain. Both arose from household positions. In 1537 Sadler had an annual rent of £20 as a gentleman of the chamber.[11] This was subsequently raised to £50 in 1540, ostensibly to support the dignity of his knighthood, according to an entry in a book of household payments.[12] The other office, that of the secretaryship of state, was far

---

[1] PRO, C 66/700, pt. 8, m. 29*a*.   [2] *Notes*, p. 284.

[3] PRO, E 101/222/7 and 11; 223/6, for claims of 192, 194 and 200 days in 1535, 1536 and 1540 respectively.

[4] PRO, E 101/222/11, m. 1*a*.   [5] Elton, *The Tudor Revolution in Government*, p. 101.

[6] Riding money went as low as £13. 11*s.* in 1536 and as high as £20. 16*s.* in 1543.

[7] PRO, E 101/224/2, m. 3*b* and 222/11, m. 1*b*.

[8] PRO, E 101/223/15, no. 7.   [9] *Ibid.* no. 5.

[10] PRO, E 101/222/11, m. 1*a*; BM Add. MSS. 35824, fo. 31*a*, gives a total for 1541 of £85. 6*s.* 10*d*.

[11] PRO, C 66/671, pt. 4, m. 5*a*.

[12] BM Add. MSS. 45716, fo. 13*b*; Lansdowne MSS. 2, fo. 34.

more lucrative in terms of the official salary and guaranteed fees. Leaving aside for the moment the profits of the signet and gratuities arising from Sir Ralph's influence over the process through which the Crown dispensed its favours, the secretary of state's office was lucrative. He was one of the few household officers to have a fixed salary *ex officio*.[1] A neat sum of £100 was granted for the 'supportation' of the many burdens of the position.[2] Of course, collecting one's salary was another matter, as we learn from the fact that in 1543 his salary was three years in arrears.[3]

The total annual average of salaries from 1540 to 1547 was about £350. The fact that Sadler lost the secretaryship in 1543 made no difference in the total expectation from salaries, since the mastership of the great wardrobe, his gift in exchange for the secretarial seals, carried £100 p.a., as we have already noted. Hence, the yield for the sub-period 1543–7 was equal to that for the years 1540–3.

Other sources of a non-recurrent character are more difficult to gauge. Perquisites and allowances were often irregular and impossible to evaluate in terms of annual averages. Grants of livery, bouge of court,[4] and board wages,[5] as well as certain other items, can only be estimated. In the same way, some other casual payments defy exact calculation. Given these disclaimers, we can nevertheless attempt to indicate the range of the annual yield.

Livery and perquisites turn out to be more estimable than one might suspect. Robes and furs were owed Sadler in his capacity as keeper of the hanaper and by virtue of his wardrobe position. The former were worth £15 p.a., while the latter were worth £2. 6s. 8d.[6] The issues were made by virtue of special warrants from the lord chamberlain himself.[7] Extraordinary allowances came Sadler's way for the green and white

---

[1] Aylmer, *The King's Servants*, p. 161.

[2] PRO, E 315/250, fos. 37, 38a and E 323/2B, fo. 52a as well as no. 315/252, fo. 44b.

[3] PRO, E 315/235, fo. 31b and BM Add. MSS. 35823 for the enrolments of the grant and PRO, E 323/2B, fo. 52b, for the arrearages.

[4] For an analysis of the bouge see *The Manuscript of William Dunche*, ed. A. G. W. Murray and E. F. Bosanquet (Exeter: William Pollard, 1914), a household account book giving the full particulars of such matters.

[5] The amount spent by the clerk of the kitchen to feed any member of the household entitled to eat at the king's charge. It seems possible that commutation for money was allowed in the early sixteenth century.

[6] PRO, E 351/3026, fo. 62a, for furs *ad festum natalis*.

[7] All liveries were given under special warrants signed by the lord chamberlain; for examples see PRO, LC 5/38.

Tudor liveries which he was expected to wear *ad festum natalis* and other ceremonial days.[1] Other available perquisites were more valuable. Sadler had rooms at court for which commutation was not allowed, which means that we can place no value on them. But allowances were made for his own personal servants, a thing obviously valuable to a harried diplomat and administrator who had to quarter and feed a numerous body of his own agents in the course of doing the king's work.[2] We can assume that these benefits, along with the 'taking' in kind allowed to the managers of offices handling materials appreciably augmented the profit potential of office.[3] That such practices might encourage jobbery was well known, especially in connection with the wardrobe, which had a terrible reputation in the seventeenth century.[4] Even beyond the 'taking' and servants' allowances, in themselves of great worth, Sadler received specific sums for intelligence work and other current expenses of a singular kind on an *ad hoc* basis.[5]

Such sums, vague as they are, hardly compared to the allotments for bouge allowance which was worth £22. 7s. 11d. until 1542, at which time an increase to £33. 19s. 1d. was made,[6] much to the chagrin of William Dunche, the clerk of the kitchen, who noted the increased cost of the secretary's breakfast, quarters, lights and warming coals.[7] From Dunche's accounts we also learn that Sadler collected bouge for each of his positions concurrently, which meant an additional £22. 7s. 11d. for the wardrobe office in 1543.[8] The total bouge allowance was £43. 11s. for the period 1540–2 and £54. 12s. 1d. from 1543–7. The overall average for 1540–7 was £48. 16s. 6d.

Board allowances dwarfed those for bouge of court. The mess provided for the secretary and his staff was regulated by the household ordinance of 1539,[9] as was also the case for the master of the wardrobe and the grooms of the royal chamber.[10] Morning and evening meals on a lavish scale, often consisting of five or six meat and fowl choices, as

---

[1] PRO, SP 1/161, fos. 147–8.
[2] BM Add. MSS. 45716, fo. 10b. The hanaper also had special rooms.
[3] Aylmer, *The King's Servants*, pp. 172–3.
[4] *Ibid.* p. 42, for the terrible reputation of the wardrobe.
[5] PRO, E 315/255, fos. 85, 105–6; 233/2B, fo. 52b; C 66/730, pt. 9, m. 27b, all provide information about such allowances.
[6] BM Add. MSS. 45716, fo. 5a. [7] *Ibid.* fos. 52a–54a.
[8] *Ibid.* fos. 31a–32b.
[9] *Ibid.* fo. 10b; a single 'mess' served six people.
[10] BM Lansdowne MSS. 2, fo. 34b.

well as eggs, butter, milk, cheese, fish and delicacies from the king's kitchen, were served.[1] There is no clear evidence that commutation was allowed. That would have been a considerable privilege, since the secretary's mess was worth £378. 9s. 3d. p.a. and the wardrobe keeper's allotment was £359. 7s. 6d.[2] An ambiguous reference, however, may well indicate that Sadler took advantage of such a conversion right.[3] Whatever the case, these sums included the allowances made for the secretarial staff, which was taken to include six men in the morning and twelve at the evening meal. Special diet money was also paid to those working under extraordinary commissions, although regular board wages might also be drawn at the same time. Thus, while surveying the state of the royal revenue in 1546 Sadler drew £244.[4] His diet money for the time of the great embassy from 1543–5 was a staggering £1,792. 9s. 4d.[5] We also have to add the special Star Chamber diets given to the attendant lords and councillors in the 1540s.[6] These bring the annual average for diets from 1540–7 to £656. 4s. No wonder Sadler grew more portly with each passing year; even less wonder that the financial machinery groaned and grumbled in 1545!

All sources of income described thus far derived either directly or indirectly from the Crown. The total annual average of such income for the years 1540–7 came to something like £1,000–1,100. That large sum was equalled, if not surpassed, however, by the income arising from the exploitation of the fee system and accompanying gratuities. These opportunities for profit-making were then part of a well-formulated system certainly an outgrowth of the medieval habit of government which regarded office in almost a proprietary sense. Today we should view the same practice as corrupt, although some public officials, such as notaries and lawyers, are still paid fees by clients, despite the fact that technically they are officials of the court. Indeed, for most Tudor office-holders fees and gratuities were more vital than were salaries and perquisites, which were usually small and sometimes non-existent. The fees in question were regulated by custom in part and

---

[1] The sumptuous menus are in Dunche's book, BM Add. MSS. 45716, fos. 39 a–43 b.
[2] BM Add. MSS. 45716, fos. 12 a and 39 a; Lansdowne MSS. 2, fo. 34 b.
[3] *Ibid.* fo. 12 a.
[4] PRO, E 315/254, fo. 80 a and 255/1 B, fo. 85 a.
[5] PRO, E 101/674/2, fo. 10 b; no. 351/211, mm. 13 a–b; C 66/730, pt. 9, m. 27 a.
[6] PRO, E 407/52–5, Star Chamber diets, 1540–3. See BM Add. MSS. 38134 for Star Chamber diets, Trinity 1545 to Hilary 1547; I owe this reference to Dr G. R. Elton.

often had the sanction of law. Originally, such payments to officialdom were in the nature of gratuities to the clerks and scribes, given to speed the administrative process or for other reasons related to the routine of patronage. In time, however, habitual gratuities became fees to which the clerk in question had a right in the eyes of the common law. As that idea finally developed, additional gratuities came to be superimposed on the traditional fees, thus multiplying the profit potential of any office. Hence there was a continuing distinction normally made between fees and gratuities, the latter often becoming exaction forced on unwilling victims of public process.

Over and above both fees and gratuities, outright bribes existed. Here we enter a tricky and delicate area, for modern notions of bribery were hardly current in the Tudor age. Today, any public servant who takes money or goods for a service connected with official duties is deemed guilty of peculation. For a sixteenth-century official to do so was simply to demonstrate his grasp of the morality of the time. Unless the gifts in question could be proved to be the motive for an action, no charge of bribery or of selling justice would be brought to light. Witness the classic case of Bacon, who was of the same mind as an earlier lord chancellor, Sadler's friend Wriothesley, who made the celebrated remark that 'everie manne solde the kinge that solde justice'.[1] Of course, by 'solde' Lord Wriothesley meant that profit was the spring of action. Sadler himself was acutely conscious of the issue involved in the system, as a Stuart writer noted in quoting Sir Ralph on the problem at hand:

He that giveth rewardes embaseth a man; he that teketh obligeth himselfe; who is so most rewarded is least. Since honour hath lost the value of a rewarde, men have lost the merit of virtue; and both become mercenary; men lusting after the wealthe that buyeth service, rather than after the qualities that deserve it.[2]

Given that stern sentiment, it will be instructive to follow Sadler's own manipulation of the fee system and its attendant possibilities for profit, with the sweets that salved conscience.

Obviously, we cannot hope to formulate an exact annual average for the income derived by the exploitation of local revenue offices. Never-

---

[1] BM Sloan MSS. 1523, fo. 30b.   [2] *Ibid.* fo. 29a.

theless, there is some basis in fact for claiming that such profits could be gross. As the Crown's local agent, a steward or bailiff presided over the manor court, collected fines and duties,[1] granted franchises and other rights, enforced suit of mill and, in general, kept a close check on royal tenants. Opportunities for profit were enormous, often being a function of the scruples and inventiveness of the officer involved.[2]

Perhaps we can gauge the lucrativeness of the situation from a letter addressed by Thomas Styldoff to Thomas Cromwell.[3] It seems that Sadler had been named high steward of a Crown manor near Chaussey, with all the rights thereunto pertaining. Styldoff did not wish to encroach on Sadler's rights, but in the past he himself had always held the courts baron and leet within the manor and taken the profits in his capacity as under-steward. Sadler had sent his own agent to do that task, with the result that Styldoff faced ruin due to the consequent loss of income. So much for the details. If we assume Styldoff to be a solid yeoman, or even one of the impoverished gentry, and the presumption ought to be that he had such rank, that Sadler's action had so endangered his income to evoke a protest to Cromwell is worth noting. His letter to Cromwell was accompanied by a small gift; fortune smiled on the bountiful. It was even worth his while to sue at law to recover his old rights, although the sum could hardly have been enormous. Yet it is only by multiplying the Styldoffs and Chausseys by tens and twenties that the worth of small offices can be appreciated. Recently Professor MacCaffery has brought to light an example in which we see the steward of a single manor making 500 marks a year by working steadily at the exploitation of his position.[4] While we cannot assume that Sir Ralph would keep the full income, since he exploited minor offices by deputy, nor that such opportunities as MacCaffery chronicles were typical, we have no reason to suppose that either the exploitation or the yield were beyond Sadler's capacity and intention.

Yet such profits did not amount to much, when set beside the formidable returns from positions in the machinery of central government. There the fee system worked to perfection. Where the favours

[1] Sums exacted when a new 'taking' or lease was drawn.
[2] *Elizabethan Government and Society*, p. 124.
[3] PRO, SP 1/159, fos. 64*a*–65*a*, Styldoff to Cromwell, 12 Apr. 1540.
[4] The figure stems from the 1580s: see MacCaffery's paper in *Elizabethan Government and Society*, p. 124. Even after allowing for an inflation of 200–300 per cent, what an opportunity!

dispensed were greatest, the rewards were sweetest. Fortunes were built on the basis of a single high office or on the humble lintel of a strategically placed clerkship. Needless to say, Sir Ralph Sadler, who was the incumbent of two chancery clerkships, master of the great wardrobe, treasurer for the wars against Scotland, and who also served in the king's chamber and was secretary of state, was a man matchlessly placed t o make office profitable.

A portion of all chancery fees went to the keeper of the hanaper. In the sixteenth century the amount was fixed at 2s. 6d. for every document sealed in chancery.[1] The particulars of the hanaper's business enrolled by the comptroller show that such fees were payable for all writs, warrants, licences and exemplification.[2] The comptroller's elaborate accounts also show that fees so due were rarely waived,[3] so that for all practical purposes the total number of entries in the particulars is a reliable guide to the value of such fees. Between 1540 and 1547 the annual average number of entries is over a thousand, from which the keeper and his staff had about £125 as their share of the profits arising from the application of the great seal.[4]

The traces left by gratuities and *douceurs* are by the very nature of the exchange rather faint. But the estimated yield for any office is within our grasp, provided that we adhere to a rather circumlocuitous but fruitful method of calculation. Late Tudor and Stuart officials often put capital values on their offices, expressing the sum in terms of annual rents or, in other words, a certain number of years served as the divisor of the capital sum. By that system they meant to express the assured annual income that a prospective purchaser might realise from the office in question. A summary of such valuations has recently come into print in the work of Dr G. E. Aylmer.[5] Since his information is drawn primarily from the period 1600–42, we must allow for the passage of two generations and for the consequent inflation of the era 1540–1640,

---

[1] PRO, C 66/700, pt. 8, m. 9, 'feoda debita et consueta'.

[2] PRO, E 101/222/8, a large parchment of twenty-five membranes, the keeper's *compotus* was based on these particulars kept by the comptroller of the hanaper. I would like to note that these particulars have value for biography, since they often supply the defects of signet, privy seal and other warrants.

[3] Remission of fees was, of course, a primary form of good will and patronage, whether directed to a friend and superior, Cromwell, for example, or to one's wife: see PRO, E 101/223/1, m. 7a for examples.

[4] PRO, E 101/222/9; 223/4 and 11; xxxx 225/4 and 8.

[5] Aylmer, *The King's Servants*, pp. 204–10, 217, 221–3.

which multiplied prices in about a four-to-one ratio. Making the proper allowances, we can use Dr Aylmer's figures on a trial basis.

In 1630 the estimated annual value of the notaryship in chancery once held by Sadler was £1,500–3,000.[1] Allowing for the inflation, and using the lowest of Aylmer's figures, we find the office worth £400 p.a. *c.* 1540. In 1620 the hanaper clerkship was said to be worth about £800 p.a., a figure very solidly based on an actual sale of that office for £2,400 at three years purchase.[2] Accounting for the inflation of the intervening period, the office should have been worth about £200 p.a. to Sadler in the mid-sixteenth century.

That last figure inspires some confidence in our rough hewn method. I have already demonstrated that for the period 1540–7 Sadler received an average income of £65 from slated rents and about £125 from the profits of writing and sealing. The total of £190 p.a. accords well enough with our estimate of £200 developed by the use of Aylmer's figures. Thus the combined income from the two chancery offices must have been something about £600 beyond the assured salaries and perquisites. That the gratuities for the notaryship were greater than those arising from the hanaper post seems likely, since the former office had some role in obtaining action in suits while the latter did not.

Unfortunately, we cannot follow even so rough a method with regard to the wardrobe. No figure for the sale of that office from a nearly contemporary period is available. What can be said with some confidence is that the master of a spending department in the household was not wanting in opportunities to enrich himself. Sadler could easily command gratuities for the letting of contracts. Further, consider the audit system which prevailed with regard to the wardrobe. If Sadler found himself working with a surplus at the end of an accounting period, he might invest the arrears for private profit, on the understanding that he would eventually have to get his quittance from the Crown. The wardrobe, with surpluses often in the thousands of pounds, provided ample scope for such operations.[3] The same was true of the hanaper, which often showed arrearages of more than £1,000

[1] *Ibid.* p. 210.

[2] *Ibid.* pp. 217, 222. In 1571 Hales, contesting Sadler's right to the profits of the hanaper, told Leicester that he had offered £500 down and £100 p.a. for life to Sadler, who refused, allegedly on the grounds that he had better offers, one for £400 down and £200 p.a. for life: see BM Add. MSS. 32091, fos. 248*a*–250*b*, January 1571.

[3] Aylmer, *The King's Servants*, p. 167.

during Sadler's tenure.[1] Finally, it is worth noting that the keeper of the hanaper could account to the master of the great wardrobe in order to secure his quittance. That practice may well account for the active role played on the London money market by Sadler and other household officials.[2]

Much of what has been said so far is based on solid figures balanced with an informed sounding of the depths of speculation. But in the case of Sadler's most lucrative office more precise information exists in some measure. An almost exact figure is available for secretarial fees, gratuities and *douceurs* by virtue of the nature of the patronage process at work during the period. Since the secretary stood at the head of the long line of officials one had to pass in order to tap the bounty of the Crown, his office was the most attractive abyss of spending into which a suitor could plunge in looking for some reward.

In Sadler's case we are singularly lucky. His signet register, a docket book recording all grants passing the signet between 1540 and 1542, is the first such source to survive intact until the present day.[3] From its pages a calculation of fees arising from the control of the signet is possible. Beyond that, by knowing the volume of business handled, we can make a reasonable estimate of the range of gratuities and *douceurs*.

For the period covered by the register Sadler received £201. 2s. 7d. p.a. as his share of the profits from the application of the signet. Monthly sums ranged from a low of £3. 12s. to an upper extreme of £65. 11s. 4d.[4] Included in the total figure were small monthly remittances from the chancery clerks[5] and a portion of all sums paid in excess of the established fees.[6] The record, innocent enough at first glance, also provides a good introduction to the matter of gratuities. It is difficult to believe, for example, that the clerks of the bishop of Llandaff were ignorant of the fact that they had sent five times the required sum for the sealing of a perpetuity. The signet clerk receiving the money simply noted that it

---

[1] PRO, E 351/3025-6. Sadler's wardrobe accounts showed overages of £2,137 and £1,149. His hanaper accounts were often enough glossed 'remanet clare': see E 101/223/13 and 224/14.

[2] BM Add. MSS. 35818, fos. 36a–38b, where loans and trade in foreign currencies are registered by Gervase Cawood, Sadler's receiver-general. Relatively little has been done with the surviving household account books of Tudor officials, including the excellent early specimen of Thomas Heneage's accounts in PRO, E 192/2.

[3] BM Add. MSS. 35818. Walsingham's docket book is the next in the series.

[4] The low came in Aug. 1540, and the high in May 1541.

[5] BM Add. MSS. 35818, fo. 8b.

[6] *Ibid.* fos. 54b–55a.

was to be divided between the two secretaries and the clerks in the usual manner, as if it was routine to handle such sums in excess of fees through the clerks themselves, without recourse to the secretaries.

Suggestive as that entry is, we must know something more about the monies paid for the forwarding of suits, for the obtaining of the king's ear. In that regard, the simplest form of gratuity was the direct payment for a favour already granted. Five or six pounds was the normal tariff, according to Miss Evans, who also stated that the sums often ran as high as £20 or £40.[1] Her statement is fully supported by the evidence found in the single volume of Wriothesley's papers in the Public Record Office[2] and by the researches of students investigating the regulation of patronage in Burghley's household. Sadler's own correspondence supplies further corroboration, as does an account book kept for him.[3] What follows, therefore, is only a sampling of the evidence, since a full account would double the length of this chapter without materially enhancing the conclusions.

We can begin with the most direct evidence about which we have any knowledge. Lord Lisle once promised Sadler £40 for expediting the grant of Fetherstone priory, remarking that he would rather give Sadler that sum than a penny to some unidentified third person[4] 'who nevar dyd me gud'.[5] One Robert Kenark sent £10 to promote the grant of two chantries.[6] Sir Richard Southwell, solicitor of the Augmentations, offered Sadler an unspecified sum to be 'humble suitor to the kinges maiestie for me bihaulfe'.[7] In a more complicated case, Richard Sanford begged one of the grooms of the privy chamber, a certain John Gates,[8] to act as an intermediary for him with Sadler, who was then to

---

[1] Evans, *The Principal Secretary of State*, p. 211. Folger Shakespeare Library, Losely MSS. 170: in this brief page we have a memorandum made by Sir Thomas Cawarden's agent of fees owing to the signet clerk for the granting of the keepership of the revels to Cawarden in 1541. Beyond the normal exaction for the issuing of the warrants under the signet, £3. 5s. was clearly owed to the secretary's clerks.

[2] PRO, SP 7/1.

[3] I wish to thank Drs Alan Smith and Richard Barnett for information about the household of Lord Burghley. Here Cromwell's own dealings will repay very careful study: BM Cotton MSS. Cleopatra E IV, fos. 14b and 220b, shows Cromwell receiving bribe offers of £400 (not to dissolve Furness Abbey; 200 marks (not to dissolve the priory of Great Malvern); the first fruits of any former monastic lands granted by Cromwell to Charles Elyot: and £200 not to dissolve yet another abbey!

[4] This is possibly a reference to Wriothesley.

[5] PRO, SP 3/9, fo. 54, Lisle to Sadler, undated.

[6] PRO, E 326/B 8194.   [7] PRO, SP 1/127, fos. 209–10.

[8] PRO, SP 1/243, pt. 3, fo. 269b, undated.

help Sanford get a certain parcel of land. Gates was to tell Sadler that Sanford would 'gyve full twentie poundes for your paynes'.[1]

All of these cases have this much in common: it is impossible to cite a single instance as a clear-cut bribe. We lack the crucial information. We cannot say that the sum offered influenced Sadler's course of action and therefore are in no position to speak of corruption. In the light of the ambiguity of the evidence, moderation is necessary in judging the actors. If we cannot speak glibly about corruption, it is none the less important to find out how widespread the giving of gratuities was.

In the absence of a large number of letters sent by indiscreet men, an analysis of a single manuscript throws some light on this difficult question.[2] Sadler's personal account book for the years 1540–2 survives among the books of the Hardwicke Papers in the British Museum. From that book, it is evident that many persons, high and low alike, as well as a number of corporations, tried to protect their influence at court by issuing annuities in lieu of a single gratuity. In effect, such persons and groups gave retainers to Sadler, apparently in the hope of some future disposition to plead their causes. Why else would a certain Mr Cooke pay £20 p.a.?[3] Or take the case of William Hill, who conferred on Sadler £2 p.a. for life.[4] How do we evaluate such a payment? The case of Lord Lisle is easier to parse. Sadler did many favours for Lisle.[5] In return, Lisle gave him gifts and an annuity,[6] which ended in an agreement to pay Sadler £10 p.a. for life.[7] John Dudley, later to be so much a factor in Sadler's career, as the earl of Warwick and duke of Northumberland, made a similar patent for £10 p.a.[8] The patents made by various religious communities are more difficult to interpret, unless we infer that they thereby hoped to stay the inevitable by befriending one of Cromwell's agents. Sadler held annuities from the Guild of St Peter and St George at York (£2. 6s. 8d),[9] John Oliver and the fellows of King's College, Oxford (£6. 13s. 4d.),[10] the abbot of Westminster (£6. 13s. 4d.)[11] and the unusually large sum of £40 p.a. from the community of monks at Gisborough priory, Yorkshire.[12]

---

[1] PRO, SP 1/243, pt. 3, fo. 270.
[2] BM Add. MSS. 35824.   [3] *Ibid.* fo. 33 b.   [4] *Ibid.* fo. 34 a.
[5] The evidence for the Lisle–Sadler relationship is scattered throughout the Lisle Papers in the PRO, SP 3/3–9 and 14. See also SP 1/87, *passim*, as well as vols. 105, 114, 137 and 140.
[6] PRO, SP 3/5, fo. 16; 3/8, fo. 51.   [7] BM Add. MSS. 35824, fo. 34 a.
[8] *Ibid.* f. 34 b.   [9] *Ibid.*
[10] BM Add. MSS. 35824, fo. 35 a.   [11] *Ibid.* fo. 33 b.   [12] *Ibid.*

Ironically enough, the annuities paid Sadler by ecclesiastical bodies were assured him by rulings of the court of Augmentations once the great dissolution began. The Guild of St Peter and St George was gobbled up, but the annuity was paid,[1] as was that owed by St Frediswude's College,[2] where Sadler had once served as high steward.[3] If the grantee produced his patent, the court was bound to pay, issuing the necessary fiats for the settlement of the claim, including any arrears that might be outstanding. Thus Sir Ralph collected a paltry £7. 10s. 4d. in arrears on a grant made by the monks at Berking, Essex,[4] and the not so paltry arrears in excess of £100 based on a patent of the abbess of Nuneton priory, Warwickshire.[5]

Whatever patronage might fall to Sadler as secretary of state enhanced his profit-making position. But he was also a member of the privy council deputed to serve on the commissions erected for the sale of Crown lands under the administration of the court of Augmentations.[6] How far gifts prompted Sadler's action in that capacity is a matter for mere speculation. Certainly, letters from men like Richard Sanford might move Sadler to favour a suit in return for £20. The land was going to be sold to somebody, and a gift might well determine the recipient. But then the case of Lord Lisle comes to mind, with its stark reminder that Sadler's words were 'not holie watre'. Lisle got very little help for his occasional gifts and the £10 annuity. He lost nearly every suit in which he had Sadler's favour, prompting Lisle's London factor John Husee to complain that Sadler was a double-dealer. At any rate, *douceurs* were a sure gain to the taker but a gamble to the donor.[7]

Apparently enough suitors were willing to gamble to make the secretaryship worth between £500 and £700 p.a., exclusive of salaries and signet fees. That figure for the 1540s is based in part on the known market price of the office in the early Jacobean period.[8] It is also based in part on the details gleaned from Sadler's register, especially from the

[1] PRO, E 315/105, fo. 72 *b.*   [2] PRO, E 315/104, fos. 172 *a–b.*
[3] PRO, E 315/104, fo. 174 *b.*   [4] PRO, E 315/94, fos. 137 *a–b* and enclosure.
[5] PRO, E 315/102, fo. 137 *b.*   [6] *L & P,* XXI, ii, 200 and 332; XXI, i, 970 and 1,166.
[7] PRO, SP 3/8, fo. 51; 1/240, pt. 1, fo. 273 *a.* See PRO, E 315/113, fo. 32, for an offer of £110 made to Sadler, on condition that he get Selby abbey from the Crown and sell it to a third party.
[8] *CSPD,* James I, 1623–1625, clxiv, 7, estimates the office at £2,000 p.a. Chamberlayne, *Angliae Notitia,* II, 10, made the same guess in 1603. Manningham, *The Diary of John Manningham,* p. 31, claimed the value in 1601 was £3,000. Aylmer, *The King's Servants,* p. 205, gives a range of £2,800–4,000, based on sales in 1618 and 1628. Evans, *The Principal Secretary of State,* p. 211, shows Windebanke making £6,000 just before the Great Rebellion.

unique memoranda listing suits earmarked for approval in behalf of the great and the little men of the kingdom. If we take July 1540 to July 1541 an ordinary business year at the signet, we find that 329 writs and perpetuities were granted under Sadler's seal, including 59 warrants for grants of extended value and 270 ordinary warrants. At the same time, Wriothesley's register listed 586 grants, of which 111 were of extended value.[1] For the following year the figures in Sadler's register were 61 perpetuities and 292 ordinary warrants.[2]

Against the background of the available evidence and the practices of the Elizabethans recently catalogued by historians, the interpretation of the figures in Sadler's docket book is possible. It is clear that the office had to be worth a small fortune to Sadler. The sheer number of processed grants alone argues for a considerable income, supporting easily the estimate of from £500–700 in gratuities. Sanford's offer of £20 and Lisle's of £40 still doubts and raise the issue of the estimate being far too low. Perhaps an estimate of £700 is only half what the office was worth. Whatever the true income was in pounds, shillings and pence, our method of estimate has at least demonstrated the enormous profit-making potential of high office in concrete terms.

The various sources of income, exclusive of revenue from his own lands, reached a very large total in Sadler's case. Our own account, based throughout on data supplemented by conservative estimates where the material thins out, can be summarised in this way. Crown salaries were worth £350 p.a. Livery and bouge yielded £66. 3s. 2d., while messes were worth nearly £650 p.a. Fees and favours given by seekers after Crown patronage connected with minor offices was worth perhaps £600 p.a. The secretaryship and control of the signet was worth about £900–1,000 p.a. from all sources. The total annual average for the peak years of the period 1540–7 was in the neighbourhood of £2,600.

That figure can best be appreciated against the background of annual income estimates made by the commissioners for the Henrician subsidies, the Tudor equivalent, in a rough way, of the modern tax on income. Miss Helen Miller has shown that thirty-nine Tudor peers were taxed in 1534 on annual incomes averaging £921, which figure

---

[1] BM Add. MSS. 35818, fos. 8–43b. In part Wriothesley's greater volume is explicable by Sadler's absence on mission in Scotland. Figures in Sadler's register also provide Wriothesley's totals for each month.

[2] BM Add. MSS. 35818, fos. 44b–66b.

included revenue from real estate. Only fifteen incomes exceeded £1,000. In 1545 the average was down to £3,300.[1] It was Miss Miller's opinion that the assessments were scrupulously made, wholesale fraud in such matters being reserved for the Elizabethan commissioners.[2]

Sadler's own assessment is therefore a matter of some interest. While we cannot controvert the general data used by Peyton and Miller in their research, we must point out that Sadler's income was grossly under-evaluated, even if we consider only the land revenues treated below, with no attention given to official income. In 1545 he was listed at £306 clear annual income, putting him far down the list of nobility and court-connected gentry. That was less than the £350 paid him by the Crown in salaries, although it seems that fees enjoyed a tax immunity, which was simply another way of making office pay.[3] In the Elizabethan period no less a light than William Cecil set the pattern, since his assessment never rose beyond 200 marks, while his income has been estimated at over £4,000 p.a. by modern scholars, as well as by his household biographer, and that from land alone! When the lord high treasurer cheated on his tax, what the underlings did ought to occasion no surprise.[4]

The picture drawn here of Sadler's profits from office raises a capital question. What did he do with the wealth so gained? Was he a 'typical' court-connected gentleman? Did he invest his gain in the storied land market of the mid-sixteenth century? Further, what effect did office have on the general style of his life? Henry's son Sir Ralph did indeed have a fair inheritance from his father; but it was in the form of affinity not affluence. The latter was the product of the former.

[1] Helen Miller, 'Subsidy Assessments of the Peerage in the Sixteenth Century', *BIHR*, xxviii (1955), 18 ff. By 1566 the average fell to £503; in 1586 it was a mere £311. Miss Miller found jobbery, but not an impoverishment of the aristocrats.

[2] S. A. Peyton, 'The Village Population in the Tudor Lay Subsidy Rolls', *EHR*, xxx (1915), 240. Peyton upheld the early Tudor assessments, claiming that the assessors were not often corrupted and that the method of assessment was fairly good.

[3] PRO, E 179/69/32. Sadler's friends Sir Francis Bryan, Sir Anthony Edwards, Sir Anthony Wingfield, Sir George Herbert and Sir Anthony Denny were all rated higher than Sadler. In 1546 Sir Ralph's assessment rose to £356, according to PRO, E 179/69/56, fo. 3b. Roger Schofield, 'Parliamentary Lay Taxation, 1485–1547', supersedes Miller and Peyton. His unpublished doctoral thesis (Cambridge, 1963), stresses that assessment was upon either lands or goods, whichever had the greater worth.

[4] Peck, *Desiderata Curiosa*, I, i, 35. See also the fine essay by Lawrence Stone, 'The Fruits of Office; The Case of Robert Cecil, The First Earl of Salisbury, 1596–1612', in *Essays in the Economic and Social History of Tudor and Stuart in Honour of R. H. Tawney*, ed. F. J. Fisher (Cambridge University Press, 1961), pp. 89–117.

9

PLACE AND PROFIT: SADLER AND
THE HENRICIAN LAND MARKET

*...with favorable terms for all sufficiently rich, or 'influential, or mean,
to get in on the ground floor'.*

R. H. TAWNEY, *Religion and The Rise of Capitalism*

Sir Ralph Sadler acquired great wealth and some influence during the
last phase of Henry VIII's reign. The practices by which he got that
wealth and made that influence work for him pose some vital questions.
What effect did acquisitiveness on a grand scale have on Sadler's pattern
of life, as he advanced steadily among the gentry? Mentioning the
gentry necessarily obliges us to treat related issues. What exactly was
his place as an investor in land? How did he operate in the currents of
the market for monastic lands? What relationships are discernible
between his position as an office holder and his acquisition of great lands
in several regions of England? Any effort to answer these questions puts
us squarely in the middle of the current 'storm over the gentry'.
Hence, we must at the outset disclaim any intention to solve the novel
problems occasioned by much heat and the considerable light generated
by scholars working in that field. But at the same time it is part of the
intention of this chapter to illustrate the conditions under which great
estates could be acquired by a courtier-official, whatever other scholars
may make of the typicality of Sadler's ventures.

The context of the entire problem is, of course, the discussion begun
early in the current century by Tawney's researches into the deepening
crisis of English agrarian life and the dark picture of the gentry which
emerged from his work. Tawney believed that a sweeping redistribu-
tion of real wealth was carried out by a minority of courtiers and
bureaucrats lacking in every virtue, a minority bent on the use of fraud
and violence, if need be, to accomplish the desired end. The 'furor of
land speculation'[1] touched off by the dissolution brought in its wake,

[1] R. H. Tawney, *The Agrarian Problem in the Sixteenth Century* (London: Longmans, 1912),
p. 381.

according to Tawney, 'an orgy of interested misgovernment on the part of its principal beneficiaries...'[1] As a result of that corruption, a small circle of men plunged England headlong into the abyss of agrarian unrest and crisis. The dizzy fall ruined the yeoman, accompanied by a 'sinister hum as of floating of an immense land syndicate, with favourable terms for all sufficiently rich, or influential, or mean, to get in on the ground floor'.[2]

Tawney was spurred on by the investigations of the noted Russian scholar Alexander Savine, whose writings about the disposal of monastic lands broke new ground in the understanding of Tudor social and economic history. Savine's main contention was that between 1540 and 1547 two-thirds of the newly acquired Crown lands had been granted away. Some of the land was alienated in the form of gifts, but such parcels accounted for but 41 grants in a total of 1,593 surveyed. In addition to the gifts, which Tawney viewed as ill-gotten gains, land worth about £70,000 p.a. was sold to nearly one thousand grantees. It was the breakdown of the statistics of sales that so aroused Tawney, since 209 of the 'best placed persons' received advantageous terms on the best lands, according to Savine's data. Thirty-eight peers supposedly acquired spoils for only three or five years purchase, while nearly one hundred courtiers paid a mere nine years purchase. A group of nearly fifty royal servants bought lands at 9·6 years purchase, roughly the same rate at which a number of bureaucrats came by their lands. To give further substance to the idea of looting, one has only to consider that 617 non-court connected persons purchased lands worth £29,500 p.a. for a sum of £457,230, a rate equal to nearly twenty years purchase.[3]

Savine was no less fervent than Tawney in his strictures against those who got the bulk of the land, but he also pointed out that there were good explanations why monastic estates came to the hands of men 'who knew not only to whom they should address themselves, but knew also what particular estates to ask for...'.[4] Long before the

[1] *Religion and the Rise of Capitalism* (London: John Murray, 1948), p. 138.
[2] *Ibid.* p. 143.
[3] These figures are gleaned from Savine, *The English Monasteries on the Eve of the Dissolution* (Oxford: Clarendon Press, 1909), *passim*. A convenient tabulation is presented by Fisher, *The Political History of England*, v, 497–9.
[4] Savine, *The English Monasteries on the Eve of the Dissolution*, p. 260.

dissolution, Savine wrote, 'economic initiative had, on the monastic territory, to a considerable extent passed from the monks to the gentry'.[1]

Tawney largely disregarded Savine's *caveat*, further crystallising his case against the gentry in a study of their rise as a social class. They rose, he explained, because they applied more rational techniques of exploitation on their newly acquired lands than did the aristocrats or the yeoman. The gentry were the true rural bearers of that ethos introduced by Calvin and described by Weber and Troeltsch. They ruthlessly exploited rents and entry fines, much to the deprivation of the small farmer and farm labourer and the disgust of the nobility. Such groups would not or could not keep pace. Thus the gentry rose at the expense of all other groups traditionally associated with the well being of the land. In the gentry Tawney saw and despised the prototype of the rationalistic, urban bourgeoisie of the unhappy age of the industrial revolution. Tawney catalogued their purchases, their rampant speculation on a great buyers' market, their ruthless handling of large manorial units and their downright villainy and corruption.[2] In addition to certain social and intellectual issues, Tawney's arguments, in which Sir Ralph Sadler and his heirs figured prominently, rested on a certain image of the market for monastic property, a method for estimating social mobility which entailed the counting of manors, the nature of the movement of rents and the analysis of the ethos of Protestantism.[3]

Hence there can hardly be an intelligent discussion of Sadler's place in the Tudor land market or of his progress among the gentry without mention of the matrix of work done by Tawney and his critics. The very questions we ask about Sadler arise naturally from the context of the Tawney thesis. What lands did Sadler acquire? When and how did he do so? What did he keep and what did he alienate? How can we account for the choices made? Did he indeed speculate on a booming market? How did he exploit the lands he kept? Was he much involved in urban holdings, in the 'takings' and trade in London house properties?

[1] Savine, *The English Monasteries on the Eve of the Dissolution*, p. 261.

[2] Tawney stated that view firmly in his now famous 'The Rise of the Gentry', *EcHR*, XI (1941), 1–39.

[3] Tawney's conclusions, which have ever since determined the basic shape of the controversy about the land market, rested on a survey of some 2,700 manors.

Finally, what of Sadler's building programme and the consolidation of his holdings in certain recognisable groupings?

Tawney's view that corruption was the keynote in the humming activity of acquisition does not seem to hold up well in Sadler's case. Patronage and friendship rather than fraud seem to have aided Sadler more than anything else. The pattern of advancement was clear as early as 1537 when Sadler, complaining about his debts, remarked that Furness abbey lands went to men no more deserving than himself.[1] He wanted to get in on the ground floor in the race to acquire former monastic lands. His inquiries and dolorous letters run through the 1530s without abatement, a good example being his 1538 letter to Wriothesley in which he praises Cromwell for his aid in obtaining some Warwickshire lands. He readily acknowledged that the key to success was 'the lettre you procured me' from Cromwell to the prior of the Gray Friars at Coventry.[2] Friendship gave him the inside track in more ways than one. John Hales pursued the Coventry inquiry through one of the surveyors of Augmentations, John Hanby, who promised that Sadler would soon have a 'book of sale' for the lands desired.[3] That was the basic pattern: reliance on Cromwell and the Cromwell affinity until that great minister's fall. Almost up to the time of his death Cromwell's memoranda were filled with notes to 'remembre Rafe for one monasterie', along with Dr Kern on one occasion[4] and Wriothesley on another.[5]

These memorials indicated the role played by simple patronage. But even Cromwell's notes were not infallible signs of success. In April of 1539 Sadler noted with alarm that his suit for lands at Robertsbridge went for naught, that he was losing out to Sir William Sydney. *Mora trahit periculum* were his words on that occasion, as he complained that the delay or failure of the grant would 'somewhat touche mi poore honestie as yt ys bruted in the cuntrie that the kinges maiestie hath geven yt to me'. What in fact aroused his anxiety was that he had anticipated the grant and had already taken possession of Robertsbridge. A recovery suit faced him, if Sydney was the grantee.[6] Obviously

---

[1] *L & P*, XII, ii, appendix 44, Sadler to Cromwell, Oct. 1537.

[2] PRO, SP 7/2, fo. 40, Sadler to Wriothesley, undated.

[3] PRO, SP 1/138, fo. 73, Hales to Hanby, Sept. 1538.

[4] Cromwell's private agent in Flanders and Cleves in 1539, sent in part to arrange the Cleves alliance (*L & P*, XIV, ii, 424).

[5] BM Cotton MSS. Titus B I, fo. 469; see also *L & P*, XIV, i, 424–7.

[6] PRO, SP 1/151, fo. 243, Sadler to Cromwell, Apr. 1539.

Sydney was more villainous and corrupt than Sadler, since he secured the lands, said to be worth between £150–200 p.a.[1]

Of course there was a note of avarice and anxiety in the Robertsbridge incident. It is difficult to negate the avarice displayed by Sadler and by other courtiers, bureaucrats and members of the aristocracy, for that matter. They were anxious for profit, an anxiety that did not pass away with Sadler's patron Cromwell in 1540. In that year, however, his own accession to the principal secretaryship gave him a basic hold on patronage which he used to good advantage. A routine request for the particulars of lands he was interested in was enough to set the machinery in motion for the secretary of states. Such requests survive, along with the corresponding particulars of the surveyor of Augmentations, for Standon,[2] Stratford-le-Bowe,[3] Selby abbey,[4] Westbury-on-Trym,[5] and Whytmore Park, Coventry.[6]

Any man might send such requests to the Augmentations office. Sadler was in a position to do more. He might send a kind word or two through the surveyor or auditor's friends, a practice suggestive of the very nature of the governmental process of the sixteenth century rather than any special viciousness. Here is a typical letter illustrating Sir Ralph's transactions with Augmentations:

Mastre Hanbye I hertely commende me unto you and so thanke you for your paynes many tymes taken for me. I nowe desire you that I may use the same agen and that you wyl send unto me written in a parchment the particulares of the manor of Allesborre in the cuntry of Wigorn,[7] parcel of the possessions of the late monastery of Pershore. Whensoever it may do you plesure ye shal fynde me as redy to gratifie you as may other your frendes. Thus fare ye hertely well. From mi house at Westmynster the xith daie of Decembre in the xxxviii th yere of the kinges maiesties reigne. Your lovyng frende Syr Rafe Sadleyr.[8]

What this letter shows is the easy confidence of a man close to the source of power in a monarchical society, a man who can trust a friend

---

[1] *L & P*, XIV, i, 906 (7). Robertsbridge in Sussex was a very rich plum. Sadler's confidence was doubtlessly related to Cromwell's being high steward there.

[2] PRO, E 318/967, 9 June 1545.   [3] PRO, E 318/969, undated.

[4] PRO, E 318/966, 22 June 1540.

[5] PRO, E 318/968 and E 305/F 29, the actual deed of purchase and exchange, 10 Dec. 1546.

[6] PRO, SC 12/38/29, undated.   [7] The official designation for Worcestershire.

[8] PRO, SP 1/227, fo. 45, Sadler to Hanby, 11 Dec. 1546, the often mentioned auditor of Augmentations.

and who in turn is in a position to return favours for the people at Augmentations. There is no hint of furtive or conspiratorial deals. If corruption was intended, the parties were quite blasé about it. More likely, it seems, we are simply seeing the evidence that the Tudor system operated by virtue of the reciprocity of fee and favour institutionalised. Although this is not to deny that there were instances in which corruption on a conscious level was involved in Sadler's dealings, it is to say that the few instances in which we have good grounds for suspicion cannot explain away the normal operation of Tudor government.

With these considerations in mind, we can turn to the major issues, trying to arrive at some just conclusions about the scope and nature of Sir Ralph's activities in the land market, with the hope that the data will shed some light on the validity of the work of the critics of Tawney and his defenders.

Sadler's activities in the Tudor land market was a steady one, yet it was punctuated by periods of heightened attention, especially in 1539–40, 1544 and 1546–7. His earliest acquisitions were made in 1536, when he got the manors of Lowhall and Highall, Essex, and Lesnes and Fauntes in Kent. From then until 1540 he bought or was given little land. In the year of Cromwell's fall he attained from the Crown thirteen parcels of land, including a dozen manors and their appurtenances. Among these were the rich lands of Stratford-le-Bowe in Middlesex, formerly the possessions of the Knights of St John of Jerusalem, and the great priory of Selby, Yorkshire. 1541–2 was a period of very limited acquisition, although a compact group of five manors was acquired, three of them in Hertfordshire. 1544 was another great year of acquisition, as Sadler added thirteen new manorial groupings, including another five Hertfordshire properties and a very large holding in the western Midlands. Then another couple of years went by with little activity until 1546–7, the year of the king's death, at which time Sadler's activities reached their peak, with the acquisition of massive holdings in Gloucestershire, Warwickshire and Worcestershire.

Viewed as a sequence of periods of expansion followed by the relative inactivity of digestion, Sadler's operations showed a rhythmic beat. When viewed from the geographical perspective, Sadler's holdings formed two compact groups and some outlying lands. There was a

Home Counties complex centred in Hertfordshire and Middlesex, which included parts or the whole of some twenty-five manors. There was also the great mass of lands in the Avon–Bristol region, comprising the largest single estate built out of former monastic lands in the Shakespeare country. Tawney noted that fact, remarking that for many decades Sadler's heirs were considerable landholders there.[1] Apart from the two major complexes, Sadler held woodlands, messuages, manors and other parcels in twenty-five English and Welsh shires.[2]

Obviously any survey of these holdings is itself a complex task. With the aid of particulars of purchase, leases, evaluations and details supplied by such sources as the *Valor Ecclesiasticus* of 1535, as well as other contemporary compilations, however, we can provide chronological and regional summaries based on the counting of manors.[3] In that way we can work toward a compact analysis of Sadler's activities in the light of our general knowledge of the nature of the market for monastic property.

In 1536 three properties came to Sadler, perhaps to help support the burdens of his new position as groom of the king's chamber. Highall and Lowhall were parcels of Walthamstowe priory impropriated in Bruton priory for administrative purposes before the dissolution.[4] Sadler's grants were in the form of leases for twenty-one years; they were worth £48. 3s. 4d. and £15. 0s. 8d. p.a. respectively and were a gift for loyal service to Henry VIII.[5] Lesnes and Fauntes were also parcels of Bruton priory[6] and were likewise rewards for faithful service.[7] That patent is badly mutilated, and the values cannot be stated. Nor do alternative sources of information help much, although a list of the lands of William Brereton, one of the grooms attainted for complicity in the adultery of Anne Boleyn, does exist and includes the

[1] *EcHR*, XI, 28.

[2] In alphabetical order: Berks., Bucks., Devon, Denbigh, Dorset, Essex, Glamorganshire, Gloucs., Hants., Herts., Kent, Lancs., Lincs., Middlesex, Montgomeryshire, Norfolk, Northants., Northumberlandshire, Oxford, Somersetshire, Surrey, Sussex, Warwicks., Worcs., and, lastly, Yorks.

[3] Since I am here discussing a single family the dangers inherent in the count of manors method discussed by J. P. Cooper, 'The Counting of Manors', *EcHR*, 2nd ser. VIII (1956), 377–89, do not apply.

[4] PRO, SC 6/1123.

[5] PRO, C 66/700, pt. 8, m. 1, 13 March 1536. In 1559 Sir Ralph's grant was confirmed: BM Additional Charters 26024.

[6] PRO, SC 6/1108.

[7] PRO, C 66/670, pt. 3, m. 32b.

Kentish parcels.[1] The nearest contemporary report was that made in a rental survey of the manor in 1542, at which time the yield was £37. 4s. 6d.[2] The small manor was reported to be very beautiful and subsequently became Lady Sadler's lying-in retreat.[3]

The centre of the Home Counties complex, Standon manor, at Standon in Hertfordshire, was gathered in by a grant in 1540.[4] Sadler had first-hand knowledge of the great head manor, since he had served as high steward there when the lands formed part of Jane Seymour's possessions.[5] He knew that Standon, with its supporting manors, Plasshes and Popeshall among others, was a very rich property. It had long been a favourite retreat of English royalty.[6] In 1540 it consisted of 7,738 acres of arable, 30 acres of water, numerous buildings and improvements which raised the total value of the estate and a scenic view of the River Rib.[7] The entire holding was given to Sadler for life, in return for which he surrendered two annuities worth £46. 13s. 4d. p.a. It might be argued that the purchase price was high, since he died in 1587. But any consideration of the annual yield of the Standon complex puts the sacrifice in perspective. Standon was worth £65. 12s. 11d. in 1540.[8] Plasshes and Popeshall together were worth nearly £100 clear a year, according to Chauncey, the famed Hertfordshire antiquarian.[9] Tudor accounts confirm the evaluation of Chauncey to a very fine point.[10] When in 1545 the original grant for life was altered to one in tail male, Sadler found it not to his liking and sued for a regrant in fee simple. The Crown was willing, providing that an additional payment of £450. 4s. 9d. was made, estimated to be six years purchase. That fact in itself explains Sadler's willingness to part with the large sum, since between 1540 and 1545 Standon's yield was up to £75. 0s. 9d.[11]

About Standon in Braughin hundred, in the rolling north-east corner of Hertfordshire, hard by the River Rib, Sadler built a small empire. In

---

[1] Brereton held the lands until his attainder, at which time Sadler acquired them: see *L & P*, x 878, no. 3.

[2] PRO, SC 11/927.   [3] PRO, SP 1/125, fo. 116.

[4] PRO, C 66/700, pt. 1, m. 1*b*, 11 Dec. 1540.

[5] BM Royal MSS. 7F xiv, fo. 79*a*; PRO, SC 6/1147.

[6] *VCH Herts.* iii, 353.   [7] *Ibid.* p. 347.

[8] BM Royal MSS. 7F xiv, fo. 79*a*.

[9] Sir Henry Chauncey, *The Historical Antiquities of Hertfordshire*, 2 vols. (London, 1700), ii, 228.

[10] PRO, SC 6/1111 and 1147; *VE*, i, 44, 93, 412.

[11] The request to purchase in fee simple, along with the full particulars, is in PRO, E 318/967. The original letter patent is in Herts. County Record Office, General MSS. AS 204. The final regrant is in PRO, C 66/753, pt. 14, m. 6*a*.

addition to Plasshes and Popeshall, Sadler acquired a dozen other holdings in the area before 1547. Queensbury Manor in nearby Odsey hundred was added in 1540.[1] In 1535 it was worth £12 p.a., according to Dugdale.[2] In 1542 Sadler gained the minor property of Benge, for which I have found no contemporary evaluation.[3] But the terms of the grant imply that it was worth £20 p.a. In that year he also got the valuable properties of Temple Chelsyn and Temple Dynsley, formerly possessions of the rich Templars, by capital purchase at £843. 2s. 6d.[4] A very small part of the land was held *in capite*, as the twentieth part of a knight's fee, with a rent of £4. 9s. 4d. reserved to the Crown each year.[5] Whatever the intention of the reservation, and we ought not to overlook the likelihood that the Crown hoped to catch Sir Ralph in the snares of wardship, Sadler was long-lived. Finally, before 1547 Sadler bought or received in free gift seven other Hertfordshire manors worth about £200 p.a.[6]

The almost princely appanage in Hertfordshire comprised fifteen manors, thousands of acres and dozens of buildings, among them tenements, messuages, and mills. Yet this complex, worth thousands of pounds in capital investment, formed only a part of the Sadler holdings in the Home Counties. Sir Ralph also held the manor of Aston, Berkshire, by purchase in 1544[7] and Slacksted in Hampshire, bought at the same time.[8] These small farms were worth £10. 1s. 6d. together. In Surrey Sadler acquired three manors in 1544. Ewell was worth £3. 9s. 9d.[9] The dual manor of Bansted and Walton *super montem*, however, was worth either £42 or £48 p.a., depending on which of two contemporary accounts one credits.[10]

---

[1] *L & P*, xiv, i, 403 (44).

[2] William Dugdale, *Monasticon Anglicanum*, 6 vols. new ed. by John Caley, Henry Ellis and Bulkeley Bandinel (London: Longmans, 1817–30), iv, 119. See also *VCH Herts*. iii, 251.

[3] *L & P*, xvii, 220(48).

[4] PRO, C 66/707, pt. 7, m. 33.

[5] Herts. County Record Office, General MSS. AS 204.

[6] The following properties are referred to; all figures in parentheses represent values and references. Sopwell Manor (*VE*, i, 451: £40. 7s. 2d.); Ansty Manor (PRO, SC 6/1,119: value obliterated); Barwick-on-Rib (*L & P Addendum*, i, i, 981 (22): £12. 11s. 6d.); Holywell Manor (PRO, SC 6/1,119: £30. 14s.); Wylkeley Manor (PRO, E 315/218, fo. 155b: £11); Hitchin Lordship (BM Royall MSS. 7F xiv, fo. 80a: £87. 14s. 8d.) and Walden Regis (*VCH Herts*. iii, 35, no value given.

[7] *L & P*, xix, i, 278 (68). [8] *VCH Hants*. iv, 444.

[9] PRO, E 315/235, fo. 94b, 25 June 1542.

[10] BM Royal MSS. 7F xiv, fo. 81a (£48) and PRO, E 315/213, fos. 49a–49b (£42), a detailed rental and survey of the joint manor.

None of these holdings was as important as the Middlesex property which Sir Ralph came by at this time. To the Hackney lands acquired earlier by inheritance and purchase,[1] Sadler added very important holdings after 1540. A singular acquisition was the near-palatial Brooke House, which was bought for £1,000 in 1547.[2] Less spectacular and only slightly less profitable in the long run was his purchase of the entire complex of lands of Stratford-le-Bowe in fee simple in 1540. The property was rated at £129. 10s. 6½d. p.a.,[3] with the terms of purchase at twenty years, or a total capital outlay of £2,591. 0s. 6d., plus incidental expenses based on reserved rents. The significance of the Middlesex lands lies partly in the capital expenditure and partly in their nearness to the rapidly expanding London. Such outlays of capital point back to the great profits of office. The further profit implicit in ownership of lands near the great city raises the question of Sadler's interest in urban lands, one which will be treated after the completion of this survey.

Before dealing with the Avon–Bristol complex, it would be well to look at the less nucleated holdings acquired in scattered transactions. In 1541 Sadler gained some small parcels in Lincolnshire[4] and Northamptonshire[5] worth £15 p.a. combined. Six months earlier he had purchased from the crown the major part of Selby abbey, Yorkshire, a great Benedictine house, with its appurtenances at Bragton and Snathe priories in the city of York.[6] The total price was £736, according to a somewhat ambiguous entry in an Augmentations Office account book.[7] The difficulty occurs because the annual value of the Selby estates is clearly stated to be £129. 6s. 8d., which would imply a mere

[1] Hackney Public Library, Thyssen MSS. Y 150/1, mm. 11d and 15a; Y 235/7; Y 235/22; M 90/1.

[2] Sadler bought the property in Aug. 1547, with John Hales as co-purchaser, from Sir William Herbert, to whom it had been granted in July 1547. The property once belonged to Thomas Cromwell, who made large-scale improvements there in 1535-6. Sadler also had a good house near the parish church and other property there, including some arable. See PRO, C 54/451, for the Hales-Sadler purchase. For the general area of Hackney and Sadler's interest there see F. W. Shepherd (ed.), *The Survey of London; Parish of Hackney, I: Brooke House* (London: Athlone Press, 1960), pp. 58–60.

[3] See the patent of 14 Feb. 1540 and that of 21 Apr. 1540 in PRO, C 66/685, pt. 8, m. 18a and 700, pt. 8, m. 13. The particulars for purchase clearly state the value to be £120. 19s. 4d. p.a. clear (E 318/969). How the discrepancy came about it is impossible to say. What is certain is that the price paid was that listed in the patent. On this and all related technical points see Richardson's volume on the court of Augmentations.

[4] PRO, E 315/213, fo. 15b, 23 Feb. 1541.   [5] PRO, SC 6/1127.

[6] PRO, E 318/966 supplies the particulars; the grant is in C 66/688, pt. 3, m. 14.

[7] PRO, E 315/1, fo. 109a.

$5\frac{1}{2}$ years purchase. Sadler's anxious inquiries about the Selby properties may well have been prompted by just that fact. Furthermore, the commissioners for the valuation of 1535 thought Selby to be worth £829. 4s. 4d., a figure repeated in a steward's survey of 1540.[1] Here we have good reason to suspect something beyond the normal operation of the patronage system, especially since Sadler resold the property to Leonard Beckwith, who was the Augmentations Office surveyor responsible for the low evaluation. Finally, Beckwith was involved in a defence of his integrity in regard to his work in Yorkshire, especially with regard to Selby. Providentially, Sadler managed to secure the king's commission to hear the charges against Beckwith, who easily secured his quittance at the hands of his old friend. Short of the most damning positive evidence, one could hardly construct a better case for the existence of some of the peculation unfortunately exaggerated by Tawney. Yet there is more to the Selby purchase than meets the eye. In this instance Sadler used his secretarial influence to obtain property desired by a third party, the true middleman and speculator, Henry Whitereason of Hackney, a Sadler friend and sometime attorney. Oswald Sysson, the leasee of most of the Selby lands, told another tale, incriminating Beckwith, who in that version was the prime mover. At any rate, Sir Ralph apparently received the sum of £100 and a horse, disguised as an entry fine, for his part in the arrangement.[2]

Warwickshire was also a target for investment. In the early 1540s Sir Ralph obtained a considerable amount of land there, including the White Friar's Property in Coventry, worth £83. 12s. 6d.;[3] the manor of Nuneton, valued at £253. 9s. 3d. p.a.;[4] the great house known as 'le Habyte', worth £36. 13s. 4d.;[5] and Welford-on-Avon, a small manor worth only £4. 13s. 4d. p.a., acquired in 1546.[6] Sadler also bought Haselor Manor for £900[7] and the large woodlands included in Whytmore park, which were purchased at a capital outlay of £213. 3s. 4d.[8]

[1] *VE*, v, 12–14.
[2] PRO, SC 12/17/54. For the Sadler–Whitereason–Sysson–Beckwith exchange see G. W. O. Woodward, 'A speculation in monastic lands', *EHR*, LXXIX (1964), 778–83.
[3] PRO, C 66/753, pt. 14, m. 6, 22 March 1544; *VCH Warwicks.* II, 323–4.
[4] PRO, E 303/17/376, 1 Sept. 1540.
[5] Formerly the house and manor of the prioress. The mansion was sold to Sadler 26 Apr. 1541: PRO, E 315/212, fo. 128. Sadler's deed survives in E 303/17/376.
[6] *VCH Warwicks.* v, 193; for the value see *VE*, III, 96.
[7] Warwickshire Record Office, Warwick MSS. 259.
[8] PRO, SC 12/38/29.

The gentleman whose father once counted the Warwickshire profits of the Belknaps had become a great Warwickshire landlord.

This collection of Avon valley lands was augmented at the king's death in 1547. In that year Sadler completed a deed of purchase and exchange with the agents of Edward VI that dwarfed his other transactions. The whole of the huge college of Westbury-on-Trym, with holdings in Warwickshire, Gloucestershire and Worcestershire, was granted to Sadler in exchange for several Sadler parcels and a cash settlement. According to the patent issued in the exchange, the entire deal was a fulfilment of the old king's personal desires to reward Sir Ralph.[1] More likely than not that statement hides or otherwise obscures the facts, which amount to this: the exchange was the price worked out by Paget and Somerset in their efforts to secure his support in the veritable *coup* that followed Henry VIII's death.[2] As a member of the Privy Council and being also the most powerful commoner in Hertfordshire, able to raise a small army from among his tenants, his support was badly needed by the new government. Even the old three-cornered friendship was not a sufficient guarantee for the arch-plotters of the initial Edwardian settlement. The justifying clause in the deed of 1547 is perhaps an example of the kind of jobbery that Tawney always suspected, but that is, of course, mere speculation.

Whatever the explanation of the grant's existence, the particulars of the exchange are very impressive. Sadler surrendered seven manors worth some £308. 18s. 3d. p.a. and received from the Crown fifteen manors, municipal lands in Worcester, Bristol and London, several farms in Essex, numerous advowsons and other sources of ecclesiastical income—in all holdings worth £433. 18s. 3d. p.a.[3] The difference in annual value was rated at fifteen years purchase, which meant that Sadler was out of pocket £1,846 to the commissioners of the exchange.[4] On a cash basis, the entire transaction was worth £6,510, the calculation being based on fifteen years purchase. Few deals of the entire period, even those carried off by Tawney's 'syndicates', rivalled Sadler's exchange and purchase of 1547. He thereby acquired a position of eminence in the Avon–Bristol area equal to that he enjoyed in Hertfordshire. He had no betters and few peers about that county.

[1] PRO, C 66/733, pt. 12, m. 2*a*, 22 March 1547. See Strype, *Memorials*, II, i, 123.
[2] Pollard, *England under Protector Somerset*, pp. 22–9.
[3] PRO, E 318/968.   [4] PRO, E 305/F 29, 10 Dec. 1547.

One technique for comprehending Sir Ralph's place in the land market is simply to evaluate his transaction in terms of possible capital outlay. From the figures given above, it is likely that he made investments worth better than £10,000 in ready capital. An even more incisive method of interpreting the nature of his undertakings would be to fit his activities into a more generalised picture of the land market of the 1540s. In that way we can overcome the problems inherent in the mere aggregate capital investment, which is very difficult to gloss in modern terms. At the same time, we can thus provide some insight into the process of his rise among the gentry.

Sir Ralph's activities do not fit into the pattern drawn by the earliest scholars of the land market after the dissolution. In that pattern any turnover was taken to imply rampant speculation, especially when the lands dealt off were widely scattered. Although Sadler did acquire lands which on a superficial view had no intrinsic connection and were widely scattered geographically, a detailed look reveals the real unity in such holdings. They were chiefly parts of ecclesiastical estates which had formed common administrative units during an era in which the Crown had not yet rationalised the accounting system on a county basis. The Bruton priory lands spoken of above are a good example of such a non-nucleated holding extending over several counties and united for sale by the history of their administration. The same is true of the Stratford-le-Bowe lands. No matter how scattered the holdings might be geographically, they were up for sale as parcels of revenue units, a fact not obvious to the mere cataloguer of manors on a county basis. In the matter of Sadler's alienations, the same holds true. Consolidation and the reduction of administrative expense prompted the surrender of some of the lands of Bruton and Stratford in favour of the development of the more nucleated complexes. Alienation was also a technique for the support of the building programme at Standon.

Like many another purchaser of lands in the 1540s, Sadler ran up debts in order to pay for Crown lands. Luckily, some of the notes of payments due the court of Augmentations have survived; they testify to Sadler's instalment buying.[1] J. P. Cooper has demonstrated that this common practice was often necessary, since in most instances monastic lands were under long leases and therefore not immediately exploitable.

---

[1] PRO, E 315/1, fos. 109, 110a; 203, fo. 74b.

Place and Profit: The Henrician Land Market

The mere speculator stood much less chance of making a profit than did the man who held fast to the land for a generation or more, paying off debts and raising rents when leases expired.[1] In that connection it is worth noting that Sadler retained until his death[2] the greatest part of the lands acquired after the dissolution, either in his own right or in the form of estates created for his sons and daughters.[3] The total of his alienation, in terms of manorial units, was something less than 20 per cent.[4] Faulty genealogy and some misconception of the nature of the disposition of the former monastic lands raised the bogey of speculation, a spectre not very pertinent to Sadler's activities.

That is not to say that Sadler did not hope to turn a quick profit here and there. If we turn to his urban holdings rather than to manorial properties, alienations bear a different interpretation. Between 1539 and 1542 Sadler bought and sold a large number of messuages and plots of city lands, most of which were connected with Stratford-le-Bowe.[5] Since he retained the compact rural holdings of that rich manor, the selling of the valuable urban properties must bear closer inspection, before any talk of speculation is justified. A good part of his urban property was sold shortly after acquisition to his good friend and legal agent Henry Polsted.[6] Sadler also dealt part of the land to John Mychell,[7] his father-in-law.[8] This was especially the case with regard to some Hackney lands. Such transaction within the circle of one's friends and relatives suggests patronage rather than speculation. It looks very much like a case of Sir Ralph, who enjoyed court favour, helping less well-placed people. Surely his sale of a large London house to Sir John

[1] Cooper, *EcHR*, VIII (1956), 387.

[2] See his will in PCC Register 23 Spenser.

[3] For lands deeded to Henry Sadler's use: *VCH Herts*. III, 425; Chauncey, *The Antiquities of Hertfordshire*, I, 528; for Thomas Sadler see *VCH Worcs*. I, 157; *ibid*. IV, 158; for the lands deeded to Edward Sadler see Chauncey, *The Antiquities of Hertfordshire*, II, 179 and 309, as well as *VCH Herts*. III, 10 and 25.

[4] A substantial part of that figure went to his sons and to his daughters. It must also be remembered that he sold or exchanged a good deal of land with the Crown, often at a good profit. Hence the count of manors will lead to errors, if simple alienation is not checked against other relevant data.

[5] PRO, E 210/D 10497; C 66/685, pt. 8, mm. 29 and 22; C 66/704, pt. 4, m. 34, and 707, pt. 7, m. 32.

[6] PRO, E 326/B 5608; E 326/2 B, pt. 1, fo. 51 b and E 326/B 5609 and 5685.

[7] Hackney Public Library, Thyssen MSS. Y 150/1, m. 15 a, and Y 235/22.

[8] Lady Sadler's father's name was John Mychell. He was a merchant from Great Hadham, Essex. In the deeds cited in n. 7 above Lady Sadler is the grantor and John Mychell the grantee. The rents charged were less than nominal.

Dudley, on request, supplies no evidence of speculative lust.[1] And what are we to make of the sale of a mansion in Cannon Row to Sir Thomas Smith in 1547 for 200 marks?[2] After all, Smith was an important politician, not wholly without connections in his position as secretary of state to Edward VI.

Shrewd investment for profit and speculation are different things. Sir Ralph wanted profits, even huge ones, when they could be had. He was not above getting Brooke House for £1,000, only to sell it within six months to Sir Wymond Carew for £1,200.[3] Nor was he immune to the temptation of similar deals in York,[4] Bristol[5] and Warwickshire house properties.[6] Furthermore, he was not overly concerned with the decline of hospitality that might accompany such sales, if we can credit the testimony of a Yorkshire man who complained that Sadler sold to those who 'woulde kepe but small hospitalitie there' for the local poor accustomed to alms from the profits of church holdings.[7] Such reservations aside, these sales are evidence of Sadler's astuteness, since city lands were generally unencumbered by long leases and were in great demand, especially in London, where the population was growing rapidly. The market for such holdings was strong.

An interesting pattern emerges from a consideration of rural holdings which Sadler alienated. Little land closely related to the complexes of Hertfordshire and the Avon counties was sold. Some alienations in Surrey,[8] Essex[9] and Hampshire took place.[10] In Yorkshire Sadler sold a number of parcels of land to Beckwith under suspicious circumstances,

[1] The report is in BM Royal MSS. 7C xvi, fo. 151, 11 Aug. 1540. Sturge, 'The Life and Times of John Dudley', p. 350, states that Dudley got the house.
[2] Strype, *Sir Thomas Smith* (Oxford: Clarendon Press, 1820), p. 31.
[3] The example of Brooke house is of singular interest. After the purchase made jointly with Hales (see p. 197, n. 2, above), Hales in turn released his claim to the property in Oct. 1547 to Sir Ralph (Warwick Castle, The Earl of Warwick's MSS., Class OG. 308, Warwick 6628), thus giving Sadler a neat estate in the suburbs of London. But in February Sadler sold the house to Sir Wymond Carew for £1,200, which price also netted the entire manor, with all appurtenances (Warwick Castle, The Earl of Warwick's MSS. Class OG. 308, Warwick 6629).
[4] *HMC Various Reports*, ii, 57; *L & P*, xiv, ii, 742.
[5] The Bristol Archives Office, The Council House, Bristol, has some unaccessioned deeds (1960) showing Sadler's activity in that area. One item is worth noting, since it is an illustrated deed showing Sadler kneeling to receive from Henry VIII the land on which the modern city is built. Other MSS. relate to Sadler's holdings in Almondsbury, Clifton, Olveston, Turkdean, Upton, Sodbury, Bedon, all in Gloucs., and Ashley, Allesborough and Gorversley in Worcs.
[6] *VCH Warwicks.* ii, 323–4.
[7] PRO, SP 1/155, fo. 178, Sir John Negyll to Wriothesley, 26 Dec. 1541.
[8] PRO, E 326/B 7151; *VCH Surrey*, iii, 317.
[9] *L & P*, xix, i, 147 (77); xvii, 284 (6); xiv, i, 580 (69).   [10] *VCH Hants.* iv, 444.

as we have already noted.[1] But he never sold an acre of Hertford lands. He did part with some very valuable parcels in Coventry; but these were sold to his agent John Hales, after much very active seeking by the latter.[2] Some Worcestershire lands were surrendered also, including the manor of Astley[3] and that at Shelve,[4] as well as a number of smaller properties, not often in excess of a few virgates or half a hide.[5] Sales there were. But in three of the cases just mentioned the date of sale was 1556. In a fourth the sale took place in 1563.[6] Lands held for a dozen years or a score of years and then sold to a friend, John Hales again being the buyer, afford scant evidence to buttress a theory of speculative madness.[7] Even the sale of the large manor at Haselor to Fulke Greville in 1553 for £900 fails to support a theory which sees Sadler as a 'mere land speculator' in so far as Warwickshire is concerned.[8] Haselor was Sadler's a full decade before he sold it to Greville.

A congeries of reasons existed that better explain the pattern of purchase and alienation than does the idea of speculation. Fundamentally, Sadler's large-scale purchases and exchanges resulted in an over-extension of his resources. This created a need for ready cash with which to pay notes due in Augmentations. It also made it difficult for Sir Ralph to foot the bills accumulating in connection with the building of Standon, where he chose to erect a great house to mark the process of his rise. In 1546, just as the building grew out of the ground, outstanding notes on transactions made in 1540 matured also.[9] One manor resting on such a note was sold with specific mention of the fact that Sadler was hard-pressed to make a payment to the crown.[10] Furthermore, the bulk of the other alienations fall into two distinct groups, chronologically speaking. The urban lands were sold chiefly in 1541–2, when Sadler had taken on the huge aggregation of Hertfordshire lands.

---

[1] *L & P*, XVI, 379 (40).

[2] Warwick Record Office, Miscellaneous MSS. DR 127.

[3] *VCH Worcs.* IV, 232.   [4] *Ibid.* III, 395.

[5] *Ibid.* pp. 56, 185, 268; *VCH Warwicks.* V, 193.

[6] *Ibid.* IV, 167.

[7] Warwick Record Office, Warwick MSS. 259

[8] W. B. Bickley, *Abstracts of the Bailiff's Account of Monastic and other Estates in the County of Warwick* (London: Dugdale Society, 1923), xviii. Mr A. C. Woods of the Warwick Record Office writes of Sadler: 'It is my impression that Sadler's Warwickshire lands are largely the result of speculations in ex-monastic property' (Woods to Slavin, 8 March 1961). While I obviously cannot agree with Mr Woods, without his learning and generosity I should have no conclusions at all about the estates in question.

[9] See p. 200, n. 1.   [10] PRO, E 326/B 7151.

The outlying manorial properties were sold primarily in 1544–5, while Standon was under construction and while the purchase of Westbury-on-Trym was being planned. It needs to be stressed, therefore, that a superficial view of alienations will reveal little or nothing of the situation in which a rising gentleman found himself. It tells us even less about the reasons for buying and selling that might exist in any particular case. It seems that rational exploitation and consolidation were more vital in explaining Sadler's sales than was a fever to turn a quick profit.

There are several documents which enable us to say something about the use to which Sadler put the land he acquired, while also throwing some light on how he hoped to make them profitable. For Stratford-le-Bowe and other parcels in the Home Counties, Gervase Cawood kept account books in his capacity as Sir Ralph's receiver general.[1] Certain Yorkshire properties were surveyed for Sir Ralph and the results remain available today at Westminster cathedral.[2] A *compotus* relative to several Gloucestershire and Warwickshire manors survives in the Bristol City Archives Office.[3] In addition, a number of court cases and stray items throw some light on Sadler as a landlord.

From the Selby documents and other scattered manuscripts we can see how carefully Sadler attended to the exaction of feudal and manorial dues.[4] Views of court baron and court leet, as well as of frankpledge, reveal that Sadler kept a very close check on all matters related to rents, reversions, tithes, oblation and other spiritual dues, advowson rights of presentation, franchises, goal and gallows, rights of fair and markets, inquiries into the yields of mines and other subsurface rights and all the incidents of tenure, especially wardship, relief, heriots, escheats and boon work.

When tenants failed in any particular Sadler quickly claimed his due. In a chancery suit, he claimed that two tenants owed him an ancient

[1] BM Add. MSS. 35824.

[2] Westminster Cathedral Archives, Selby MSS. Se/CR/18–20; also Add. MSS. 2. I owe these references and my stay at Westminster Cathedral to Dr Kevin McDonnell of Queen Mary's College, London University.

[3] Bristol Archives Office, Unaccessioned MSS., item 'The *Compotus* of Sir Ralph Sadler's Gloucestershire and Warwickshire lands'.

[4] Some Westbury-on-Trym documents are in BM Stowe MSS. 671, fos. 251–67 and Harleian MSS. 7089, fos. 440–58. The Selby court rolls are at Westminster Cathedral Archives, Selby MSS. Se/CR/18020. Temple Chelsyn and Standon court baron accounts and views of frankpledge are preserved in Oxford University Library, Ancient Charters, Rolls 4–8.

rent of twenty-four bushels of salt which they refused to pay.[1] They charged that Sadler mouthed blatant falsehoods, traversing his claim that the abbots of Pershore had ancient payment of that kind, also demanding damages for the false charges.[2] Here was grist for the mill of those who wrote about the habits of the gentry as rack-renters and destroyers of the common man, using political influence to crush legitimate complaints. Unfortunately for that view, despite the fact that no decision survived in the case of Hunt and Squery *v.* Sadler, Sir Ralph was in the right. Among the particulars of Pershore is a direct affirmation of the rent claimed by Sadler and paid to the abbots by the last pre-dissolution tenants.[3]

Sadler's lawful conduct in that case can in no way provide us with a rule of thumb in discussing other suits, however. When he sued Wriothesley, asking the chancellor's help in protecting rights he claimed as lord of Astley manor against William Solway, the resultant evidence casts an unfavourable light upon Sadler. He demanded an increased entry fine upon the death of Solway's father. Sadler claimed that Solway's failure to pay constituted a forfeiture of his rights to the land. Consequently, Sir Ralph had leased the farm to a certain John Combes, who gladly paid the greater entry fine. Solway answered with a suit of *novel disseisin* in lands rightfully his by inheritance. Sadler, for his part, readily admitted that he was a rack-renter, justifying himself on the grounds that the custom of the manor allowed such increases over a period of years 'whereof the remembraunces of man is not to the contrarye...'.[4]

That Sir Ralph was a self-confessed rack-renter, the bane of the poor in the inflationary Tudor century, throws an interesting light on yet another case of great complexity. Alice Mercer, a tenant at Standon, sued for redress of grievances against Sir Ralph and Lady Sadler. Mrs Mercer was a widow who had spent the best part of her life helping her husband to improve their small farm. Then, upon her mate's death, she was left with the homestead and its appurtenances with which to support herself and several young children. But at that time Sadler had demanded an increased entry fine of £2, despite a lease agreement

---

[1] PRO, C 3/159/1, fo. 1, undated. [2] *Ibid.* fo. 2, undated.
[3] PRO, E 315/61, fo. 36a.
[4] PRO, C 1/1156/1, a file containing the bill of complaint and the traverse. I use the term 'rack-rent' in its technical sense, as the economic rent of a piece of land.

prohibiting such exactions. Despite the fact of her tenure of the land since 1537, she noted that Sadler 'of hys infeasyable covetous mynd extort powre and devillishe intent most cruelly forsiabley and wrong-fully dyd entre into the premysses' and dispossessed her. She was summarily ejected without warning. Her children had 'noe place where to putt theyre poore heades'. Further, Sadler's retainers destroyed the house and drove away the chattels. She, being a poor but honest woman, had no recourse save an appeal to the masters of Requests, especially since Sadler 'was a manne of suche powre...if she went withoute her graces[1] ayde she cold not prevayle agenst hym and scarcelie for the veray feare before thys tyme durst claim no redresse...'.[2]

It is entirely possible that Sir Ralph and Lady Sadler were guilty of the crimes alleged, and we ought not to explain away the vilest exploits of those in positions of relative power. Nor can we afford to accept such charges as evidence of the way in which Sadler exploited his land and influence. On this point we must in effect suspend judgement until we have conclusive evidence of one sort or another. At any rate, it is interesting to notice the date of Mrs Mercer's charges, during the first year of Mary's reign, and the ostentatiously Catholic tenor of the complaints, with their indictments of the Reformation and all that it entailed. That calls to mind the sobering fact that the great as well as the small were often the victims of a passionate age in which the stakes involved were the souls of men as well as their possessions.

From such hectic charges and counter-charges it is with some relief that we turn to more pacific means of exploiting resources. By doing so, we learn that Sadler went about the business of managing his huge estates in a precise way. Not only did he exact the highest entry fines and feudal dues. He also used his local stewards, collectors, ministers and receiver-generals in the Home Counties[3] and the Avon regions[4] in an exacting way. All rendered accounts to Gervase Cawood, the chief receiver for all of Sadler's lands. These documents included detailed extents of manors, itemised rents, statements of default, outstanding

---

[1] Bills sent to the Masters of that court always were in form of petitions to the sovereign.

[2] PRO, Requests 2/20/14, undated. For a similar case of ejectment: C 3/162/36; see also Charles M. Gray, *Copyhold, Equity, and the Common Law* (Harvard University Press, 1963), 65–6, for the background of the law.

[3] Gervase Cawood's book is in BM Add. MSS. 35824.

[4] Stephen Hales, brother of John Hales of Coventry, Sadler's administrative *aide*, is so named in a *compotus* of lands cited in note 7, page 198, above.

debts, records of produce sales and lists of the profits of manorial justice. Hence, Cawood's book, summarising the data of a number of estates, throws considerable light on Sadler's economy.

It was an economy well calculated to maximise revenue. Sir Ralph leased the major portion of the demesnes of each manor, keeping enough inland for the purpose of self-sufficiency. When surpluses occurred, Cawood had authority to market them for the best price, either locally or in the great London markets, depending on the location of the surplus producing units.[1] In the matter of letting farms, Sadler preferred copyholds on renewed takings to leases of any other kind. In the cities, where short-term leases were common and where rentals rose rapidly, Sadler was reluctant to grant long leases. He also regularly reduced the terms of leases at Selby and in Gloucestershire.[2] The evidence shows that he refused to be handicapped by long-term agreements in an age of rapidly rising prices and rentals. Only at Standon did he retain the demesne lands almost entirely, doubtless to support the large household there.[3] It would not be inappropriate to label his management shrewdly capitalistic.

The large *compoti* for Selby, Stratford-le-Bowe and Avon lands list hundreds of takings that illustrate the practices referred to above. Everything from small crofts to mills and other manufacturing facilities appear in these documents. Some tenants, Henry Hubblethorne for example, a very rich London alderman, leased huge amounts of land from Sadler, apparently subletting the property in question.[4] This helped Sadler to realise the full profit potential of his holdings. At Stratford-le-Bowe, where the data are unusually full, a good picture of the value of the estate emerges. For the manor and its appurtenances Sadler paid a sum equal to £120. 19s. 4d. p.a. at fifteen years purchase.[5] In the very year of the purchase, however, he farmed and otherwise exploited the property to the tune of £155. 3s. 8d., exclusive of the demesne lands, which yielded another £16. 16s. 8d., according to Cawood's ledger. The profit was something better than £50 more than the estimate made by the Crown's auditor.[6] Finally, every entry related

---

[1] BM Add. MSS. 35824, fo. 31*b*.   [2] PRO, E 315/104, fos. 222*a*–223*b*.

[3] Herts. Record Office, Standon MSS. 2–3.

[4] BM Add. MSS. 35824, fos. 11*a*–14*b*.

[5] PRO, E 318/969; *VE*, I, 137, gave the value as £121. 6s.

[6] BM Add. MSS. 35824, fos. 14*a*–16*b*.

to the Middlesex estate was checked by Cawood and an outside auditor, before being initialled by Sir Ralph himself.

Similar profits were made out of the Hackney lands and those in Essex and Kent.[1] Lands near Coventry, supposedly worth £203 p.a. to the Crown, made £233. 3s. 4d. for Sadler.[2] Selby properties for which Sadler paid at a rate based on a clear annual profit of £129. 6s. 8d. returned £137. 6s. 5d. when they were leased to one Oswald Sysson.[3]

Sadler's caution in auditing his receiver's accounts was matched by interest extended in other directions. Although he had a good and trustworthy staff of ministers charged with the management of his lands, he addressed himself to certain technological matters with genuine enthusiasm and with a fine eye towards the improvement of his estates. Of particular interest in that respect is the memorandum he prepared pertaining to Highhall and Lowhall in Essex. Sadler noted that in order to maximise profit there certain modifications had to be made in the property. His directions to the steward there were quite specific:

Fyrst, to skore the twoo great dyches that goeth along in the lane from the howse to the ryver warde. Then cause all the dyches on the northe syde of Buttchers marshe to be skored, that the water may come into the aforesayd dych of the long lane, and so into the ryver. Cause the tenants of Waltham-stowe to skowre theyr dyches on the northe west syde of Buttchers marshe. Also you must stubbe and stock Busshe marshe and Buttchers marshe, and make gud medowe of them, for Busshe marshe was, at my last beyng theyr, clene over growen wyth thornes. And you must also attend...[4]

There the manuscript becomes unreadable. But enough has survived to support the conviction that Sadler looked more deeply into his situation than to be content with mere speculation and rack-renting.

Aside from a few more figures, the trail of useful evidence is at an end. Nothing more attests to the management of the Sadler estates. For the majority of his manorial holdings no additional figures worth mention are now extant. Nor is there any great body of data illustrating Sadler's direct role in managing his lands. It is very unfortunte for this aspect of the story that no great peerage came to Sadler's family in the male line. Had that happened, we might have had at Standon a muni-ments room of some value to the social and economic historian. As it is,

---

[1] BM Add. MSS. 35824, fos. 30a–31b.
[2] See p. 206, n. 4, above.
[3] Westminster Cathedral Archives, Selby MSS. Add. 2.
[4] *SSP*, II, 28.

despite the fact that Sadler was a careful worker with years of administrative experience behind him when he became a great landholder, and notwithstanding his own claim that he had 'booked' every item involving his estates and every expense, since he first 'lyved on his own',[1] we have only the scattered manuscripts here surveyed.

Enough has survived, however, to allow some conclusions. What we have already presented, combined with our knowledge that he successfully exploited large tracts of woodland without depleting their stock of timber in an age of deforestation,[2] enables us to fit Sadler into the more generalised picture of the Tudor gentry emerging from recent studies.

The older view of the mad scramble for monastic lands motivated by speculative fever in this instance and, perhaps, in similar ones, must give way to a less dramatic thesis. The men who gained most from investment in land were those who held for the rising market of the next generation and those who practised skilful economy. Sadler did both. He successfully exploited what he held during the 1540s and early 1550s. Most of his alienations were made on the rising market of the late 1550s and the early 1560s. As Dr Habbakuk has so tenaciously maintained, the vital thing was not the buyers' market, although that existed for a time, to be sure. The major factor in successful investment in land was the curve of the income potential to which a purchaser acquired title and how well he cultivated that potential. The situation was the same with land as it was with office. If either could be acquired below the market value, one stood to maximise profit. But there was nothing automatic about it. In Sadler's case, Westbury-on-Trym is a good example of valuable holdings acquired at something like one-quarter below the going price. But only Selby promised large immediate profits through an apparently corrupt purchase agreement.

The most profitable lands were those that remained in Sadler's hands for a generation or more. He then stood to benefit from the steady rise in rents and agricultural prices at a time when labour rates were depressed. He was also in the best position to farm these lands, since they were then unencumbered by long-term leases. What Habbakuk and Dr Youings have described as the pattern of the successful entrepreneur seems to hold true in the case of Sir Ralph Sadler. Most of his purchases

---

[1] BM Sloane MSS. 1523, fo. 29*b*. [2] PRO, SC 12/38/29.

were honestly made at normal prices. Inflation rather than corruption was the chief factor benefiting the landlord with some staying power, which might be enhanced by trading briskly in urban takings, a statement made even more true when we consider that such lands seem to have been honestly under-evaluated by surveyors working for the court of Augmentations.[1] When all the pieces are put together, the picture that emerges is that of an intelligent and energetic man manipulating his capital well and utilising his high place to the best advantage. If the shadow of the rack-renter and the politician conniving to feather his own nest sometime encroaches, it never dominates.

Perhaps the picture does not flatter Sadler. But is that necessary? Skilful exploitation is not charity, a word so often on Sir Ralph's lips. Nor is desire for personal gain a concomitant of that zeal for the commonwealth which he always professed. Yet these are traits of men who are not monsters, either singly considered or taken as a class. Sadler did not owe his high station or his wealth to fraud and corruption. If his retainers did beat Dame Mercer's cows until a few of the dumb beasts died, let it be a necessary reminder that the 'new monarchy' was not really so new after all. The age of the Pastons and John Falstaff, in which fear was the twin brother of every humbly born Jack in the kingdom, died hard and was not yet consigned to the lumber room of history. Industry and intelligence were seconded then by power and prestige, which, sad to say, sometimes still took odious form. In all, however, Sadler was not an egregiously bad man, unless his wealth, which was egregious, is enough to qualify him for dishonour. Rather, as was fitting for Cromwell's man, his efficiency and passion for detail extended far beyond the council board, reaching into little corners of the pleasant valleys of the Avon and the Rib, into the counting house he built beyond the octagonal house where he kept his beloved hawks.

[1] The literature of the revisionist historians is by no means a substitute orthodoxy. Partisanship remains lively on all sides of the question, although new dimensions have been added by recent articles and lectures on the role of the gentry and middle classes in the universities and elsewhere. I have in mind here especially the work of Mark Curtis, Joan Simon and Christopher Hill. For the main work on the economic side see H. J. Habbakuk, 'The Market for Monastic Property, 1539–1603', *EcHR*, 2nd ser. x (1958), 362–80; the Cooper article already cited in *EcHR*, VIII (1956); Joyce Youings, 'The Terms of the Disposal of the Devon Monastic Lands', *EHR*, LXIX (1954), 18–38; and, finally, Eric Kerridge, 'The Movement of Rents, 1540–1640', *EcHR*, 2nd ser. VI (1953), 16–34. In addition see the early polemical works listed by Hexter in his appendix to 'Storm over the Genty' reprinted in *Reappraisals in History*. Finally, Lawrence Stone's new book, *The Crisis of the Aristocracy*, offers detailed study of most questions touched upon here.

Place and Profit: The Henrician Land Market

As a gentleman in office, Sadler exacted the full measure of his place. Given the Tudor system, he would have to be set down as a stupid man had he done less. He put to use every lever his office supplied, whether it was the chance to acquire land by gentle pressure on Mr Hanby or the more suspicious work that brought Selby and Westbury-on-Trym into his hands. While some of his peers longed for patents of nobility, Sadler had a great appetite for something more sensible. His entire career as a member of the office-holding gentry seems to confirm Trevor-Roper's thesis. Sadler rose because gain was easily within his reach as a politically well-situated man. On the inside in all matters, including the market for monastic lands, he made the most of his chances.[1] 'As fishees are gotten with baytes so are offices caught with sekyng,' wrote Sir William Cecil to Sir Ralph Sadler on 27 April 1568, just before Sir Ralph's appointment to the chancellorship of the duchy of Lancaster.[2] The same candid and witty remark applies equally to the market for lands during the 1540s.

[1] Tawney, *EcHR*, XI, 10. [2] *CSPD, 1547–1580*, p. 309.

10

THE PARADOX OF SADLER'S POSITION

I can not endure the spending of that time in designing an action which
might perform two; or that delay in performing two which might well
perform twenty.
SIR RALPH SADLER

The investigation of Sadler's career ends in a paradox. Unlike his contemporaries Cecil, Paget and Paulet, to name but a few, Sir Ralph never
gained a peerage. Despite great riches, the enjoyment of the confidence
of Henry VIII and Elizabeth I, continuous tenure of high office over a
half-century crowded with revolutionary events and the fact that he
was Cromwell's disciple and Cecil's confidant, Sadler never scaled that
ultimate peak of success in Tudor politics.

Factors of a non-political sort appear to have played a fundamental
role in that respect. Of these, none was more a vital deterrent than his
marriage. That Lady Sadler was not the ideal wife for a climbing
courtier seems clear enough when one considers that her name hardly
appears in royal household books, those oblique records of Tudor
pageantry which take the place of presence lists in the sixteenth century.[1]
There one finds recorded the activities of the court on the queen's side,
with the wives of councillors and courtiers a normal part of the royal
entourage. Lady Sadler never attended court. She might send presents,[2]
but she was conspicuous by her absence.

Sadler was at pains to explain something of a minor mystery in July
1543 when he wrote to Henry VIII begging that the king excuse Lady
Sadler from a much rumoured appointment as governess to the child
queen of Scotland. With great reserve, he rehearsed the 'bruits' and the
difficulties involved:

And whereas it haith pleased your Maiestie to appoint me and my wife for to
supply and furnish that part of the treatie...I have thought it my bounden
dutie to render unto your roiall maiestie mine humble and lowlie thankes
upon my knees that it hath pleased you maiestie to conceive suche an opinyon

---

[1] BM Harleian MSS. 6074; Add. MSS. 45716; Cotton MSS. appendix xxviii.

[2] BM Add. MSS. 45716, fo. 16a; Arundel MSS. 97, fos. 167a–170b; *The Book of William
Dunche*, pp. 5–7.

of us, as to think us mete to serve your highnes in a place of such trust and credit. And as I am bounden, so shall I not fayle to serve most willinglie, either here or wheresoever, and...to the uttermost of my poor wit and powr; assuryng you also for my poore wife, that she hath as gud a wyl to serve, according to your maiesties appointment, as any women in lyfe. But as she is most unmete to serve for such a purpos...havyng never been brought up at court, nor knowing what appertaineth thereto; so that, for lack of wit, and convenyent experiences in all behalfs, she is undoubtedlie not able to supplie the place to your maiesties honor.[1]

There were a number of reasons alleged, including the matter of her current pregnancy, but the truly interesting one was veiled. Sadler spoke of 'such impedimentes' in his wife's past life as to render her neither grave enough nor wise enough to tutor a future queen.

Behind that extraordinary letter of self-denial there is a long story which helps to explain the mysterious 'impedimentes' and other features of Sir Ralph's positive dislike for the life of the court as well as his providing a possible explanation for his not being elevated to the peerage.

Lady Sadler was at birth Helen or Ellen Mychell, the daughter of John Mychell of Great Hadham, Essex.[2] Her father was not much of a man by worldly standards. He made little impression on the subsidy-men who surveyed Dunmowe hundred from time to time, a place famous in legend for the marital squabbles of its inhabitants. After 1524, when he was rated at 40s.,[3] he disappears from the lists, presumably because he went off to London in 1528 or 1529 in order to pursue a mercantile career.[4]

Born in modest circumstances in a little Essex village about two miles from Tiltey abbey, where the young Sadler may have occasionally visited his father during the Dorset years, Mychell's girl grew up to find a hard life. Just about the time of her father's move to London, she married a man from Sevenoaks, in Kent, named Mathew Barre.[5] Her husband was also apparently a man of slender resources.[6] And by virtue

---

[1] *SSP*, I, 229-30. [2] London, Inner Temple Library, Petyt MSS. 535/6, fo. 336b.

[3] PRO, E 179/108/161, m. 5a.

[4] PRO, E 179/108/346, m. 3b. The move to Hackney is implied in BM Harleian MSS. 7089, fos. 450a–b; see also Hackney Public Library, Thyssen MSS. Y 151, m. 13d.

[5] BM Stowe MSS. 671, fo. 251a.

[6] The Barres of Sevenoaks were not rated in the subsidies levied between 1524–47, according to the lists and rolls preserved in PRO, E 179/124/208, 216, 222, 223, 262 and E 179/125/269, 271, 282 and 287.

of that seemingly innocent act she managed to produce the most vexing situation faced by Sadler and his biographer.

According to the oldest account of that marriage, one written in Elizabethan times by the Jesuit historian Nicolas Sanders, a deep scandal blighted the union. Sanders reported an extremely scandalous matter, that while Barre still lived Helen contracted a bigamous marriage with Ralph Sadler. Barre had allegedly deserted his wife. She, thinking her husband dead, met Sadler while they were both in Cromwell's employ, and then married him. Her station in life was not an honourable one at the time, since she was a common laundress, according to the often gossipy Jesuit. Then the unexpected happened. Barre showed up in London very much alive, after the lapse of several years. Sadler, 'not an obscure man', contested Barre's claims. While noting that Matthew's uxoriousness came a little late in the day, Sanders was really amazed at what passed for justice during the English Reformation: a special commission awarded Helen Mychell Barre to Sir Ralph, utterly confounding her true spouse as well as the laws of matrimony.[1]

Protestant historians went immediately to the defence, for Sadler was a minor religious hero, Knox's mentor in 1560, and also the victim of Jesuit vilification. Bishop Burnet, for example, in his justly famous *History of the Reformation*, wrote as follows:

This is, as far as I can learn, a forgery from the beginning to the end: and it seems that Sadler, that was a privy councillor in Queen Elizabeth's time, did somewhat that so confounded Sanders, that he resolved to be revenged of him and his family, by casting such aspersions on him. I find no footing of any such story. Sure I am, there is nothing concerning it in the records of the parliament. And for the business of the dissolution of this marriage for adultery, absence or any other great cause, there was so great and so strict any inquiry made into it, after the parliament was ended, in the case of the Marquis of Northampton, that it was clear that it was the first of that sort that was examined; and might perhaps, after it was confirmed in parliament in the fifth yeare of this reign...have been made such a precedent for tother cases.[2] But this of Sadler, in the first parliament, is a contrivance of the author.[3]

---

[1] Nicolas Sanders, *De origine ac progressu schismatis Angliae* (Romae: Bartholomae Banfadoni, 1586), pp. 279–80.

[2] The problem of divorce in the 1540s is the subject of an article by A. G. Dickens, 'The Marriage and Character of Archbishop Holgate', *EHR*, LII (1937), 428–42.

[3] *History of the Reformation*, V, 593–4.

Scott and other nineteenth-century historians accepted the existence of some parliamentary process touching Sadler's marriage, but they persisted in considering Sander's tale a malicious slander.[1] Led by Froude, they believed that the papist historian had 'collected in his book every charge which malignity had imagined against Henry VIII and his ministers...and used them' to colour the truth.[2] Stoney, the least of these writers, but of some interest because of his descent from Sir Ralph, admitted that Lady Sadler was the wife of Barre, also crediting the kernel of the tale, that Barre was alive when the second marriage took place. Yet he percipiently spoke of her as a woman of 'undoubted credit and respectability, hardly a laundress'.[3] For him the partisan issue was one of social standing!

The woman called Margaret Sadler by Stoney was Ralph Sadler's wife. That her real name was Helen or Ellen cannot obscure that fact, though Tudor genealogists and heralds knew little about her and seem to have added to the confusion surrounding her. Their ignorance was an embarrassment to their craft, and Hertfordshire visitations were either silent about Lady Sadler[4] or else reported in error on her identity.[5] An entry typical of the more complete but erroneous variety, with glosses added in a later hand, is more than ample to demonstrate that point: 'Sir R. Sadler m. Margarette daughter of— Mychel.[6] A common laundress to Cromwell who Sir R. in the absence of her first husband married, that is M. Barre a tradesman in London.'[7]

The true and the false are so equally mixed in such reports as to set a problem for Sadler's career as well as for our understanding of the actual background of a peculiar piece of parliamentary business that escaped Burnet. Happily, some chancery manuscripts help to set the record straight.

In 1544 Sadler was in the north, caring for the treasure expended on the Scottish campaign of that year. He returned to London in 1545, there to confront a man who under the influence of drink had proclaimed himself the true husband of the privy councillor's wife. Lord

[1] *SSP*, I, iv; Stoney, *Memoir of the Life and Times of Sir Ralph Sadler*, p. 13; Chalmers, *Biographical Dictionary*, XXVII, 28–32.
[2] *History*, X, 550–1.
[3] Stoney, *Memoir of the Life and Times of Sir Ralph Sadleir*, p. 14.
[4] BM Harleian MSS. 1234, fo. 153; 1504, fo. 3; 1546, fos. 3b, 4, 4b and 5.
[5] *Ibid.* 1547, fo. 27; 1565, fo. 61b.   [6] *Ibid.* 1565, fo. 61b.
[7] This last portion was added in a nineteenth-century hand.

Chancellor Thomas Wriothesley's man had heard the boast, reported it, and subsequently seized Barre, who was kept in custody until Sadler returned to question him in person. Barre insisted that what he claimed was true, that here indeed was a clear case of bigamy and that he intended to have his own.[1]

A commission was duly appointed to investigate the conflicting claims. Heading that body was Thomas Cranmer, Sadler's friend and political ally. Sitting with him were the Conservative bishops of Worcester and Chichester, Heath and Day. Although the three did not agree in basic matters of ecclesiastical polity,[2] they were joined by the royal commission in the hearing of a cause with political and doctrinal overtones.[3] After taking evidence and the testimony of witnesses including that of the parties involved, they issued a report concluding that a true and lawful marriage did exist between Barre and Lady Sadler, as was proved by local records and the fruit of Mrs Barre's womb in the shape of two children fathered by Barre. That being the case, the bishops learnedly confessed themselves perplexed by the ambiguous marriage had between Sadler and his consort. They admitted themselves open to a more detailed inquiry, thus avoiding a decision for a time.[4]

While no implications of great legal moment came forth as a result of the commissioners' work, the more particular interests of Sadler and his *wife* were vitally affected, since they had had seven children who were now clearly bastards, barring some unexpected remedy. The old canon law was not operative in England by that time, and the Henrician church had no code of its own. Some solution had to be found, if equity was to prevail, since Sadler apparently was the victim of an honest error, while his supposed wife was the victim of an evil man who perhaps hoped to profit from her improved circumstances.

In such circumstances recourse was had to parliament. It cut the badly knotted marital ties with a deftness peculiar to its expanding powers. On 10 December 1545 the Lords' *Journal* contained a note of the first reading of a 'bill for R. Sadaler'.[5] On the 14th the Lords heard

[1] *L & P*, xx, ii, 850(19), 23 Nov. 1545.
[2] Smith, *Tudor Prelates and Politics*, p. 306.
[3] *L & P*, xx, ii, 910(78), 29 Nov. 1545.
[4] PRO, C 84/785, no. 1.
[5] Great Britain, *Journals of the House of Lords, 1509–1577* (London, n.d.), p. 273, col. b.

the second and third readings and passed the bill with nobody dissenting.[1] On the very next day the bill was sent to the Commons.[2] There the bill was apparently amended, for on the 19th Sir Anthony Browne and other councillors carried the bill back to the Lords for reconsideration.[3] Finally, after five days of rather obscure movement back and forth between the two Houses, the bill was read a third time as amended and approved by the Commons, securing passage as 'an acte for Sir Ralphe Sadler knighte'.[4] During the final stages Sadler, himself a veteran councillor and parliament man, expedited the movement of the bill in person.[5]

The act in question resulted from a private bill and as such was not necessarily enrolled with the public statutes. Enrolment was upon request of the beneficiary. On this occasion Sadler had good reason to spare both expense and publicity. Nor was it ever published with the other *Statutes of the Realm,* while the existence of some process for Sadler is noted there. That in itself explains Burnet's error in fact and also sets Stoney's *apologia* in context, although nothing in print demonstrates the true nature of the settlement effected by Parliament. In fact only the efforts of William Petyt, that shrewd collector of parliamentary curiosities which might be useful to a Williamite hoping to illuminate the great power of the parliament, have preserved intact from a chancery exemplification 'the unprecedented case of Sir Ralph Sadler, anno xxxvii Henrici VIII'.[6] Subsequent copies of the document in late Stuart hands appear to rest on Petyt's text rather than the original chancery manuscript.[7] The latter still exists however and was found among a bundle of unrelated papers.[8]

All versions agree on the basic facts. Barre told the whole truth. He had deserted his wife. She inquired about him and searched for him for a number of years before giving up hope, at which time she began to consider entering a nunnery as a cure for her despair. Dissuaded from that choice by a friend of Thomas Cromwell, she sought and obtained

[1] *Ibid.* p. 274, col. b.　　　　　　[2] *Ibid.* p. 275, col. a.
[3] *Ibid.* p. 278, col. b.　　　　　　[4] *Ibid.* p. 279, col. a.
[5] *Ibid.* pp. 279, col. a to 280, col. a.
[6] London, Inner Temple Library, Petyt MSS. 535/6, fos. 335–50b.
[7] BM Stowe MSS. 671, fos. 251–67; Harleian MSS. 7089, fos. 440–58.
[8] PRO, C 89/2/29 and C 89/6/2. Together these manuscripts form the whole of the text of the bill. Apparently, they were torn apart before the time at which they were catalogued during the eighteenth century. The Petyt copy and those in the BM show no significant differences.

the favour of the king's secretary, gaining employment in his house-hold. There she met Sadler. After a year or more he confessed his love for her and, seeing that she was an 'honest woman', by which it seems he meant to accent her account of the birth of her children, he married her. All of the details of Helen Mychell Barre's unhappy past are fully rehearsed: her humble origins, her husband's profligate ways and the plight of a deserted mother in a society not given to too much pity emerge in often lurid lights.

Such a past was a sufficient motive for Lady Sadler's avoidance of the court of Henry VIII. While it is fair to note that she bore seven still living children by 1543, as well as two who had died in their infancy, that cannot be taken to explain her situation, since many another courtier's wife raised a large family while playing her part in her husband's fortunes. Hence, while Sanders lacked an adequate warrant for the assertion that she was a menial, her defenders erred on the other side. Beyond any fault attributed to her by virtue of the real scandal, she was neither well born nor well educated. Her single accomplish-ment with regard to society was her good marriage. And that statement reveals the paradox of her position as well as Sadler's.

Since Cromwell obviously had Ralph's interest at heart throughout Sadler's long apprenticeship, and since Cromwell was anything but a sentimental maker of love matches, how did Ralph's disadvantageous marriage come to take place? That the two met in his employ and called on him to bless the fruit of the union had between them by standing god-father to two sons who in succession were given his name only confirms the puzzlement.[1] Cromwell knew the value of a good marriage as well as any man, even William Cecil.[2] Sadler, for his part, was no sentimentalist either, if we can judge from the marriages he arranged for his daughters.[3] Jane, the youngest of the Sadler girls, went to her father's friend and senior, Sir Edward Baeshe, the high Henrician official and subsequent member of the Elizabethan naval board.[4] That

[1] BM Cotton MSS. Titus B I, fo. 343, undated (1536?).

[2] Conyers Read, *Mr Secretary Cecil and Queen Elizabeth* (New York: Knopf, 1955), p. 34.

[3] This statement is based on uncatalogued material made available to me from the files of the History of Parliament Trust Offices, Tavistock Square, London: see the trays on the Tudor Parliaments marked 'Sir George Horsey, Sir Edward Elrington, Sir Thomas Bolles and Sir Edward Baeshe, Sadler's sons-in-law'. I wish to thank Sir John Neale and Miss Helen Miller for their kindness in this matter.

[4] Baeshe was born in 1506 and died in 1587. Under Henry VIII he was chief victualler to the navy. He served as an M.P. for Preston, and was one of Sadler's nominees in the duchy of Lan-

leaves us with the impolitic reason of congeniality to Sadler's tastes. He had a natural disposition to shy away from the court and to mask his private life. While there may be something paradoxical in imagining a highly successful bureaucrat with a flair for diplomacy and intrigue who at the same time disliked frivolity and abhorred masks and revels, Sadler seems to have combined a quiet uxoriousness with Tudor politics. Thus Standon was something more than a country seat for a rich bureaucrat-courtier; it became a retreat verging on isolation for his family, a place in which he and his family could stand apart from events they felt unsuited for and the scandals that broke around their heads in 1545.

Standon had been a part of Sadler's life for a long time. In 1537 he served Jane Seymour as high steward there.[1] Holding fast to the past after the queen's death in that year, he availed himself of the right to use the manor house, for in 1539 Audley reported visiting Standon to see Sadler's wife.[2] By 1540 the newly minted secretary of state had exchanged two annuities for the former royal manor.[3] Shortly thereafter he began the lengthy process of integrating the ancient lands of the estate into a major complex of Hertfordshire lands, all the while making use of the old manor house.[4] Whenever the rigours of royal service allowed, Sadler spent time on the banks of the Rib with his wife and children. He hated to be apart from them. Every day away was a year, he once remarked.[5]

As Sadler became a dominant man in Hertfordshire, not only in terms of his local position but in terms of his service as a knight for the shire and a privy councillor, he simultaneously built his estate at Standon. It was a relationship profitable for him and the Crown as well, since 'perusing the shire to any advantage' in money matters was impossible without him.[6] All the while Sir Ralph planned to obtain a regrant of Standon in fee simple, which he finally managed in 1544.[7] Soon after his return from Scotland in 1545 he commissioned his agents

caster. He exhibited Puritan sympathies during Elizabeth's reign, while serving as a navy board official, according to Dr Clifford Davis of Wadham College, Oxford.

[1] BM Royal MSS. 7F xiv, fo. 79.
[2] PRO, SP 1/153, fos. 118–19, Audley to Cromwell, 12 Sept. 1539.
[3] L & P, xvi, 379 (26), 11 Dec. 1540.   [4] VCH Herts. III, 347.
[5] PRO, SP 1/97, fo. 56, Sadler to John ap Rice, 28 Sept. 1535.
[6] PRO, SP 1/170, fo. 122a, Robert Dacres to Sir Anthony Denny, 13 March 1542.
[7] PRO, E 318/967.

to undertake the building of a great mansion on the site of the old manor, high on the stony hill from which the place took its name.[1]

Standon House, set hard by the River Rib, was built on a scale grander than that intended by Sadler.[2] Although the details have been lost it is clear that he wanted a house of stature without desiring a conspicuous place. The results of the labours of 1545 were very conspicuous.[3]

The new house was of the courtyard type so popular in Tudor architecture. It was completed in a little over a year, as is attested by the yellow stone still standing in the gateway, '1546' staring out at the visitor from the encircling motif of Tudor roses and the Sadler arms. Beyond that gate stood a little Hampton Court, perhaps the work of Edward Thorpe, the great Tudor domestic architect.[4] The large brick building was nearly square, with huge castellated towers at the corners. Tall, octagonal double chimneys and a clock and bell tower stood in the centre of the main wall. Judging from the plan and a number of views of the house preserved in the Hertford Record Office, there were upwards of fifty rooms in the three-storey house topped with Spanish tiles above pink walls ornamented in yellow carved stone insets which employed the motif of the gateway: Tudor roses flanked by Sadler's arms and crest.[5] It was the home of a rich gentleman, in fact of an aristocrat.

Within the walls were gathered all the trappings of aristocratic life. Inventories of the principal rooms taken in the late sixteenth and early seventeenth centuries testify to the opulence of the furnishings.[6] The common dining room was large enough to accommodate three great carved Spanish oak tables, two other tables, fifteen 'olde Turkie chaires', two Turkish carpets, a pair of ivory inlaid chess tables set with elaborate men, other gaming facilities and a number of other pieces. The walls were richly hung with seven tapestries 'with scenes' unfortunately not further described. In the family dining room there were

[1] Chauncey, *The Antiquities of Hertfordshire*, I, 419.
[2] Fuller, *The Worthies of England*, II, 41.   [3] *VCH Herts.* III, 354.
[4] 'An Old English Country House: Standon, Herts.', *The Burlington Magazine*, LXXXII (1943), 110–14, an unsigned article.
[5] Hertfordshire Record Office, Minet Collection, Miscellaneous Drawings, VI, 55 ff. Other fine drawings by 'Mr Oldfield' are in BM Add. MSS. 36366, fos. 223–30. The earliest engraving of Standon was done in the late seventeenth century by Jan Drapentier; it is in Chauncey, *The Antiquities of Hertfordshire*, II, 440–1.
[6] The late sixteenth-century inventory is printed in the article cited in n. 4 above. The *SSP*, II, 601–12, prints a 1620 inventory.

a dozen tapestried chairs of ordinary size and three 'grete tapestrie chaires'. The walls there were decorated with five hangings depicting the tale of 'Tobie and his dogg'. A richly tapestried billiard chamber, hung throughout in cloth-of-silver, stood adjacent to the dining room. Nearby was the royal chamber, adorned with three tapestries showing 'the marriage of the Queene of Scottes', a fitting memorial to a diplomat's failure. Both Mary of Scotland and Elizabeth used that room, in 1551 and 1578.[1]

In the long gallery, a room used on occasion by Elizabeth's Privy Council for very important business,[2] there were seven great maps, a large collection of uncatalogued books, some histories and chronicles, and a great collection of sculptured heads of the kings of England *en roundeaux*, among them Henry II, Richard II, the Lancastrians, Henry VII and Henry VIII.[3] There were also fifteen paintings, including a number of royal portraits, among them the double portrait of Mary and Elizabeth as young girls, two of Sadler himself, probably the work of the Elizabethan court painter Marcus Gheeraerts. That room also housed the famous Holbein portrait of Thomas Cromwell currently in the Tudor Room of the National Portrait Gallery in London, but still to be seen at Standon in Lord Chesterfield's time.[4]

Sadler's private study was richly covered with carpets from Turkey and various hangings. Of greater interest to the historian, perhaps, was the presence of a 'grete Englishe *Bible*' near his desk. Nearby were the domestic offices and the chapel. The worship-chamber was stark, even austere, with a pulpit and plain table for services, twenty-six low-backed chairs, eighteen service books and a *Bible*, but lacking in decoration of any kind whatsoever. It was a chapel decidedly low church in appearance, even Puritan, confirming everything we know about the religious sensibility of its builder. Between the chapel and the study was the library. Much to my dismay, however, the inventories fail to specify one volume by name in that 'large librarie of bookes'.

Dozens of other rooms, exclusive of the domestic offices flanking the courtyard on the west side and extending far beyond the main line of the house on the south side, were also described in the inventories. One

[1] Strype, *Memorials*, II, i, 502 and 199.
[2] A number of council letters printed in *SSP*, *HP* and *CSPD* are dated from Standon.
[3] Oxford, Bodleian Library, Gough MSS. fo. 188, 1786, Robert to Gough to ?
[4] *HMC Portland MSS.* IV, 49, 1733, George Virtue to earl of Oxford.

of the noteworthy features was the octagonal falcons' house, where Sir Ralph kept the birds he loved so well, breeding them and training them for the hunts he conducted as Elizabeth's falconer.[1] The descriptions of Standon's contents close with long lists of possessions that afford other glimpses of the wealth there assembled, not the least being the 1,316 ounces of gold and silver plate.

All in all the evidence of these documents supports well enough what we already knew of Sadler. The material possessions were suited to his newly won position in Tudor society. The chapel was what we might have expected. The historical-mindedness revealed in collections of maps, histories and chronicles, as well as in the portraits and busts, fitted well with his employment. The great Holbein reaffirms his loyalty to a great man, also serving to put Sadler's career in perspective, since it was flanked by the heads of the Tudor Henries and nearby could be found scenes of the life of Mary, queen of Scots, and portraits of the Tudor queens themselves.

Sir Ralph lived at Standon in a manner suitable for the master of so great a manor. Surrounded by his growing children, a house full of servants, hundreds of tenants and the villagers of the largest vill in Braughin hundred, Sadler was truly a successful courtier-politician.[2] Some men among his tenants showed his badge and livery, for he was allowed one hundred retainers above household servants.[3] Perhaps those men, sporting the motto 'I serve only the King' on their sleeves, also served Dame Mercer and her cattle the ill-fare she complained of in 1554. Perhaps they helped him with the burgesses of Standon borough, which he actually owned.[4] They no doubt helped to fill the local church, which he controlled then and lies in now, where plainsong still echoes over the Rib.[5] For the rest, not much remains of that vanquished splendour. The bustling market he once managed is now a railroad junction.[6] Little of the wealth that caused Lord Walter Aston to desert Tixhall in Staffordshire for Standon is still visible. Where the munificent Astons entertained Drayton, sparrows play today.[7]

[1] *VCH Wilts.* IV, 362.
[2] PRO, E 179/220/144; 121/160–75, subsidy rolls for Braughin and adjacent hundreds.
[3] PRO, C 66/715, pt. 5, m. 4.
[4] PRO, SC 12/1567, minister's account for Standon, 1545.
[5] Chauncey, *The Antiquities of Hertfordshire*, II, 443–4. [6] *VCH Herts.* III, 348.
[7] George E. Cockayne, *Complete Peerage of England, Scotland, Ireland, etc.*, rev. ed. V. Gibbs, 13 vols. (London: Macmillan, 1910–49), I, 286.

Lord Aston's tenure of Standon beginning in 1660 serves well to introduce our summing up. Ironically, Sadler's heir through his granddaughter Gertrude was a royalist and a Catholic whose only talent was in wasting the estate gathered by an ancestor whose strong 'precision' learnings would no doubt have discomforted his heir.[1] Sadler's faith and service were mocked by the course of time in which Standon became an entry for priests smuggled into England from Rheims and Douai. Even to the third generation the sins of the fathers were visited upon the sons. Aston broke Sadler's corporate hope for posterity: he neither knew God nor served Him. In his service of Mammon he failed to heed the maxim carved in wood behind the master's chair in the great hall: 'Waste not, want not, spare not.' Only that last phrase sounded at Standon in the seventeenth century.[2] Unlike Sir Ralph, who attended to the villagers and saw to it that the parish was well administered by officers of his own choosing, Aston did not keep the old ways, failing even to serve the customary dinner on St Thomas's feast in emulation of Christ.[3]

The contrast between gatherer and spender marks other paradoxes and ironies of Sir Ralph's career in Henrician politics as well. He was a most cautious and circumspect man who played an important role in four reigns. Yet he married impetuously. Personally frugal and given much to the rigours of outdoor life and horsemanship, he shied away from court. Yet he built lavishly at Standon and may even have thereby incurred the royal displeasure on account of the resemblance to Hampton Court. Sadler was not vindictive in politics when enemies went under, as Gardiner did in 1550, for example. But he exacted the last ounce from his copyholders and tenants on 364 days of the year, only to feast them royally on the other day. Unable to disguise his deep distrust and hatred of papists, he none the less advised more than one sovereign to tread cautiously in religious affairs, whatever his personal predilections might be. When souls were concerned, *circumspecte agatis* was always his motto.

In major policies he was moderate. That moderation which was the

---

[1] Mathew Parker, *The Correspondence of Mathew Parker*, ed. John Bruce and T. Perrowne (Cambridge University Press, 1853), pp. 423, 427–8, for the archbishop's complaints about Sadler's sympathy for the Puritans.

[2] Hertfordshire Record Office, Miscellaneous MSS. 'Cussan's MS. History of Hertfordshire', II, 205.

[3] *Ibid.* p. 204.

dominant note of his career was the opposite of lack of conviction, however. Nor did it mask a lack of courage, as his Elizabethan career amply demonstrated. He simply never tried to out-do his fellows. Though blessed with good features—he was a slender man of fair size, with light brown hair and blue eyes and regular ways—he resisted the affectation and foppishness of the court.[1] When the defects of his marriage became public knowledge, he acted sensibly and honourably, thereby confirming a liability. What would a Richard Rich have done? Concise and effective as a writer of diplomatic dispatches, he laboured to hide his deep wit and gift for plain and effective use of his native tongue. Unspectacular but sound, his state papers echoed his life and it has therefore been his fate to remain bound within the dusty covers of those folios.

His virtues were those of moderation in all things, if virtues they were in an age of excess. An onlooker in 1543 or in 1547 might have marked Sadler for greatness in the kingdom's political life. He was Cromwell's man, secure in the king's favour, rich, skilled and confident. He was years ahead of some other Henrician careerists on the political ladder, for examples consider Petre and Cecil. Yet he gave way to them in a short time. He was reluctant to assert himself and lacked the quality of being dramatic. He had enough to be trusted, to be an intimate of kings and prime movers of great affairs. But he lacked the ineffable stuff that made for greatness. Most of all, he lacked the aggressiveness that every first-rate politician commanded in that tough age. Of his wit and wisdom there can be doubt only for him who overlooks the many volumes of his correspondence.

Suffice it to say that wit and wisdom were coupled with moderation at a time when these were subordinate virtues. Under Henry VIII only those who took the greatest risks figured in the greatest rewards. Like Cromwell and his mentor Wolsey, one had to grasp at the brass ring, even at the risk of losing one's seat, or, worse still, one's head. Sadler never reached for the top prize, and when it threatened to fall into his lap, in 1540, he failed to make the most of his chance. Since he had

[1] Mr Roy Strong of the National Portrait Gallery in London is of the opinion that the portraits of Sadler defaced by a 'stylist' in the nineteenth century were the work of the court artist Marcus Gheeraerts the Elder, without ruling out the possibility that Gheeraerts the Younger painted them. I would like to thank Mr Strong and his friends in the Department of Prints of the British Museum for their help in finding and criticising the extant drawings and portraits of Sadler.

industry and intelligence as well as a good understanding of the machinery, there must have been some great lack in him that will help to explain the limited role he came to play in Tudor politics. Perhaps we can disguise our ignorance by saying that he lacked the passion for politics that distinguishes the successful statesman. For any consideration of either his diplomacy or his domestic administrative career leads unavoidably to one conclusion: he was never an independent statesman of note, although he remained for more than half a century a valuable councillor and administrator.

He had an honourable career but not a great one. He could not 'endure the spending of that time in designing an action which might perform two; or that delay in performing two which might well perform twenty'.[1] That was an admirable attitude for an underling. Greatness in Tudor politics required that time be spent designing actions without altering the actions' pace, the making of plans amidst the confusion and welter of events only half understood and never brooded about excessively. One could not sacrifice the one to the other and succeed to Cromwell's inheritance, which was no place for a man permeated with zeal for reform but fearful of exceeding his instructions. Sadler was not likely to risk censure or invite criticism, for such were the ways that led to Esher or Tower Hill. And Sir Ralph Sadler had always before his eyes the vision of the great cardinal garnered in his youth as well as his more mature recollections of Cromwell. *Laus deo*: within those limitations, he would make his way.

[1] BM Sloane MSS. 1523, fo. 29*a*.

SELECT BIBLIOGRAPHY

The following list of books and articles is intended to direct the reader to the principal modern works helpful in understanding special and general problems of the Henrician era. Only in a few cases is a book listed for its content in terms of primary or contemporary materials. The notes for this study are quite specific for such purposes.

Adair, E. R. and F. M. G. Evans. 'Writs of Assistance', *EHR*, xxxvi (1921), 356–72.

Allen, P. S. 'A 16th Century School', *EHR*, x (1895), 738–44.

Anglo, Sydney. 'Le Camp du Drap d'Or et les entreveres d'Henri VIII et de Charles-Quint', *Les Fêtes de la Renaissance*, ed. Jean Jacquot, 2 vols. (Paris, 1960).

—— 'Public Spectacle in Early Tudor Policy, 1485–1547', unpublished Ph.D. thesis, London University, 1958.

Anon. 'An Old English Country House: Standon, Herts.', *The Burlington Magazine*, LXXXII (1943), 110–14.

Aylmer, Gerald A. *The King's Servants* (London, 1961).

Baldwin, W. T. *William Shakespeare's Small Latine and Lesse Greeke*, 2 vols. (Oxford, 1944).

Behrens, Betty. 'Treatises on the Ambassador Written in the 15th and 16th Century', *EHR*, LI (1936), 616–27.

Bindoff, S. T., Hurstfield, Joel and C. H. Williams (eds.). *Elizabethan Government and Society: Essays Presented to Sir John Neale* (London, 1960).

Brewer, John S. *The Reign of Henry VIII from his Accession to the Death of Wolsey*, 2 vols. (London, 1884).

Brown, P. Hume. *The History of Scotland*, 3 vols. (Cambridge, 1911).

—— 'The Scottish Nobility and their Part in the National History', *ScHR*, III (1906), 157–70.

Busch, Wilhelm. *Der Sturz des Cardinals Wolsey* (Leipzig, 1890).

Cameron, Annie I. *The Scottish Correspondence of Mary of Lorraine, 1543–1560* (Edinburgh, 1927).

—— *The Warrenden Papers*, 2 vols. (Edinburgh, 1931–2).

Cavendish, George. *Life of Cardinal Wolsey* (London, 1885).

Collinson, Patrick. 'The Puritan Classical Movement in the Reign of Queen Elizabeth', unpublished Ph.D. thesis, London University, 1957.

Cooper, J. H. 'The Counting of Manors', *EcHR*, 2nd ser. VIII (1956), 377–9.

Dickinson, Gladys. *Two Missions of Jacques de la Brosse* (Edinburgh, 1942).

Dickinson, William C. *Scotland from the Earliest Time to 1603* (London, 1961).

Bibliography

Dodds, M. H. and Ruth Dodds. *The Pilgrimage of Grace and the Exeter Conspiracy*, 2 vols. (Cambridge, 1915).

Donaldson, Gordon. *The Scottish Reformation* (Cambridge, 1960).

Elton, G. R. 'The Evolution of a Tudor Statute', *EHR*, LXIV (1949), 174–97.

—— *England under the Tudors* (London, 1955).

—— 'A Further Note on Parliamentary Drafts in the Reign of Henry VIII', *BIHR*, XXVII (1954), 198–200.

—— *Henry VIII* (London, 1962).

—— 'Parliamentary Drafts, 1529–1540', *BIHR*, XXV (1952), 117–32.

—— *Reformation Europe, 1517–1559* (London, 1963).

—— 'Thomas Cromwell's Decline and Fall', *CHJ*, X (1951), 150–85.

—— *The Tudor Constitution: Documents and Commentary* (Cambridge, 1960).

—— 'The Tudor Revolution: A Reply', *Past and Present*, no. 29 (1964), 26–49.

—— *The Tudor Revolution in Government* (Cambridge, 1953).

Emmison, F. G. *Tudor Secretary: Sir William Petre* (Cambridge, Mass., 1961).

Evans, F. M. G. *The Principal Secretary of State* (Manchester, 1923).

Ferguson, Charles. *Naked to Mine Enemies* (Boston, 1958).

Fisher, F. J. *Essays in the Economic and Social History of Tudor and Stuart England in Honour of R. H. Tawney* (Cambridge, 1961).

Fisher, H. A. L. *The History of England from the Accession of Henry VII to the Death of Henry VIII, 1485–1547* (London, 1928).

Foxe, John. *The Acts and Monuments of John Foxe*, ed. S. R. Cattely, 8 vols. (London, 1837–41).

Froude, James A. *The History of England from the Fall of Cardinal Wolsey to the Defeat of the Spanish Armada*, 12 *volumes* (London, 1862–70).

Gairdner, James. 'The Fall of Wolsey', *TRHS*, 2nd ser. XIII (1899), 75–102.

Gammon, S. R. 'Sir William Paget: The Master of Practises', unpublished Ph.D. thesis, Princeton University, 1953.

Gladish, Dorothy. *The Tudor Privy Council* (Retford, 1915).

Gray, Charles M. *Copyhold, Equity, and the Common Law* (Cambridge, Mass., 1963).

Habbakuk, H. J. 'The Market for Monastic Property, 1539–1603', *EcHR*, 2nd ser. X (1958), 362–80.

Hannay, R. K. 'The Earl of Arran and Queen Mary', *ScHR*, XVIII (1921), 258–76.

—— 'On the Church Lands at the Reformation', *ScHR*, XVI (1918), 52–72.

—— Harvey, Jane and Marguerite Woods, 'Some Papal Bulls Among the Hamilton Papers', *ScHR*, XXII (1924), 25–42.

Harriss, G. L. 'Medieval Government and Statecraft', *Past and Present*, no. 25 (1963), 8–39.

Hexter, J. H. *Reappraisals in History* (Evanston, 1961).

Bibliography

Hill, Christopher. *Puritanism and Revolution* (London, 1958).

Holdsworth, William S. *A History of the English Law*, 14 vols. to date (London, 1910–64).

Hughes, Philip. *The History of the Reformation in England*, 3 vols. (London, 1950–54).

Inglis, John A. *Sir Adam Otterburn* (Glasgow, 1935).

Kaulek, Jean. *Correspondence politique de MM. Castillon et de Marillac, 1537–1542* (Paris, 1885).

Kerridge, Eric. 'The Movement of Rents, 1540–1640', *EcHR*, 2nd ser. VI (1953), 16–34.

Lang, Andrew. 'The Cardinal and the King's Will', *ScHR*, III (1906), 410–22.

Lapsely, Gaillard T. 'The Problem of the North', *AHR*, V (1900), 440–66.

Lipson, Ephraim. *An Introduction to the Economic History of England*, 3 vols. (London, 1920).

Lloyd, David. *The States-men and Favourites of England since the Reformation* (London, 1665).

Mackie, J. D. *The Earlier Tudors, 1485–1558* (Oxford, 1952).

—— 'Henry VIII and Scotland', *TRHS*, 4th ser. XXIX (1944), 93–114.

Maitland, F. W. 'The Anglican Settlement and the Scottish Reformation', *Cambridge Modern History*, II, 550–98 (New York, 1910).

Mathew, David. *The Social Structure of Caroline England* (Oxford, 1948).

Mattingly, Garrett. *Catherine of Aragon* (Boston, 1941).

—— *Renaissance Diplomacy* (London, 1954).

Maxwell-Lyte, Henry. *Notes on the History and Use of the Great Seal* (London, 1926).

Merriman, Roger B. *The Life and Letters of Thomas Cromwell*, 2 vols. (Oxford, 1902).

Millar, A. N. 'Scotland Described for Queen Magdalene: A Curious Volume', *ScHR*, I (1903), 27–39.

Miller, Helen. 'Subsidy Assessments of the Peerage in the 16th Century', *BIHR*, XXVIII (1955), 15–34.

Mousnier, R. and Fritz Hartung. 'Quelques problemes concernant la monarchie absolue', *Relazioni*, Tenth International Congress of the Historical Sciences, IV, 3–55 (Florence, 1955).

Muller, James A. *Stephen Gardiner and the Tudor Reaction* (London, 1926).

Murray, A. G. W. *The Manuscript of William Dunche* (Exeter, 1914).

Neale, Sir John E. *The Elizabethan House of Commons* (London, 1949).

—— *Essays in Elizabethan History* (London, 1958).

Nicholson, William. *Leges Marchiarum* (London, 1705).

Notestein, Wallace. *The Winning of the Initiative by the House of Commons* (London, 1926).

Bibliography

Otway-Ruthven, J. *The King's Secretary in the Fifteenth Century* (Cambridge, 1939).

Pease, Howard. *The Lord Wardens of the Marches of Scotland and England* (London, 1913).

Peyton, A. 'The Village Population in the Tudor Lay Subsidy Rolls', *EHR*, xxx (1915), 234–50.

Pickthorn, Kenneth. *Early Tudor Government*, 2 vols. (Cambridge, 1934).

Pocock, Nicholas. *Troubles Connected with the Prayer Book* (London, 1884).

Pollard, A. F. 'A Changeling Member of Parliament', *BIHR*, x (1932), 20–7.

—— 'Council, Star Chamber and Privy Council under the Tudors. Part III. The Privy Council', *EHR*, xxxviii (1923), 42–60.

—— *England under Protector Somerset* (London, 1900).

—— *Henry VIII* (London, 1902).

—— *Wolsey* (London, 1929).

Rait, Robert. 'The Scottish Parliament Before the Union of the Crowns', *EHR*, xv (1900), 417–44.

Reid, Rachael, *The King's Council in the North* (London, 1921).

Richardson, Walter C. *A History of the Court of Augmentations* (Baton Rouge, 1961).

—— 'Some Financial Expedients of Henry VIII', *EcHR*, 2nd ser. VII (1954), 33–48.

—— *Stephen Vaughan: Financial Agent of Henry VIII* (Baton Rouge, 1953).

—— *Tudor Chamber Administration* (Baton Rouge, 1952).

Sanders, Nicholas. *De origine ac progressu schismatis Angliae* (Cologne, 1585).

Savine, Alexander. *The English Monasteries on the Eve of the Dissolution* (Oxford, 1909).

Schofield, Roger. 'Parliamentary Lay Taxation, 1485–1547', unpublished D.Phil., Cambridge University, 1963.

Shelling, Felix. *The English Chronicle Play* (New York, 1902).

Shepherd, F. W. *The Survey of London: The Parish of Hackney, Brooke House* (London, 1960).

Smith, Lacey B. *A Tudor Tragedy: The Life and Times of Catherine Howard* (London, 1961).

—— *Tudor Prelates and Politics* (Princeton, 1953).

Stoney, Francis Sadleir. *Memoir of the Life and Times of Sir Ralph Sadler* (London, 1875).

Stow, John. *A Survey of London*. Edited by C. L. Kingsford, 2 vols. (Oxford, 1908).

Strype, John. *Annals of the Reformation and the Establishment of Religion*, 4 vols. in 7 parts (Oxford, 1824).

Bibliography

Sturge, Charles. *Cuthbert Tunstal* (London, 1938).

—— 'John Dudley: Duke of Northumberland', unpublished Ph.D. thesis, London University, 1927.

Tawney, R. H. *The Agrarian Problem of the 16th Century* (London, 1912).

—— *Religion and the Rise of Capitalism* (London, 1948).

—— 'The Rise of the Gentry', *EcHR*, XI (1941), 1–38.

Teulet, A. *Papiers D'État, pièces et documents inédits ou peu connus relatifs à l'histoire de l'Écosse au 16ᵉ siècle*, 3 vols. (Paris, 1852–60).

Tough, D. L. W. *The Last Years of a Frontier* (Oxford, 1928).

Tout, Thomas F. *Chapters in the Administrative History of Medieval England*, 6 vols. (Manchester, 1920–33).

Trevor-Roper, Hugh. *The Gentry, 1540–1640*, supplement no. 1 to *EcHR*, 1953.

Van Dyke, Paul. 'The Mission of Cardinal Pole to Enforce the Bull of Deposition Against Henry VIII', *EHR*, XXXVII (1922), 414–23.

Watson, Foster. *The English Grammar Schools to 1660* (Cambridge, 1908).

Williams, Penry. 'A Revolution in Tudor History? Dr Elton's Interpretation of the Age', *Past and Present*, no. 25 (1963), 4–8.

—— 'The Tudor State', *Past and Present*, no. 25 (1963), 39–58.

Woods, Marguerite. *The Balcarres Papers, 1537–1548* (Edinburgh, 1923).

Woodward, G. W. O. 'A Speculation in Monastic Lands', *EHR*, LXXIX (1964), 778–83.

Youings, Joyce. 'The Terms of the Disposal of the Devon Monastic Lands', *EHR*, LXIX (1954), 18–38.

Zeller, Gaston. *Histoire des Relations Internationales: Les Temps Modernes: De Christophe Colomb à Cromwell* (Paris, 1953).

The following very recent works of importance appeared too late to be used in this study; they throw light on the problems dealt with here without, however, necessitating any changes in the text.

Elton, G. R. 'Why the History of the Early Tudor Council Remains Unwritten', *Annali della Fondazione italiana per la storia amministrativa*, I (1964), 268–96.

Ferguson, Arthur. *The Articulate Citizen and the English Renaissance* (Durham, North Carolina, 1965).

Lehmberg, Stanford. *Sir Walter Mildmay and Tudor Government* (Austin, 1965).

MacCaffery, Wallace. 'England, the Crown, and the New Aristocracy, 1540–1600', *Past and Present*, no. 30 (1965), 52–64.

INDEX

All titles are in the English peerage, except when followed by (S.), in which case the Scottish peerage is indicated. No attempt has been made to describe estates with qualifying words such as manor, messuage, etc., since such a practice would only encumber the Index and the more complete information is in any case available in the text. In a similar manner, no elaborate system of cross-reference was attempted, since in most cases the location of items in the Index is not ambivalent. Finally, casual references to a major figure are usually not noted.

Index

Henry VIII—*contd.*
  desire to marry in France, 73; death of, 156–7; factions maintained by, 2, 42, 134, **143–5**; mendacity of, 102; relations with Margaret Tudor, 78–9; Sadler and, 47–8, 116, 118, 127, 212–13; Scotland and, 73, **94–137** *passim*
Hepburn, Patrick, earl of Bothwell (S.), 106, 110
Heralds' College, 1
Heritage, Thomas, 25
Herons of Hackney, 138–9
Hertford, earl of, *see* Seymour, Sir Edward
Hertfordshire: estates of Sadler, 193, 195–6, 202–4; compared with Avon valley holdings, 199; Sadler's position in society, 58, 199, 219
Hertford castle, 173
Highall, Essex, 193, 208
Hill, William, 184
Hilliard, Dr Robert, 96
Hobby, Sir Philip, 56
Holbein, Hans, 221
Holgate, Robert, archbishop of York, 137, 153
Home Counties: Sadler's lands in, 193–5, 204, 206
House of Commons: Sadler enters, 40; Sadler's business in, 216–17; speeches in by Sadler, 130–1
House of Lords: action on Sadler's marriage, 216–17
household offices: groom of the chamber, 174; management of, **162–71**; precedence of, 51; reputation for corruption, 166–7; secretary's fees and income, 174–5; the great wardrobe, 150, **163–71**, 181–2
Howard, Sir Henry, earl of Surrey, 156
Howard, Queen Catherine, 43, 145–9
Howard, Sir Thomas, earl of Surrey, duke of Norfolk, etc., 16, 30, 37, 41; Cromwell and, 19–21, 39, 43; his lack of caution, 80; Margaret Tudor and, 79; position in Tudor politics, 75–6, 134, 136, 151, 155–6; replaces earl of Shrewsbury, 82; Sadler and, 83, 145–9
Howard, Lord William, ambassador to Scotland, lord admiral, 147
Hubblethorne, Henry, 207
Hughes, Philip, 22, 47, 156
Hunt and Squery *v.* Sadler, 205
Huntley, earl of (S.), *see* Gordon, George
Husee, John, 30, 78

imperial alliance, the, 66–7, 143, 149
inflation and land management policies, 207, 209–10
intelligence, related to Scotland, 103

James IV, 68–9, 94
James V: alliance with France, 41, 68–9; attains majority, 41, 68–9; death of, 101; English policy of, **78–81**, 89; Henry VIII and, 129; marries Mary of Guise, 73; Tudor succession and, 86–7
James VI and I, Tudor succession and, 131
Jesuits, 214
Judde, John, underclerk of the hanaper, 168

Kenark, Robert, 183
Kenilworth, 14
Kennedy, Gilbert, earl of Cassels (S): 106, 109–10, 117
Kent, 208
Kern, Sir Edward, 191
King's Book, 150
King's College, 184
Knights Templar, 196
Knollys, Sir Francis, 56–7
Knox, John, 115; Sadler and, 214

Lancaster, duchy of, 211
Latimer, Hugh, bishop of Worcester, 42; Sadler and, 137–8
Layton, Richard, dean of York, 28–9
Lee, Roland, bishop of Coventry and Lichfield, president of the council in the marches, 38, 135; position in politics, 151; Sadler and, 137
Lennox, earl of (S.), *see* Stuart (Stewart), Matthew
Lesnes, Kent, 193–4
Lincolnshire: Neville's rising in, 140; royal progress in, 145; Sadler lands, 197
Lindsay, Sir David, 88
Lisle, Viscount, *see* Dudley, Sir John, and Plantagenet, Sir Arthur
livery and maintenance, 222
London: Guild Hall archives, 9; plague rages in, 33–4; Sadler lands, 199
Longleat, Wilts., xii
Lowhall, Essex, 193, 208
Lyngham, Richard, 56

MacCaffery, Wallace 3
Maitland, F. W., 83
Margaret Tudor, 68–9, 76–93 *passim*
Marillac, Charles de, French ambassador, on Sadler, 66–7, 141–2
Marmion, 127
Marshalsea gaol, 59
Mary of Guise, 109–23 *passim*
Mary, queen of Scots, 109, 112, 118; birth of, 99–101; English plans for, 120–1; removed from Linlithgow, 116, 123, 127–8; tapestries at Standon depict, 221; visits Standon, 221

234

Index

Mary Tudor (queen), 142, 221

Mathew, Toby, bishop of Durham, archbishop of York, 94, 99

Maxwell, Baron Robert (S.), 110

Maxwell-Lyte, Henry, 164, 174

Mercer, Alice, 210, 222; *v.* Sadler, 205–6

Merriman, Roger B., 16, 20

Middlesex, 194, 197

Milan, Italy, 70

Miller, Helen, 186–7

monastic lands: administration of before 1536, 189–90, 200; sale of, 189–90; Sadler's acquisitions of, **200–5**

Monkeith, Lord Robert (S.), 101

Montagu, Sir Edward, 135

More, Sir Thomas, vii, 24, 148

Morgan, Sir Richard, 15

Morpeth, Northumb., 106

Mountjoy priory, Norwich, 17

Murray, earl of (S.), *see* Stuart (Stewart), James

Mychell, John: father-in-law of Sadler, 213; purchases lands from Sadler, 201

National Portrait Gallery, London, 221

Neale, Sir John E., vii–viii, 3, 30

Neville, Sir John, 140

Newcastle, Northumb., 75–6, 87

North, Sir Edward, 135

Northamptonshire, 197

Northumberland, earl of, *see* Percy, Henry Algernon

Nuneton, Warws., 198; priory of, 185

offices: analysis of problems of office-holding, **159–88** *passim*; annuities from, 171–3; fees from, 173–5; gratuities and, **176–86**; legal status of fees, 160, 177–8; income from, general analysis, **171–88**; patents and tenure, 161–2; patronage and, 160; performance of duty by deputy, 159, 163, 171; perquisites, 160, 175–7; salary from, 172–3; sale of, 160; value of, annual and capital, **159–88** *passim*

office-holding gentry, 160–1, 197

Ogilvie (Ogelby), Sir Walter, 88

Oliphant, Lord Andrew (S.), 85

Oliver, John, 184

Orford, Suffolk, 20–1

Orforde, John, 50

Ortiz, Dr Pedro, imperial ambassador to the Holy See, 71–2

Ottoman Empire, 70

Pace, Richard, secretary of state, 51, 61

Paget, Sir William, clerk of the council, secretary of state, ix, 38, 50, 64, 199; early

conservative posture, 135, 153; favours imperial alliance, 66; fears France, 98; protects alleged heretics, 98, 155; role in politics, **151–7**

Palmer, Richard, 50

Panter, David, bishop of Ross, 121

Parentado: Anglo-Scottish, 102–31 *passim*; Franco-Scottish, 71–2, 81; Sadler's dilemma *re*, **111–21**

Parker, Thomas, archbishop of Canterbury, 137

parliament: and Sadler's marriage, 216–17; arena for anti-Cromwellians, 40; Sadler enters, 40; Scottish, 108, 112; Arran proclaimed regent by Scottish, 114; Treaty of Greenwich, 128

Parr, queen Catherine, 138

Parr, Sir William, earl of Essex, marquis of Northampton, 104, 109, 138; analysis of Scottish affairs, 112, 122–4; bigamous marriage of, 214; Sadler and, 123, 152

Passhe, William, 50

Paston, family of, 210

patronage; and balance of factions, 144; ambivalent nature of, 132, 133; Cromwell's clients, 133; impact of Reformation on, 159; Sadler and, viii–ix, 28–9, 57, 167, 191–3, 202–3; territorial nobility and, 132–3; Tudor government and, 158–9; Wolsey's system of, 133

Paul III (Pope), 70–3, 85, 95; negotiates northern alliance, 118; schemes for Scotland, 123

Paulet, Sir William, Baron St John, earl of Wiltshire, etc., 19–21, 135, 212

Pavia, Battle of, 70, 95, 97

Peck, Francis, 173–4

Peers, John, 56

Percy, Henry Algernon, earl of Northumberland, 33, 75–6

Pershore abbey, Gloucs., 192, 205

Petre, Sir William, secretary of state, vii, 50, 64, 146, 224

Petyt, Sir William, 54

Pexsall, John, 168

Peyton, S. A., 187

Pilgrimage of Grace, 40, 71, 75, 82

Pio, Ridolfo, bishop of Faenza, 71–2

Plantagenet, Sir Arthur, Lord Lisle, deputy of Calais, 28, 58, 158; futility of his suits, 185–6; grants Sadler annuity, 184; Lady Lisle, 183

Plasshes, Herts., 195

pluralism, **167–71**

Pole, Reginald, 71–2

Pollard, A. F., vii, 20–1, 39, 41 ,140, 143

Index

Polsted, Henry, 201
Pontefract castle, Yorks., 145
Popeshall, Herts., 195
prebends' plot, 150
privy chamber, 29, 46
privy council; churchmen and, 2; dominated by Gardiner, 140; meets at Standon, 221; political factions and, 41, 135–6, 142, 148; reviews Scottish policy, 128; Sadler and, 58
privy seal, 49–50
Protestantism: and English factions, 151, 155–6; impact of on diplomacy, 136; impact of Six Articles on, 40; in Scotland, 96; Sadler and, 123
Puritanism, 137

Queensbury, Herts., 196

Ray, Henry, Berwick pursuivant, 79–80
Raylton, Gregory, secretary to Sadler, 64–5, 137, 167, 170
Reformation, the: and clerical reform, 88–91, 98; Henry VIII's waning zeal for, 120; Sadler's views on, **136–43**; in Scotland, 126
Requests, court of, 206
retainers, 222
Rib valley, Herts., 195, 210
Rice, John ap, 28
Rich, Sir Richard, Baron Rich, chancellor of Augmentations, etc., vii, 24, 151, 224
Richard II, 221
Richardson, W. C., vii, 3, 5, 154
Robertsbridge, Sussex, 191–2
Rocheford, Lady Jane, 145, 148
Rush, Thomas, 19–21
Russell, Sir John, lord privy seal, earl of Bedford, etc., 33, 37, 136
Ruthal, Thomas, bishop of Durham, 61

Sadler, Gertrude, 223
Sadler, Henry the Elder, 2, 187; and Sir Edward Belknap, 6–7, 169; at Hackney, 7–8, 12; father of Sir Ralph, 12; his position, **10–13**; native of Warws., 7, 9; suitor to Cromwell, 3–4, 12; steward in Grey connection, 10–11
Sadler, Henry the younger, clerk of the hanaper, 161–2
Sadler, Jane, 218
Sadler, John, 14, 166
Sadler, Lady Helen (Ellen Mychell Barre), 84, 195, 218–19
Sadler, Margaret, 215
Sadler, Sir Ralph, secretary of state, etc.: accounts of life, viii–ix, chancery offices of, 33; character of career, 223–5; children of,

216; Cromwell's agent and suitor, chh. 2–4 *passim*; drafts state papers, 27–8; education of, 61–2, 92; embassies to Scotland, chh. 5–6 *passim*; exploitation of office, ch. 8 *passim*; favours French Protestants, 66; foments Protestantism in Scotland, 67; groom of chamber, 29–32; knighted, 42, 47; lands in Hackney, 8; linguistic competence, 27–8, 62–3; loss of favour in 1537, 32–7; manner of speech, 54, 62; marriage, 212–19; materials for life, xi–xii; patron of historians, 63; mission to France, 78; parliamentary career, viii; pluralism, vii, ch. 8 *passim*; political attitudes, 16, 144, 151–7; removed from secretaryship, 150; religious attitudes, 63, 66, 113, 130, 138–44; treasurer for the wars in Scotland, 215; a trimmer, 136–7
St Frediswude's College, 185
St George, Henry, Richmond Herlad, 1
St John's Hospital, Middlesex, 23
St Peter and St George, Guild of, Yorks., 185
Salerno, Italy, 65
Sampson, Dr Richard, bishop of Coventry and Lichfield, 42
Sanders, Nicholas, S.J., 214–15, 218
Sandys, Sir Edward, 7
Sanford, Richard, 183–6
Savine, Alexander, 189–90
Saxony, Germany, 143
Scarborough, Yorks., 79
Schmalkaldic League, 67
Scott, Sir Walter, 1–3, 14, 127, 215
Scotland: anti-clericalism in, 88; Auld Alliance, **68–93** *passim*; Beaton's palace revolution, 117–21; border problems, 69, 96–7, 120; Calvinists and Lutherans in, 98; council of regency, 108–9; Catholic League, 137; English policy toward, 40, 65–6, **94–100**; factional strife among nobility, 91–2, **106–31**; Reformation in, 86–91, 105–6; relations with Holy See, 68–93; Valois policy in, 76
secretary of state, the principal: analysis of duties, 26–8, 51–67; annual and capital value of office, **183–6**; apprenticeship for office, 37–8; conditions of tenure, 115, 150, 161, 192; constitutional position of, 60; division of office, 47–8; emoluments of, 174–5; fees and gratuities paid to, 49–57, 185–6; diplomatic burden of office, **59–66**; domestic security functions of, 58–9; education and qualifications for office, **60–3**; patronage control of, 48–50; parliamentary duties, 53–4; rising power of, **50–67**; secretariat of, 60–5; Wriothesley–Sadler tenure, 42, 57; *see also* signet office

Index

Selby abbey, Yorks.: accounts of, 204; circumstances of Sadler's acquisition, 192–3, 197–8, 209, 211; income and profits from, 198, 207–8

Seymour, Sir Edward, earl of Hertford, etc.: absence from court, 150; politics of, 136, 144, 151–7

Seymour, queen Jane, 33, 36, 195, 219

Shacklewood, Middlesex, 173

Shelley, Sir William, 3, 5–6

Shelve, Warws., 203

signed bills, 54–7

signet office: analysis of Sadler's register, **55–8**, 182–3; clerks of, 54–5; fees paid to, 55; gratuities paid to, 182; location of, 163; profits of, 185–6; relation to principal secretary, **48–50**; Sadler and, 25–7

signet warrants, 54–5

simony, 118

sinecurism, 159

Sion House, 146

Six Articles of Religion, 40

Slackstead, Hants., 196

Smith, Sir Thomas, secretary of state, 202

Snathe priory, Yorks., 197

Snowe, Richard, 168–9

Solway, William, 204–5

Solway Moss: aftermath of battle there, 69, 110, 122; prisoners taken at, 100; Scots defeated there, 99

Somers, John, 137, 171

Southampton, earl of, *see* Wriothesley, Sir Thomas, *and* Fitzwilliam, Sir William

Southwell, Sir Richard, 58, 102, 104, 183

speculation, monastic lands and, 201–4

Standon lordship, Herts.: acquired by Sadler, x, 1, 208, 219; borough of, 222; chapel there, 221; description of monuments there, 29, **220–3**; evaluation of manorial complex, 195; furnishings and inventories, 220–1; litigation at, 205; plans of, 220; portraits of Sadler at, 221; position in Sadler's life, 219; 222; regranted in fee simple, 219

Star Chamber, court of, 43, 100, 177

Statutes of the Realm, 217

Stewart (Stuart), Henry, Baron Methuen, 73–4, 76–7, 81, 101

Stewart (Stuart), James, earl of Murray (S.), 105

Stewart (Stuart), Mathew, earl of Lennox (S.), regent of Scotland; Angus and, 106, 120; contempt for Arran, 119; estranged from Beaton, 120; leads French forces, 116; marriage plans for, 116; Sadler and, 121

Stirling castle, 116

Stokesley, John, bishop of London, 134

Stoney, Francis Sadleir, 215, 217

Stoughton, Richard, 170

Stratford-le-Bowe, Middlesex: accounts of, 204; acquired by Sadler, 193, 197; holdings of, 207–8

Styldoff, Thomas, 179

subsidy assessments, 196–7

Surrey, 202

Swifte, Richard, 15

Swynnerton, Humphrey, 56

Sydney, Sir William, 191–2

Sysson, Oswald, 208

Talbot, Francis, earl of Shrewsbury, 57, 82

Tantallon, Scotland, 127

Taunton, Somers., 20–1

Tawney, R. H., 188–91, 193, 199

Temple Chelsyn, Herts., 196

Temple Dynsley, Herts., 196

Thirlby, Thomas, bishop of Ely, 82

Thorpe, Edward, 220

Throgmorton, William, 164

Tiltey abbey, Essex, 4, 10–11

Tithes, 204

Tixhall, Staffs., 222

Treaty of Berwick, 94

Treaty of Cambrai, 70

Treaty of Greenwich, 122–8

Trevor-Roper, Hugh, 211

Troeltsch, Ernst, 190

Tudor government: factions in, **143–59**; financial crisis of, 154–5; Henrician 'party' dominant, 134–6, 150–1, 155–6; Gardiner–Norfolk faction, **144–50**; 'New Monarchy', 39; patronage, 132–4; pluralism and office-holding, 168–71; sinecurism, 159

Tunstal, Cuthbert, bishop of Durham, 41, 104; decline in his power, 134–5; defrauded of lands, 153; optimism of, 106; Sadler and, 144, 153

Tyler, John, 56

Tylney, Agnes, dowager duchess of Norfolk, 145–6

urban lands, Sadler's holdings, 197, 202

Valor Ecclesiasticus, 194

Van der Delft, Francis, imperial ambassador, 151–5

Vaughan, Stephen, 15–16, 24, 38, 66–7, 137

Vaux, Sir Nicholas, Baron Vaux of Harrowden, 7

visitations, heralds', 215

Wales, 194

Wallop, Sir John, ambassador, marshal of Calais, 71, 134, 142

237

Index